POST-PARTUM DOCUMENT

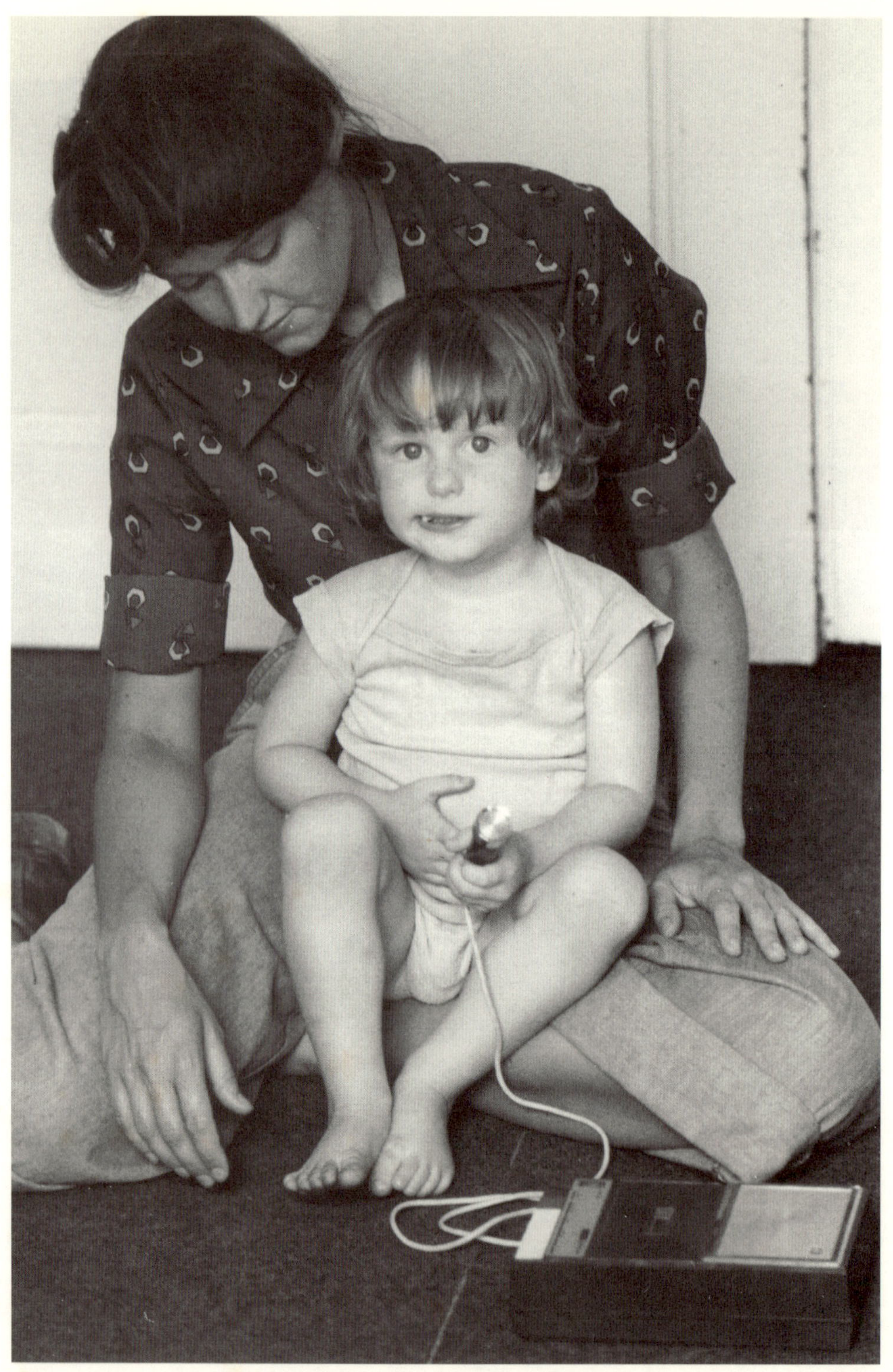

Mary Kelly and son, recording session 1975
Photo: Ray Barrie

POST-PARTUM DOCUMENT

Mary Kelly

University of California Press
Berkeley · Los Angeles · London

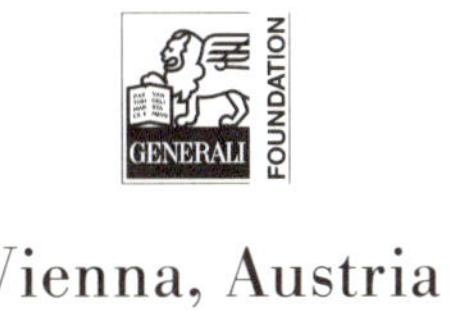

Vienna, Austria

University of California Press
Berkeley and Los Angeles

University of California Press, Ltd.
London, England

First California Printing 1999

Published by arrangement with
Generali Foundation, Vienna, Austria

Library of Congress Cataloging-in-Publication Data

Kelly, Mary, 1941 -
Post-Partum Document / Mary Kelly
p. cm.
Previously published: Routledge & Kegan Paul, 1983.
Includes bibliographical references.
ISBN 0-520-21940-6 (cl.). – ISBN 0-520-21941-4 (pbk.)
1. Kelly, Mary, 1941– Post-Partum Document. 2. Art, Modern-20th century.
3. Psychoanalysis and art. 4. Feminism in art. 5. Conceptualism (Art)–United States. I. Title.
N 6537.K42A72 1998
709'.2–dc21 98-30424
CIP

Printed in Austria

1 2 3 4 5 6 7 8 9

Contents

Illustrations

Each group of illustrations uses a code of numbers and letters for reference to the Documentation texts.

Acknowledgements

Above all, I would like to thank Sabine Breitwieser who suggested republishing *Post-Partum Document* to mark the occasion of bringing together the complete work for exhibition at the Generali Foundation in Vienna. Her initiative and dedication has been central to the realization of this project. In addition I would like to acknowledge Hemma Schmutz, Nadja Wiesener and Barbara Schröder for their collaboration on the production of the book as well as Christian Höller and Alexandra Seibel for translating the manuscript for the German edition. For coordinating the publication and distribution of the English edition, I extend my thanks to Charlene Woodcock of the University of California Press and for the German edition to Luise Metzel of Verlag Silke Schreiber. To Ray Barrie, I would like to express my appreciation for support throughout the entire project, especially for photographing the artwork for the original manuscript and supervising the reproduction of images for the reprint. My thanks to Steve Lehmer for producing the camera-ready CD Rom. I am also grateful to Juli Carson for her work on the bibliography and to Laura Mulvey, Margaret Iversen, Jo-Anna Isaak, Paul Smith and Andrea Fraser for permission to reprint their articles in the appendix, as well as Lucy R. Lippard whose foreword is still prescient. Finally, to Kelly Barrie, my thanks for collaborating a second time around.

Foreword

When I first saw the *Post-Partum Document* in London in 1977, it was incomplete but already four years underway. I saw it, as most people do initially, as a "fetish" —a more or less conventional work of art, visually refined, hung on the wall in pretty plastic boxes. I was touched by what I sensed of its content rather than by what there was to "know" about the piece—which turned out to be a great deal. The simultaneity of sensual immediacy and immediate nostalgia I recognized from my own, earlier, maternal experience. On a formal basis, I "liked" the melancholy delicacy, the visual parallels to the ephemerality of motherhood; the organic traces and talismans of the mother's individual discoveries, then the mutual discoveries, then the child's individual discoveries brought as gifts to the mother. In other words, I saw PPD precisely on the prosaic biological/autobiographical level that Kelly manipulates to subvert.

Within the context of this first encounter I was baffled by the content of the Lacanian diagrams, being mostly innocent of linguistic and psychoanalytical theory, but I "liked," again, the *sense* of rigorous analysis applied to the intimate memories of the mother-child relationship. On a general level, the juxtaposition suggested the collaged lives of women who choose both to create and to procreate, to play both masculine and feminine social roles. And finally I was moved by the intellectual refinement that I then only sensed beneath the images' surfaces. I went home and read the lengthy "Footnotes and Bibliography" booklet that revealed some of those depths. In the next four years I saw additional sections of the work, saw the piece exhibited as a whole, and read a great deal more about and by Mary Kelly, my respect increasing with each new effort.

By now I can no longer *see* the *Post-Partum Document*. In the six years since the first viewing, it has become an excruciatingly complex and demanding experience rather than merely an object of perception. The time and energy the artist has sunk into it have merged with my own learning process around it. At a 1977 feminist conference, Kelly gave a paper on art and sexual politics that made a distinction crucial to this double process, a distinction between "feminist practice" and "feminist problematic." This was not just a fancy way of dichotomizing theory and praxis. She was separating a generalized feminist art—the kind I initially perceived in the PPD (which generates questions like "what is feminist art?" thereby falling prey to the dominant culture's ghettoization and stylistic homogenization of all women's art) –from specific practices inseparable from the ideological frameworks in which they are used.

I have been asked to introduce, not to elucidate, this book version of the *Post-Partum Document*, so I can only suggest some of the issues it raises. In any case, the work itself and other, more specific essays follow this brief introduction. If any work of art should be allowed to speak for itself, it is this one, since its goal is to *give voice*. In the paper quoted above, Kelly categorized her own art as "feminine 'discourse' ('Other' art)," noting its inclusion of distancing devices such as writing and self-analysis: "Such work is scripto visual," she said, "precisely because feminine 'discourse' is trying to articulate the unsaid, the 'feminine,' the negative signification, in language which is coincident with the patriarchy; for this reason the work is always in danger of being subsumed by it, but in so far as the feminine is said, or articulated in language, it is profoundly subversive."

PPD is the story of a cultural kidnapping and a woman's passive resistance to it, made active by verbal and visual analysis. PPD outlines social interference into the "ideal" relationship of mother and child (or artist and object) in terms of desire, presence and absence. Like the best feminist art of any style, PPD cannot be fully understood outside of the feminist social structures that nurtured it. Its seeds lay in consciousness-raising, in Kelly's collaborative work on the *Nightcleaners* film and the "Women and Work" exhibition. PPD began as a more economically oriented piece about the division of labor, but, learning as she went, and eventually realising the impossibility of covering so much ground, Kelly ended up referring primarily to "the construction of sexual differences." "The whole project," she has said, "not only the visible art work but the process itself, is about the relation of writing to the mother's body... It is at the moment of our entry into language that we take up a feminine or a masculine position in the symbolic structure of our society... Learning to speak is dependent on the ability to conceptualize absence and establish differences." Thus what we have in PPD is a portrait of the mother's own emergence into sexuality, language and self-identity in a patriarchal world paralleling the "other" experience of the same phenomena by her male child.

One of the most interesting aspects of PPD relates to Kelly's image of the child as "primitive," the child's mind as microcosm of a primal society to be deciphered and then colonized by another social group—mothers, adults. (She says she has always thought of the Natural History Museum as "a vast metaphor for the exploration of the mother's body" and was trying to put "this archaeology of everyday life into that kind of framed space—an unexpected place.") The anguished battle for cultural control culminates in PPD's Part VI—entry into written language—presented as a Rosetta Stone with three levels of consciousness. The child makes the marks; the anthropologist/mother translates them and then the artist/intellectual removes herself from the experience far enough to comment on the mother's feelings at the time.

Artmaking of any kind is a means of asserting the artist's existence. This assertion need not be absorbed by the patriarchal myth of artist as individual genius. In Kelly's case, for instance, the *Post-Partum Document* might be seen as a gridded class-action suit—an assertion of the existence of a vertical class called women or mothers crossing the horizontal classes of capitalism and dominated by the vertical and horizontal classes of the patriarchy. PPD is an amalgam of numerous issues raised by feminist artists in the last 12 years. Many women will understand it immediately as "the rationalisation of a difficult experience," as Kelly put it in psychoanalytical terms—or compensation for giving birth and losing control. On this relatively obvious level, the piece joins the broad spectrum of feminist art attempting generally to rehabilitate denigrated aspects of female experience, from needlework to maternity to female sexuality and language.

On one hand, then, PPD could be said to reinforce stereotypes by identifying a woman artist by her motherhood, although eventually it becomes clear that Kelly is interrupting rather than propagating cliches. When PPD was first shown in 1976, the atmosphere was such that the mass media made a huge fuss over the "dirty nappies" and the mainstream art crowd denigrated the piece because it was just about a woman and her baby, thereby no fit subject for high culture. Feminists, on the other hand, recognized Kelly's courageous stand against the cultural repression of the mother/child experience. In 1975, unaware that PPD was underway in England, I wondered in print why there was virtually no feminist art about pregnancy, birth and motherhood except occasional subjective pictures which were often misread by the dominant culture because they resembled similar images objectified by men. I should have known why; in the early days of feminism, I had once been congratulated by a feminist artist for "courageously" allowing a magazine to publish a picture of me with my small son. She said she and the other women artists she knew always hid any trace of husband and children in a professional context. However, as a writer rather than an artist, I was not being courageous at all; I was bragging, using my son to prove I could "do everything," be a woman (mother) as well as a man (writer)—an attitude I now understand through the analysis Kelly uses of child as phallus. (In fact, despite Kelly's adamant rejection of photography in her art, a photo of herself and her son, taken by his father, artist Ray Barrie, has often appeared in the press since PPD made its debut. Interestingly, it shows her kneeling, her little son seated between her legs—being born, or being the mother's upright phallus.)

At the roots of the PPD are five intentional contradictions: (1) the displacement of the fetishization of the child" on to the artwork itself—a kind of aesthetic compensation for the unavoidable loss of the child by replacing it with the lasting presence of an artwork designed for posterity; (2) the "parody" of art commodification by the pristine and institutional presentation of the piece; (3) the intentional "conflict" between patriarchal sources (Marx/Freud via Althusser/Lacan) and the feminist analysis; (4) the "disruption" of the accustomed feminist biological/autobiographical readings; (5) the "visualization" of the mother/woman without "picturing" her, and the resolute avoidance of photography.

While on the one hand these theoretical puns enrich the piece, on the other hand they engender a certain amount of resentment on the part of an audience who either dislikes such density or doesn't get it. The rejection of the "mirror" of photographic self-portraits, the countering of subjective diary elements with objective texts is rightly seen as a criticism of feminist art dependent on those very components, and perhaps as a surrender of some compassion for other women's identity crises. Some viewers are put off by the overt focus on Lacan—a single patriarchal figure—and others wonder how much the emphasis on the verbal constitutes a denial of *visual* language, an admission of the failure of purely visual practice except as a hook into the content. Yet over the years Kelly has been irritated at the suggestion that PPD belongs in a book (though wisely, given the present context, keeping her options open). "For me," she has said, "it's absolutely crucial that this kind of pleasure in the text, in the objects themselves, should engage the viewer, because there's no point at which it can become a deconstructed critical engagement if the viewer is not first—immediately and affectively—drawn into the work. I also think that narrative can function differently in an art work because it is unexpected and controversial in that space."

Kelly acknowledges the necessity of "several possible readings" of PPD—more or less the stages I myself went through in dealing with it. Understood by different viewers on different levels, it is broadened by their multiple associations. At the same time, irony and ambiguity tread dangerous paths between communication and obfuscation. It is all very well to insist that one's use of commodification is a critique of commodification, but not all of the audience will have access to the tools for understanding this. Kelly answers such criticisms by intentionally targeting, or limiting, her audience to "the Women's Movement, other women artists and people generally interested in the issue of patriarchy." Although I think she is mistaken when she suggests that because of the breadth of the subject her audience is *wider* than that for a more generalized feminist art (such as Judy Chicago's), she makes an important point about all politically engaged art when she says "there's no such thing as a homogeneous mass-audience. You can't make art for everyone. And if you're engaged within a particular movement or organization, then the work is going to participate in its debates." The art will never be ahead of the politics, but work like *Post-Partum Document* extends the level of discourse within the art audience for all those who see the art experience as an *exchange*, a collaboration between artist and audience–the active audience an active art deserves.

Part VI is my favourite part of the *Document* because it states most succinctly the themes of the whole piece–removal, distancing, the weaning process that characterizes socialization and all relationships. Crucial to this process of removal is the subject's awareness of the ideologies that rule her experience. It is here that Kelly's work transcends the social expectations of "art." After 13 years of scrutiny of women's and feminist art, it seems to me that the most important contributions are those which provide not only an image or even a new form language, but those which delve down and move out into social life itself. These works tend, like PPD, to be intricately structural, the results of years of labor–not autonomous series, but ongoing sequences of learning, communication, integration and learning some more from the responses of the chosen audiences.

Such works concern themselves with systems critically, from within, not just as commentaries on them. Such artists (they are sometimes male as well as feminist activists), tend to be asked, as Kelly so often was, when they are going to start "some new work." Innovation is seen as stylistic and short-term, geared to the market. Artists are not supposed to go so far beneath the surface as to try to provoke change, but are merely supposed to embellish, observe and reflect the sights and systems of the status quo. Kelly has managed to bridge several interdisciplinary gaps to make a contribution to feminist thought as well as to feminist imagery. She is one of an important group of "second-generation conceptual" artists who are feminists, like Susan Hillier, Marie Yates, Alexis Hunter, Martha Rosler and Adrian Piper. They insist on the necessity for feminist artists to think, to frame, as well as to picture, and in doing so to criticize the ways in which women see and take for granted their perceptions. Other artists, such as Suzanne Lacy, Leslie Labowitz, Margaret Harrison, Bonnie Sherk, Mierle Laderman Ukeles, and Vivienne Binns, have embarked on a similar enterprise, focusing on strategic outreach into the public domain rather than on strategic theoretical analysis.

Both arms of this long-term, structural/process feminist art relate specifically to the uses and perceptions of mass, popular, and "folk or hobby" culture, especially to advertizing and to the means of presentation and representation, production and reproduction, propaganda and propagation. Thus the issue of creation and procreation within the PPD can be understood on a number of levels I haven't room to discuss here. One indication of the importance of Kelly's work is the rigor of the criticism and discussion it has provoked, and the extent to which it is infiltrating the broader feminist dialogue. Few artists can claim this for their work; few have been ambitious enough to try.

Lucy R. Lippard
New York City
1982

Preface

Post-Partum Document was conceived as an on-going process of analysis and visualization of the mother-child relationship. It was born as an installation in six consecutive sections, comprising in all one hundred thirty-five small units. It grew up as an exhibition, adapted to a variety of genres (some realizing my desire for it to be what I wanted it to be, others resisting, transgressing) and finally reproduced itself in the form of a book.

But why invoke the metaphor of procreation to describe a project which explicitly refutes any attempt to naturalize the discourse of women's practice in art? First, I want to acknowledge the way in which every artistic text is punctuated with an unconscious significance that cuts across the constraints of medium or intentionality. Second, I would like to underline one of the central and perhaps most controversial questions this particular work poses in relation to the mother's desire: the possibility of female fetishism.

Sexual identity is said to be the outcome of a precarious passage called the Oedipus complex, a passage which is in a certain sense completed by the acceptance of symbolic castration. But castration is also inscribed at the level of the imaginary, that is in fantasy, and this is where the fetishistic scenario originates and is continually replayed. The child's recognition of difference between the mother and the father is above all an admission that the mother does not have the phallus. In this case seeing is not necessarily believing since what is at stake for the child is really the question of his or her own relation to having or being. Hence the fetishist, conventionally assumed to be male, postpones that moment of recognition, although certainly he has made the passage—he knows the difference, but denies it. In terms of representation, this denial is associated with a definite iconography of pornographic images where the man is reassured by the woman's possession of some form of phallic substitute or alternatively by the shape, the complete arrangement of her body. Yet the woman, in so far as the outcome of the oedipal moment has involved at some point a heterosexual object choice (that is, she has identified with her mother and has taken her father as a love object), will also postpone the recognition of lack in view of the promise of having the child. In having the child, in a sense she has the phallus. So the loss of the child is the loss of that symbolic plenitude—more exactly the ability to represent lack.

According to Freud, castration anxiety for the man is often expressed in fantasy as the loss of arms, legs, hair, teeth, eyes, or the penis itself. When he describes castration fears for the woman, this imaginary scenario takes the form of losing her loved objects, especially her children; the child is going to grow up, leave her, reject her, perhaps die. In order to delay, disavow, that separation she has already in a way acknowledged, the woman tends to fetishize the child: by dressing him up, by continuing to feed him no matter how old he gets, or simply by having another "little one." So perhaps in place of the more familiar notion of pornography, it is possible to talk about the mother's memorabilia—the way she saves things—first shoes, photographs, locks of hair or school reports. My work proceeds from this site; instead of first shoes, first words set out in type, stained liners, hand imprints, comforter fragments, drawings, writings or even the plants and insects that were his gifts; all these are intended to be seen as transitional objects; not in Winnicott's sense of surrogates but rather in Lacan's terms as *emblems* of desire. In one way, I have attempted to displace the potential fetishization of the child onto the work of art; but I have also tried to make it explicit in a way which would question the fetishistic nature of representation itself.

Now the publication of *Post-Partum Document* prompts another question: What is the difference between them—the "original" exhibition and its bookish offspring, what loss is sustained by their inevitable separation?

As an installation within a traditional gallery space, the work subscribes to certain modes of presentation; the framing, for example, parodies a familiar type of museum display in so far as it allows my archaeology of everyday life to slip unannounced into the great hall and ask impertinent questions of its keepers. This reading relies very heavily on the viewer's *affective* relation to the visual configuration of objects and texts. There will obviously be a loss of that kind of material specificity in viewing black and white reproductions, but what I have tried to retain, in place of an accurate record or photographic substitute for the "real object," is a certain texture, a sensibility associated with its function as *mnemic* trace. In this context, it made sense to lose the frames altogether, letting them slide towards the edge of the page, becoming the size and shape of the book itself; defined by different institutions, referred to other limits (I noted that an odd size is known in the trade as a "bastard").

Indeed an exhibition may not appear to be a legitimate parent for a book.

The authority of that work is so often grounded in academic discourses which define themselves precisely by their difference from artistic practices; by definite objects, reliable sources, and logical sequences; by being read from beginning to end. An exhibition takes place, but never so completely, not from cover to cover, except in the catalogue, which is exactly why the exhibition as a system (i.e., including its associated field of publications) should be the object of art criticism rather than the utopian notion of the individual tableau. Although it is subject to the constraints of a particular site, the exhibition as an intertextual system is potentially self-reflexive.

As an exhibition, the *Post-Partum Document* is intended to construct several readings or ways through the work, indicated by the juxtaposition of found objects and commentary with a series of diagrams. These diagrams, in turn, refer the viewer to another text entitled "Footnotes and Bibliography" where the framed material as such. In book form, however, the footnotes are interspersed with the illustrations in a way which tends to close that gap, to pull the visible more firmly into the space of the readable. Typographical variation was one way of attempting to avert that kind of closure, of trying to maintain the heterogeneity and openness of the "original" (mother?). I wanted to avoid setting up an opposition between image and text. Ideally, each should hold the possibility of becoming the other, or perhaps the same, that is, "writing."

Initially the reader will be caught up in the mother's story. The first person narrative describes particular events in my own relationship with my son, from birth until age five. Events such as weaning from the breast, learning to speak, starting school, writing; but *Post-Partum Document* is not simply about child development. It is an effort to articulate the mother's fantasies, her desire, her stake in that project called "motherhood." In this sense, too, it is not a traditional narrative; a problem is continually posed but no resolution is reached. There is only a replay of moments of separation and loss, perhaps because desire has no end, resists normalization, ignores biology, disperses the body.

Perhaps this is also why it seemed crucial, not in the sense of a moral imperative, but as a historical strategy, to avoid the literal figuration of mother and child, to avoid any means of representation which risked recuperation as "a slice of life." To use the body of the woman, her image or person is not impossible but problematic for feminism. In my work I have tried to cut across the predominant representation of woman as the object of the look in order to question the notion of femininity as a pregiven entity and to foreground instead its social construction as a representation of sexual difference within specific discourses. For me, this is not a new form of iconoclasm but a shared aspiration (truly postmodernist?) to "picture" the woman as subject of her own desire.

Although the mother's story is my story, *Post-Partum Document* is not an autobiography (nor do I think of this book as an artist's monograph). It suggests an interplay of voices—the mother's experience, feminist analysis, academic discussion, political debate. For instance, in the "Documentation" and "Experimentum Mentis" sections, the mode of address shifts to the third person. Here the Mother (she) is no longer so accessible, so replete (not someone who is like you, like you once were or would like to be). For the reader this implies a moment of separation (for some, perhaps an uncomfortable confrontation with the Father) or at least a "breathing space" in the text.

The "Documentation" notes began as an attempt to explain the empirical procedures adopted in individual works and probably ended up saying more about the inadequacy of those descriptive systems. One motive for appropriating a certain pseudoscientific language in this section was to counter the assumption that childcare is based on the woman's natural and instinctive understanding of the role of mothering.

This so-called "anti-essentialist" position is taken up (with a vengeance?) in the "Experimentum Mentis" section, where maternal femininity is drawn from the perspective of Freudian and Lacanian psychoanalysis. Some readers will undoubtedly ask, why Freud, why Lacan? Why endorse their "patriarchal" authority? In one way, for me these texts are a means of working through a difficult experience—secondary revision, in the psychoanalytic sense. This is not exactly a recourse to rationality as authority. It expresses a more fundamental desire to know and to master.

Even, or especially, when I use something as eccentric as the Lacanian diagrams, they are first of all images, representations of the difficulty of the symbolic order for women; the difficulty of representing lack, of accepting castration, of not having the phallus, of not being the Phallic Mother (which is finally as significant in that order as the Dead Father). They are like blazons of a love-hate relationship with the Father (Phallic Mother?) cathected as much, perhaps more, than the memorabilia.

At the same time, I realize that these texts have other implications. They are metadiscursive. They assume a certain knowledge based on readings of and debates around specific articles. The writing is not explicitly polemical and the sources may seem somewhat ambiguous, but the reader will find that they are sited in the reference section with a key indicating the relevant "Documentation" or "Experimentum Mentis" section.

Freud's 1914 essay "On Narcissism: An Introduction," together with my reading of Lacan's "Signification of the Phallus," determined the *Document's* central concern with the mother's desire as desire for the child to be the phallus, and the coincident trajectory of narcissistic identification through which her imaginary stake is articulated. Lacan's exposition of the two end-points of the mirror phase was crucial to my understanding of the events referred to in the first two sections: "Weaning from the Breast" and "Weaning from the Holophrase." The third section, "Weaning from the Dyad" relied especially on Maud Mannoni's view of the importance of the mother's words (that is, above all, her reference to the father) in *The Child, His Illness and the Others*. Sections IV and V, "On Femininity" and "On the Order of Things," were centrally concerned with the representation of loss, not only as loss of the child but also as loss of the maternal body, and were profoundly influenced by Michele Montrelay's "Inquiry into Femininity." In the final section, "On the Insistence of the Letter," an analysis of the child's prewriting posed certain problems concerning the phonocentric (perhaps even logocentric) bias underlying notions of language derived from Jakobson's linguistics and prompted me to consider ideas which were more tangential to Lacan's, for instance Klein's essay on "The Early Stages of the Oedipus Complex." Once again there is a progression but no resolution, a theoretical elaboration but not necessarily a consistent argument (a Symbolic but "full of holes"); and here the reader will undoubtedly discover that another story unfolds, not simply my story, or the mother's story, but a kind of chronicle of feminist debate within the women's movement in Great Britain during the 1970s. The terms of my analysis are those of definite tendencies at particular moments in that history.

At the time of writing the "introduction" to the *Post-Partum Document*, in 1973, the problem of "the feminine psychology of the mother" seemed to be posed as if it were an effect of the sexual division of labor; but there was also an insistence on the "reciprocity of the process of socialization," which suggested that the notion of "subjectivity," especially one founded on Freud's theory of the unconscious, might displace the more familiar rhetoric of "ideological oppression" as indeed it eventually did. Juliet Mitchell introduced that position in *Women's Estate* and consolidated it with *Psychoanalysis and Feminism*. By the time "Experimentum Mentis I, II and III" were written in 1976, the Lacanian rereading of Freud was underway. The Patriarchy Conference in London that same year clearly indicated that the debate had shifted from the terms of sexual division to the question of sexual difference. Some readers will regard such formulations as "negative entry" or "negative place" with scepticism (or perhaps nostalgia?) but will recall the context and our first attempts to articulate a different relation to language (and to castration) for women without subscribing to the essentialist notions of a separate symbolic order altogether. In "Experimentum Mentis IV and V," 1977, those terms (and the arguments which implied that "the feminine" position was ultimately transgressive) as well as the problematic concept of patriarchy itself were abandoned. (Significantly, that year the feminist journal *m/f* was founded in order to take up and extend such debates.)

Instead the question of representation was foregrounded. On the one hand, it referred to the ideological, that is, "femininity" understood as the representation of difference produced within specific discourses, or social practices; on the other, it was used in the psychoanalytic sense as the representation of the drives with respect to aims and objects, that is "the feminine" understood as the subject's position in language, symbolic castration defined as the representation of loss.

But at this point, certain feminists began to worry about another kind of loss—losing sight of the "social," in the end, failing to understand the political relevance of the personal. Were we suggesting in some way that the psychic was the truth of the social? Could psychoanalysis simply become another political orthodoxy? By 1979, when the last part of the *Document* was completed, the movement's founding slogan "the personal is political" had been through the theoretical mill, first formulated as the subjective moment of women's oppression, then dispersed as the question of positionality in language, and finally making a reappearance in the form of the "relation between the psychic and the social." The notes to "Documentation VI" attempted to address this problem by describing the construction of the agency of the mother/housewife within the institution of the school. Yet the psychoanalytic discourse of "Experimentum Mentis VI" was unable to articulate exactly what, for instance, "social deprivation" meant in terms of the psychic economy of the mother. Perhaps there is no "relation," only "the social." If the psychic is neither outside of it nor the truth of it, but simply another level of the social inscription of subjects, then is it one which necessarily constitutes an autonomous object of discourse? Problems remain. The debate continues. The *Post-Partum Document* tells that story. For this reason I left the notes as they were originally written: to allow the gaps and inconsistencies as well as the insights to describe a process of reworking which was at the same time a shared history and to let it speak, in a certain way, for our desire to understand and change our lives.

Mary Kelly
London
1982

PPD 1973

Introduction

IN THE POST-PARTUM DOCUMENT, I AM TRYING TO SHOW THE RECIPROCITY OF THE PROCESS OF SOCIALIZATION IN THE FIRST FEW YEARS OF LIFE. IT IS NOT ONLY THE INFANT WHOSE FUTURE PERSONALITY IS FORMED AT THIS CRUCIAL MOMENT, BUT ALSO THE MOTHER WHOSE "FEMININE PSYCHOLOGY" IS SEALED BY THE SEXUAL DIVISION OF LABOR IN CHILDCARE.

The sexual division of labor is not a symmetrically structured system of women inside the home, men outside it, but rather an intricate, most often asymmetrical, delegation of tasks which aims to provide a structural imperative to heterosexuality. The most obvious example of this asymmetry is that of women engaged in social production or services who are still held socially responsible for maintaining labor power (i.e. males and children). But even more significant is the fact that the nuclear family form, under capitalism, requires more participation by fathers in housework and childcare while insisting on the social sexual division of labor. The last stronghold of the heterosexual imperative is therefore infant care. Certain tasks such as bathing, changing and attending in the night remain almost exclusively female. Yet the specificity of this labor is essential to the reproduction of the relations of production, in so far as the monolithic mother-child relationship which it welds becomes the basic structure upon which adult socialization is founded.

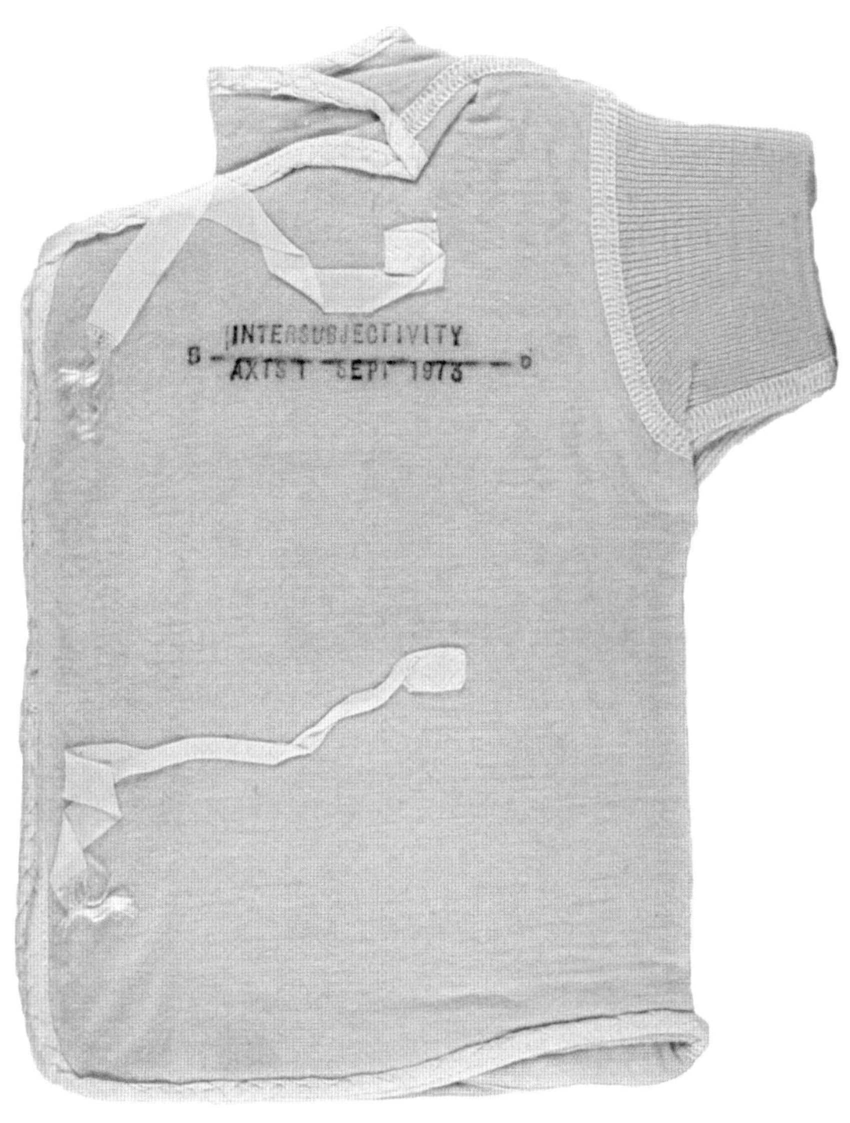
INTERSUBJECTIVITY
AXTST SEPT 1973

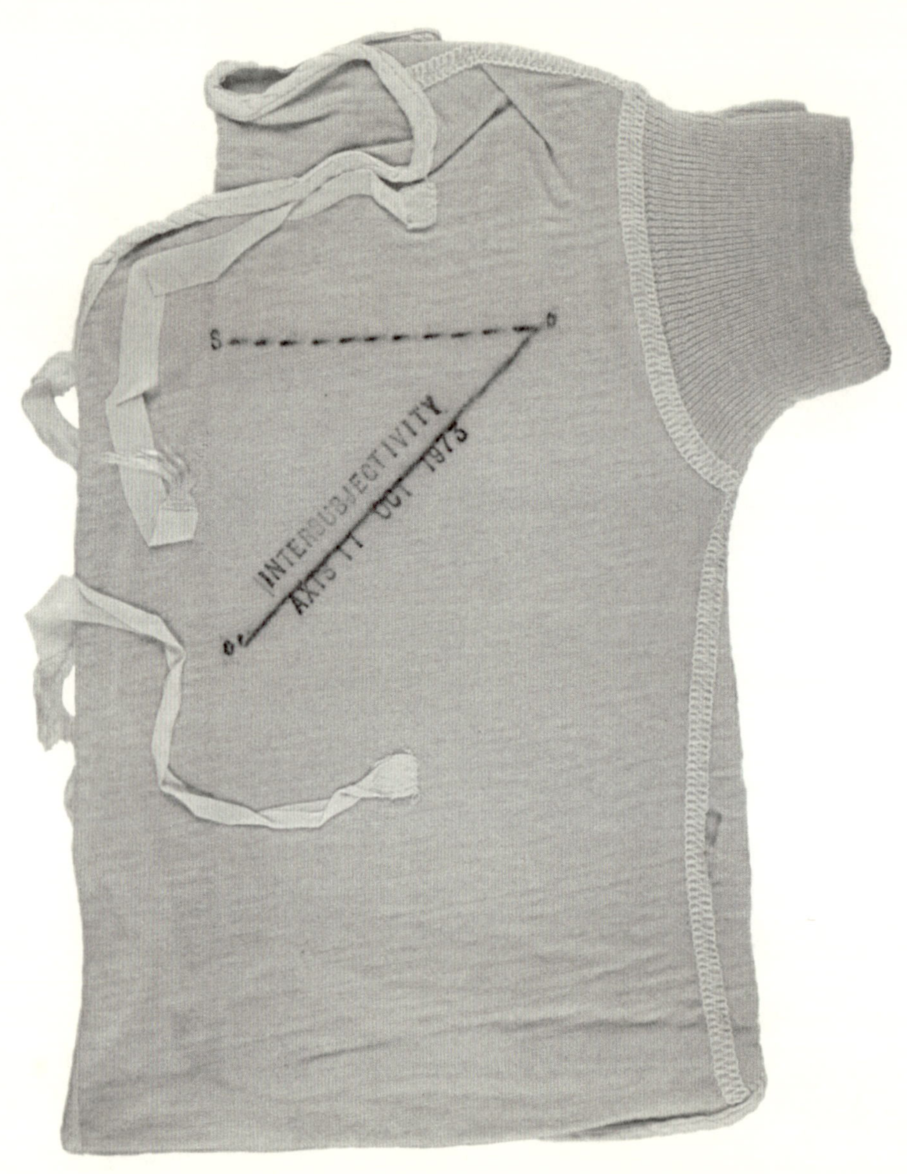
S
INTERSUBJECTIVITY
AXIS 11 OCT 1973

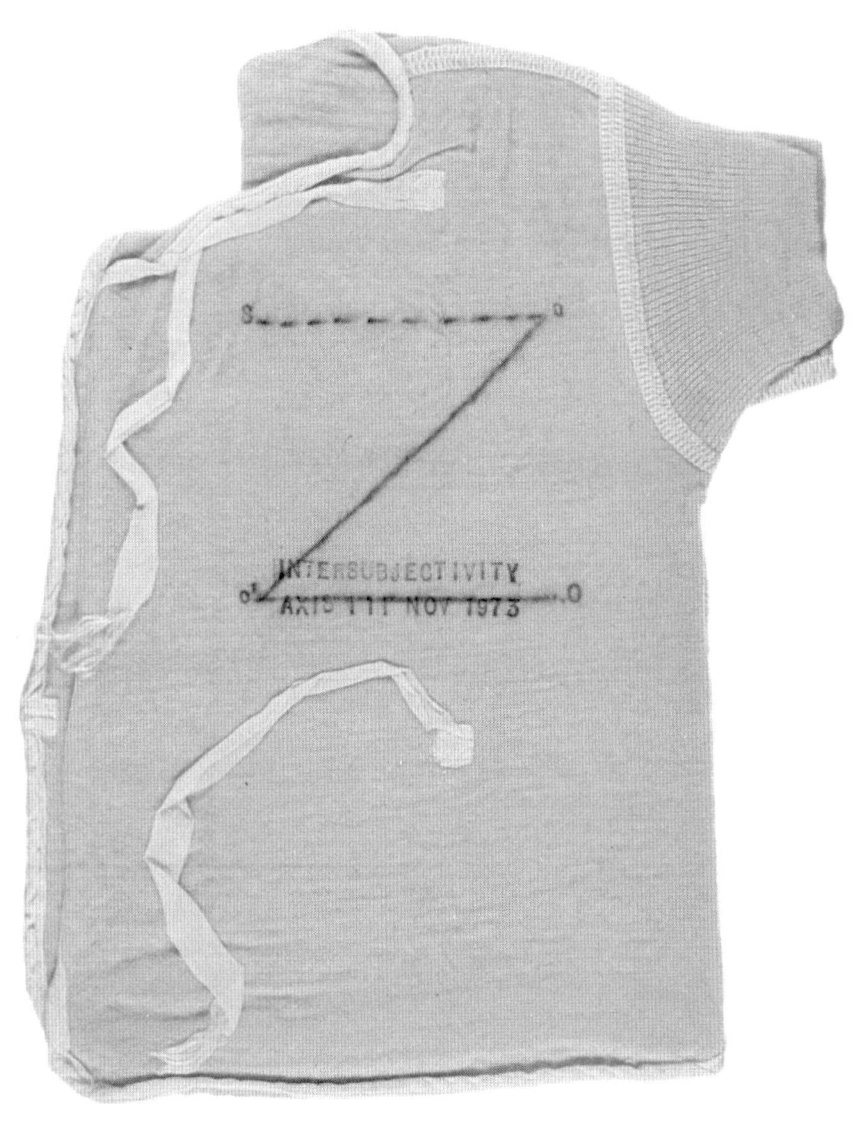
S
a
INTERSUBJECTIVITY
AXIS 1 11 NOV 1973
O

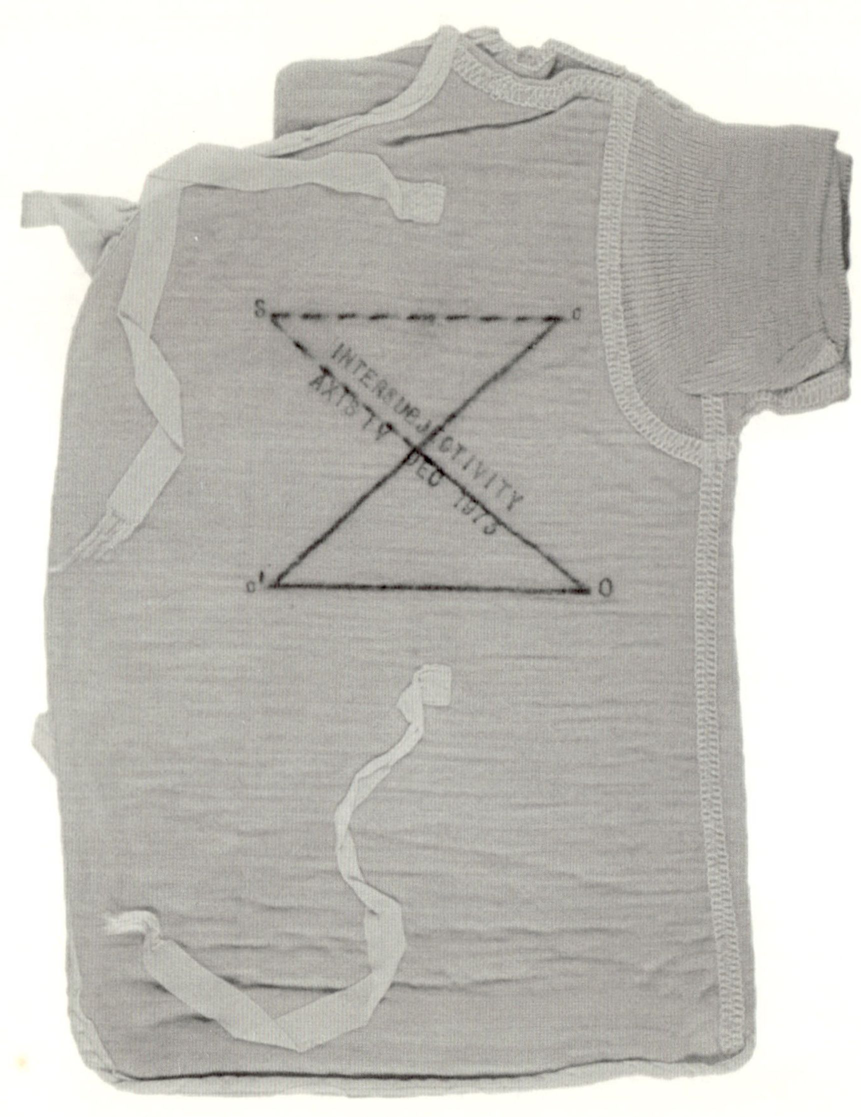
S
a
INTERSUBJECTIVITY
AXIS
DEC
a'
O

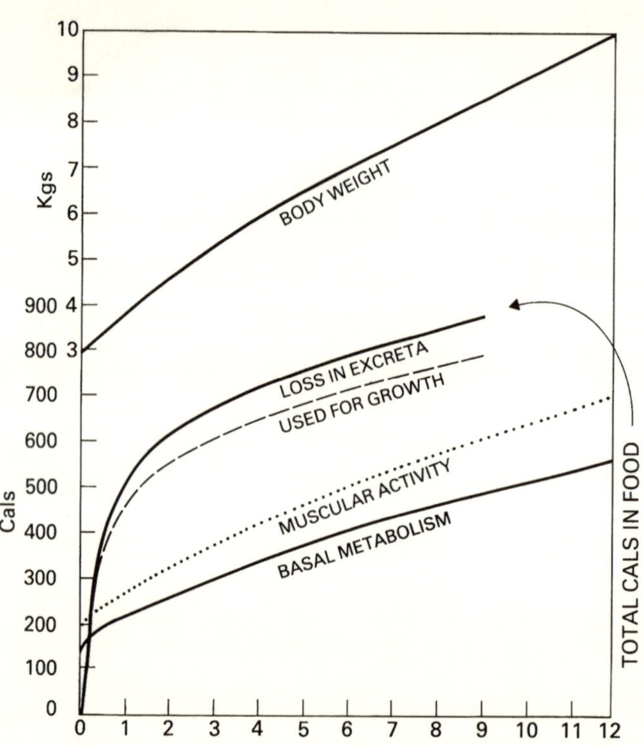

Kgs
Cals
BODY WEIGHT
LOSS IN EXCRETA
USED FOR GROWTH
MUSCULAR ACTIVITY
BASAL METABOLISM
TOTAL CALS IN FOOD
10
9
8
7
6
5
900 4
800 3
700
600
500
400
300
200
100
0
0 1 2 3 4 5 6 7 8 9 10 11 12

Documentation I
Analysed Fecal Stains and Feeding Charts

The feeding, changing process was recorded over a period of three months, January to March 1974. February, the infant's sixth month, was presented in this document because it represented the interval of most rapid change. The total amount of solids taken on February 1 was 8 tsps and on February 28 it was 30 tsps. This corresponded to a gain in weight from 16 lbs $10\frac{1}{2}$ ozs to 18 lbs $2\frac{1}{2}$ ozs. In the document on exhibition, the infant's daily nutritional intake was correlated with his stools, i.e. the stained liners, and these were analyzed according to the following key:

01 Constipated
02 Normal
03 Not Homogeneous
04 Loose
05 Diarrheal

Growth in a given genus is proportional to the potential energy of the food consumed. An infant of seven months is only able to dispose of 13 per cent of food energy for growth, the rest being lost in excreta. The introduction of solid foods is a dramatic event in so far as putrefactive organisms are consequently introduced into the essentially sterile intestinal tract of the newborn infant. Hence, the exact character of the feces of a normal infant will depend upon: (1) the kind of food and the completeness of digestion; (2) the amount of putrefaction or fermentation; (3) the amount of bile secreted; (4) the amount of fat and water remaining unabsorbed.

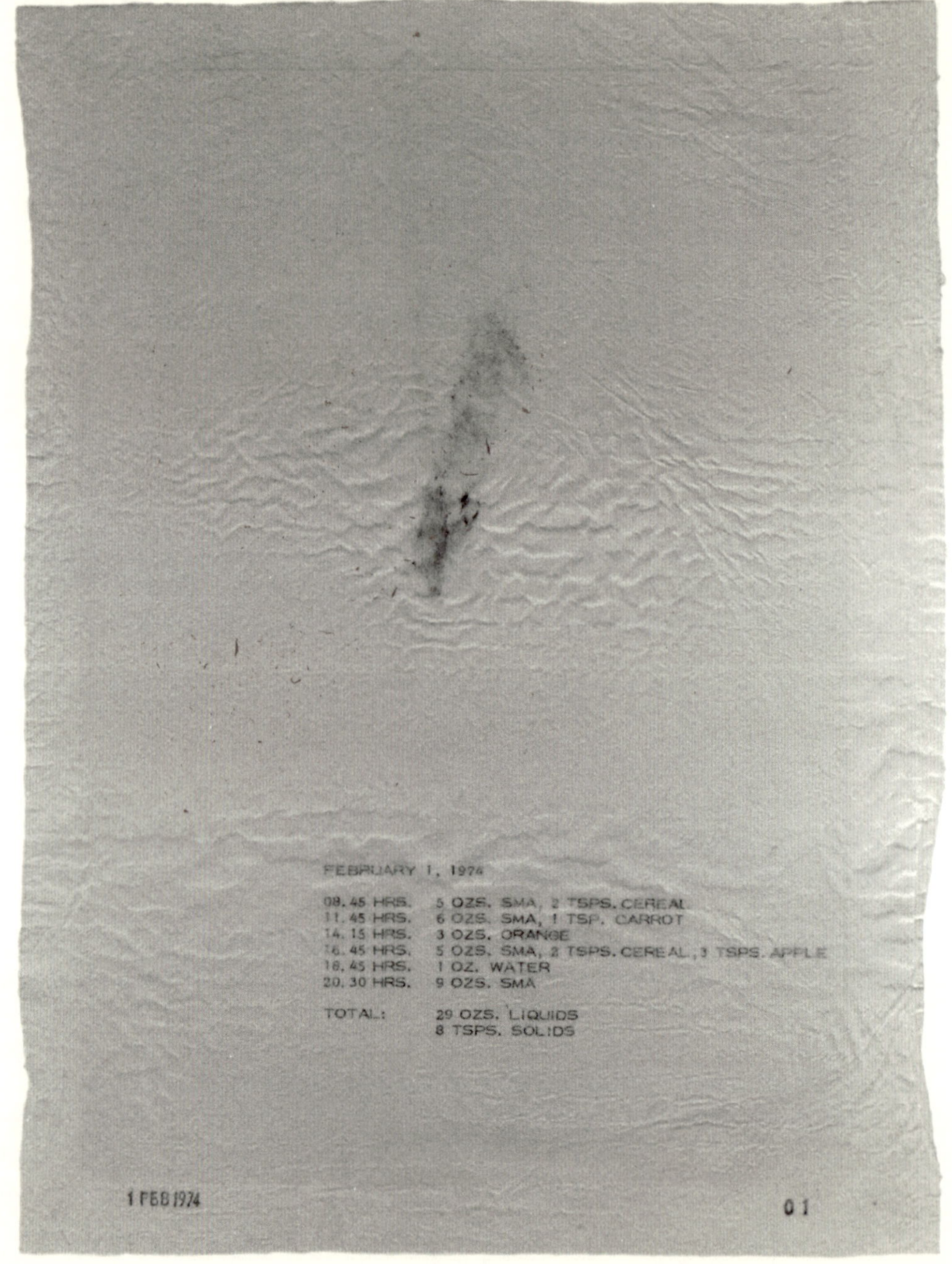
FEBRUARY 1, 1974
08.45 HRS. 5 OZS. SMA, 2 TSPS. CEREAL
11.45 HRS. 6 OZS. SMA, 1 TSP. CARROT
14.15 HRS. 3 OZS. ORANGE
16.45 HRS. 5 OZS. SMA, 2 TSPS. CEREAL, 3 TSPS. APPLE
18.45 HRS. 1 OZ. WATER
20.30 HRS. 9 OZS. SMA
TOTAL: 29 OZS. LIQUIDS
8 TSPS. SOLIDS
1 FEB 1974
0 1

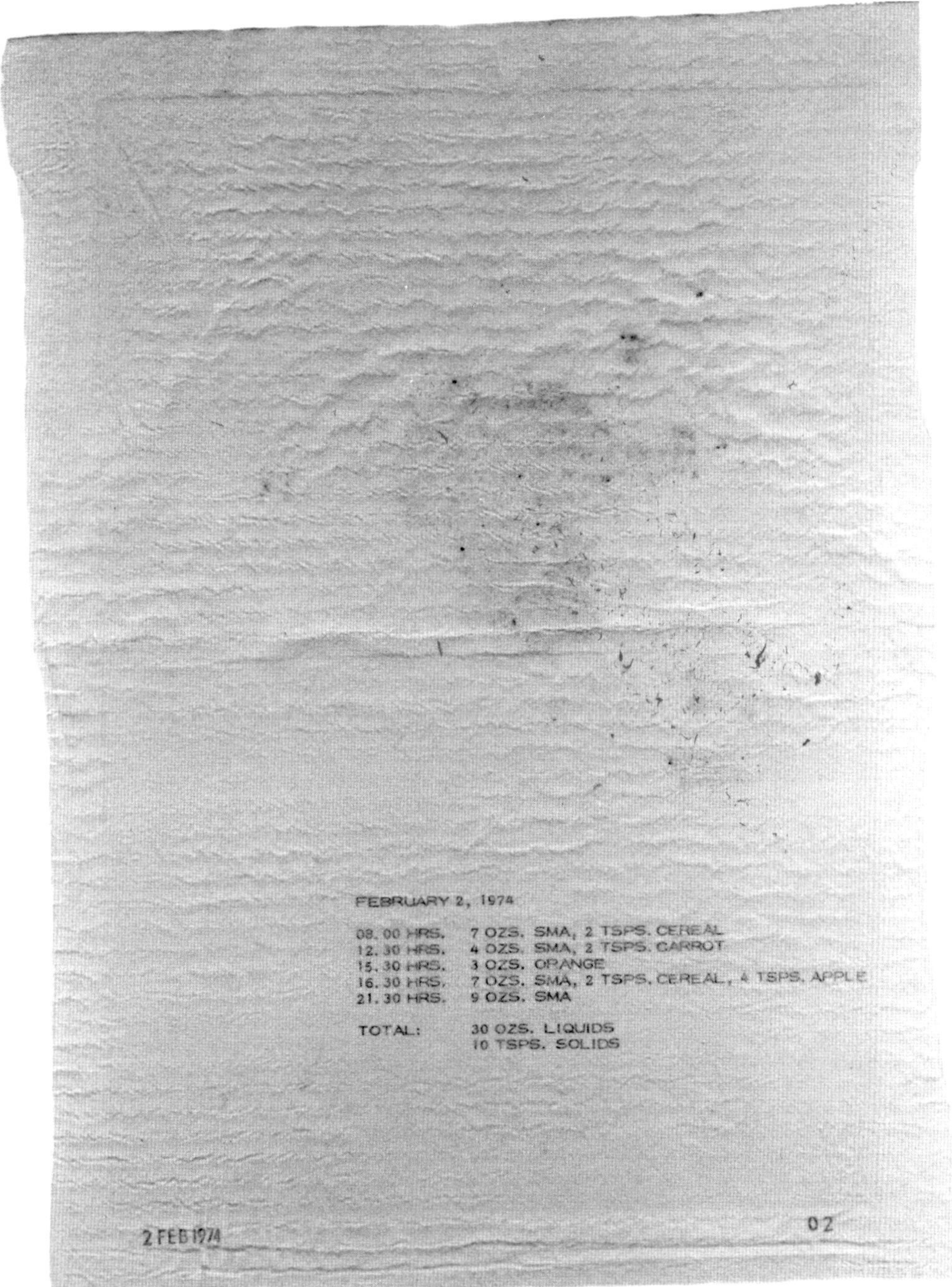

FEBRUARY 2, 1974

08.00 HRS. 7 OZS. SMA, 2 TSPS. CEREAL
12.30 HRS. 4 OZS. SMA, 2 TSPS. CARROT
15.30 HRS. 3 OZS. ORANGE
16.30 HRS. 7 OZS. SMA, 2 TSPS. CEREAL, 4 TSPS. APPLE
21.30 HRS. 9 OZS. SMA

TOTAL: 30 OZS. LIQUIDS
10 TSPS. SOLIDS

2 FEB 1974 02

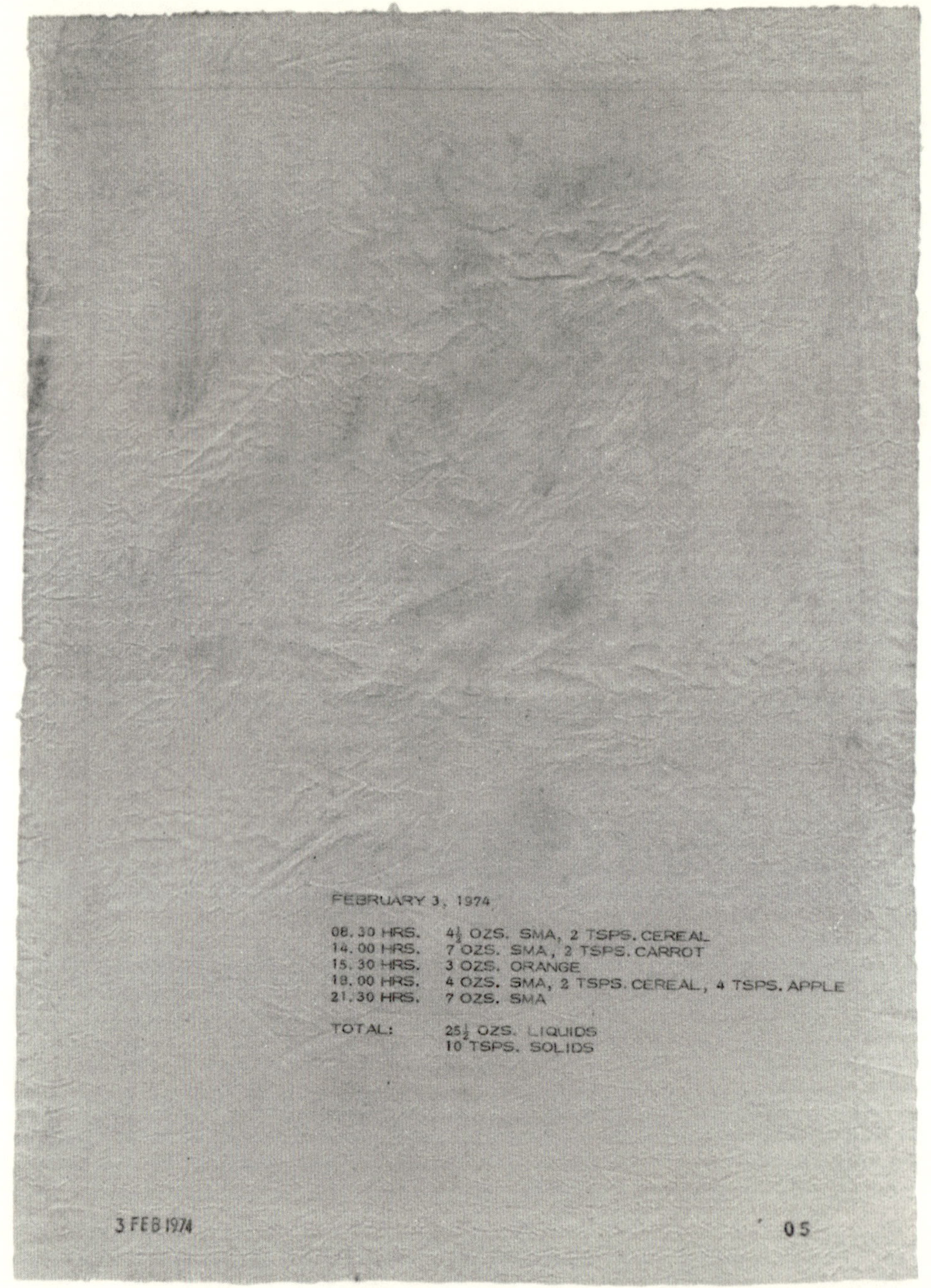
FEBRUARY 3, 1974
08.30 HRS. 4½ OZS. SMA, 2 TSPS. CEREAL
14.00 HRS. 7 OZS. SMA, 2 TSPS. CARROT
15.30 HRS. 3 OZS. ORANGE
18.00 HRS. 4 OZS. SMA, 2 TSPS. CEREAL, 4 TSPS. APPLE
21.30 HRS. 7 OZS. SMA
TOTAL: 25½ OZS. LIQUIDS
10 TSPS. SOLIDS
3 FEB 1974
05

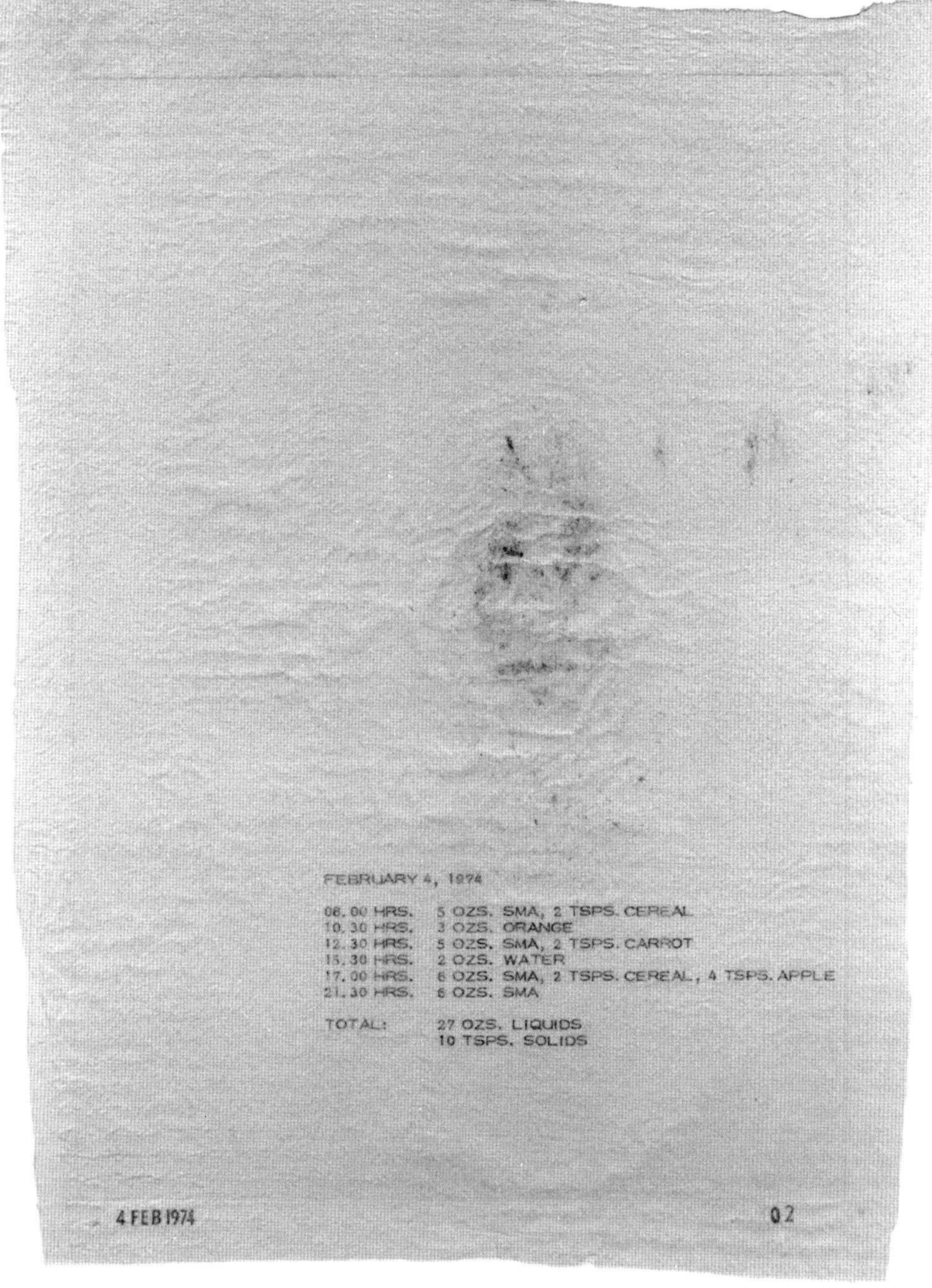
FEBRUARY 4, 1974
06.00 HRS. 5 OZS. SMA, 2 TSPS. CEREAL
10.30 HRS. 3 OZS. ORANGE
12.30 HRS. 5 OZS. SMA, 2 TSPS. CARROT
15.30 HRS. 2 OZS. WATER
17.00 HRS. 6 OZS. SMA, 2 TSPS. CEREAL, 4 TSPS. APPLE
21.30 HRS. 6 OZS. SMA
TOTAL: 27 OZS. LIQUIDS
10 TSPS. SOLIDS
4 FEB 1974
02

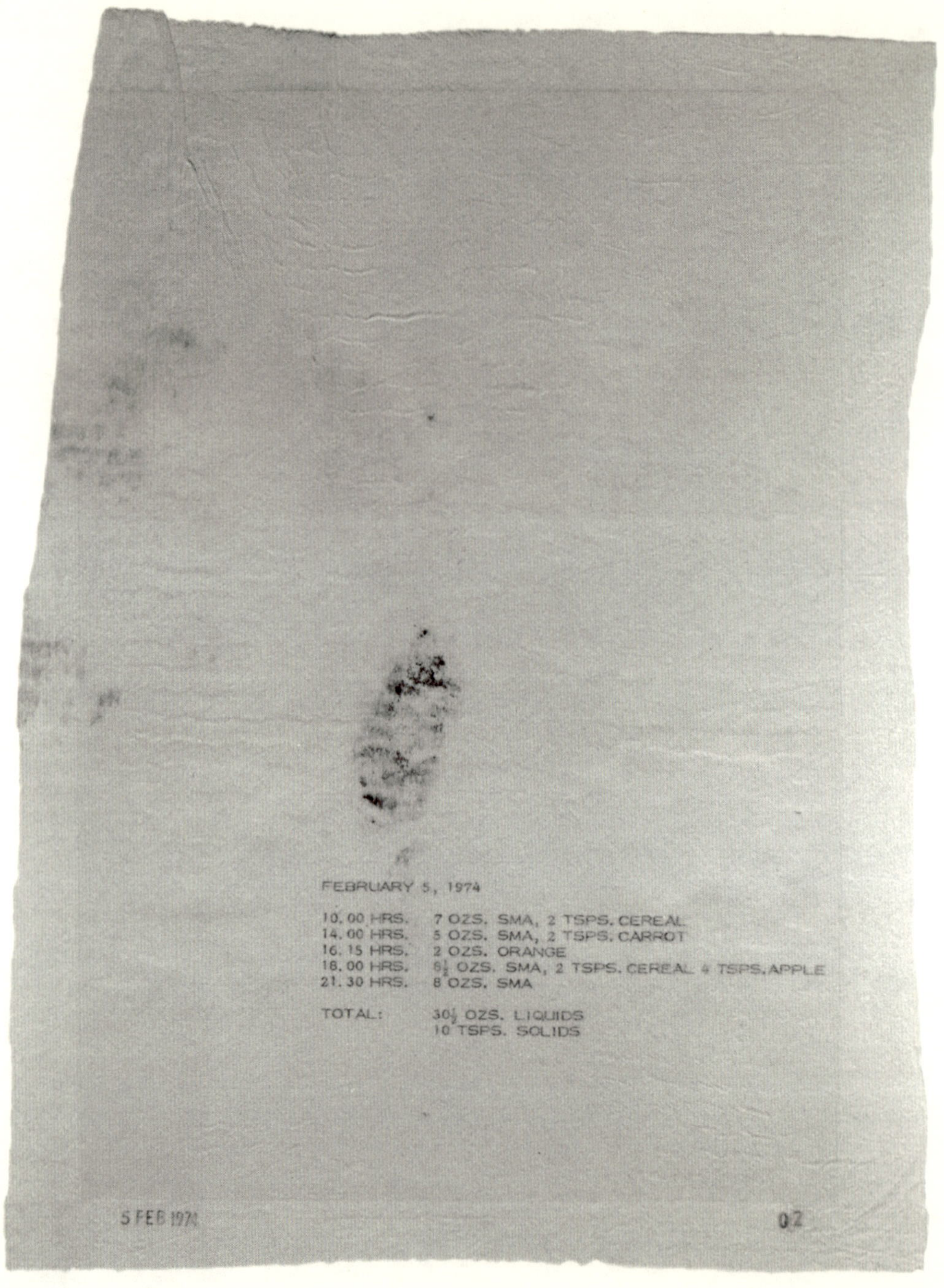
FEBRUARY 5, 1974
10.00 HRS. 7 OZS. SMA, 2 TSPS. CEREAL
14.00 HRS. 5 OZS. SMA, 2 TSPS. CARROT
16.15 HRS. 2 OZS. ORANGE
18.00 HRS. 6½ OZS. SMA, 2 TSPS. CEREAL 4 TSPS. APPLE
21.30 HRS. 8 OZS. SMA
TOTAL: 30½ OZS. LIQUIDS
10 TSPS. SOLIDS
5 FEB 1974
02

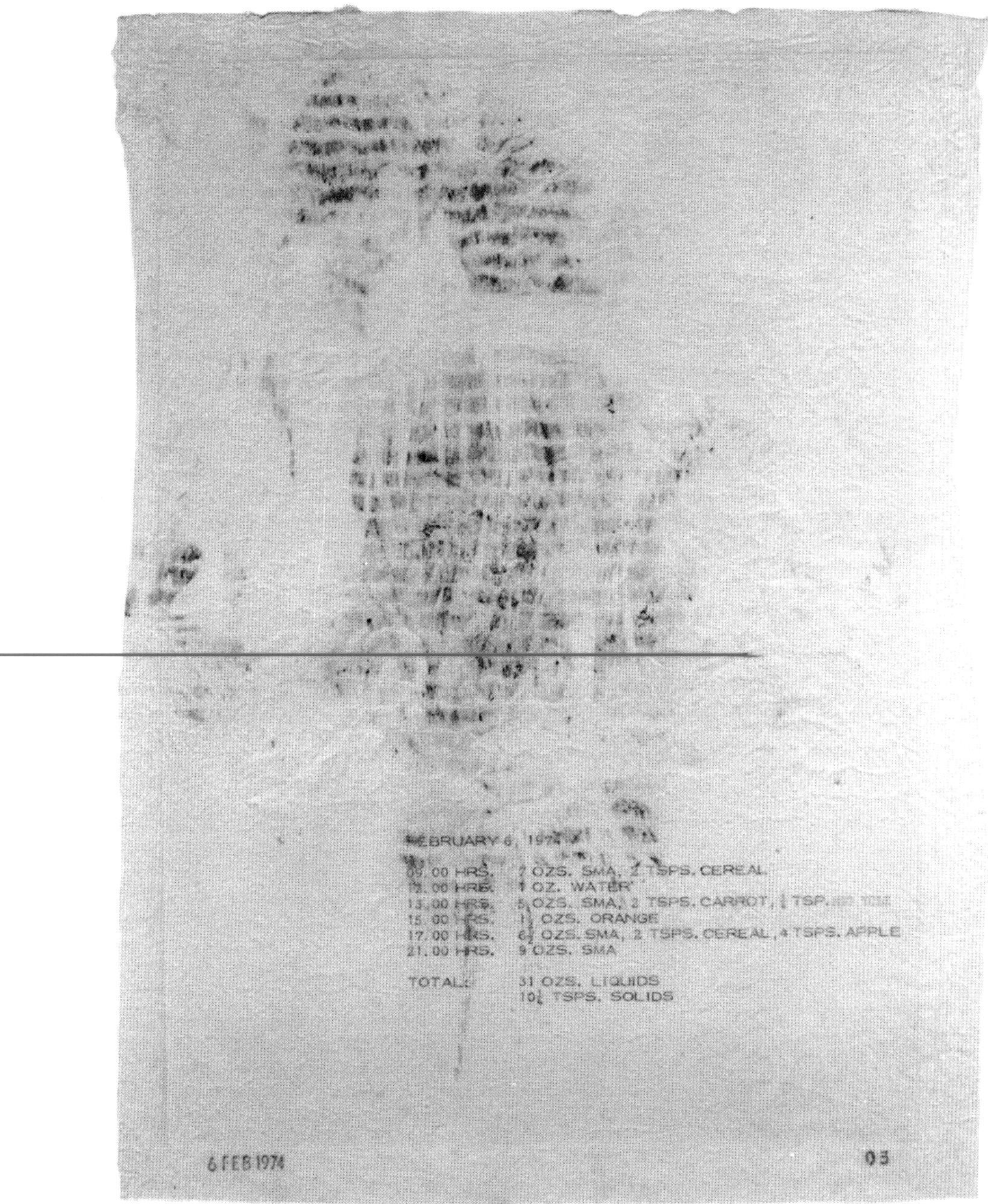
FEBRUARY 6, 1974
09.00 HRS. 7 OZS. SMA, 2 TSPS. CEREAL
12.00 HRS. 1 OZ. WATER
13.00 HRS. 5 OZS. SMA, 2 TSPS. CARROT, ¼ TSP.
15.00 HRS. 1½ OZS. ORANGE
17.00 HRS. 6½ OZS. SMA, 2 TSPS. CEREAL, 4 TSPS. APPLE
21.00 HRS. 9 OZS. SMA
TOTAL: 31 OZS. LIQUIDS
10¼ TSPS. SOLIDS
6 FEB 1974
03

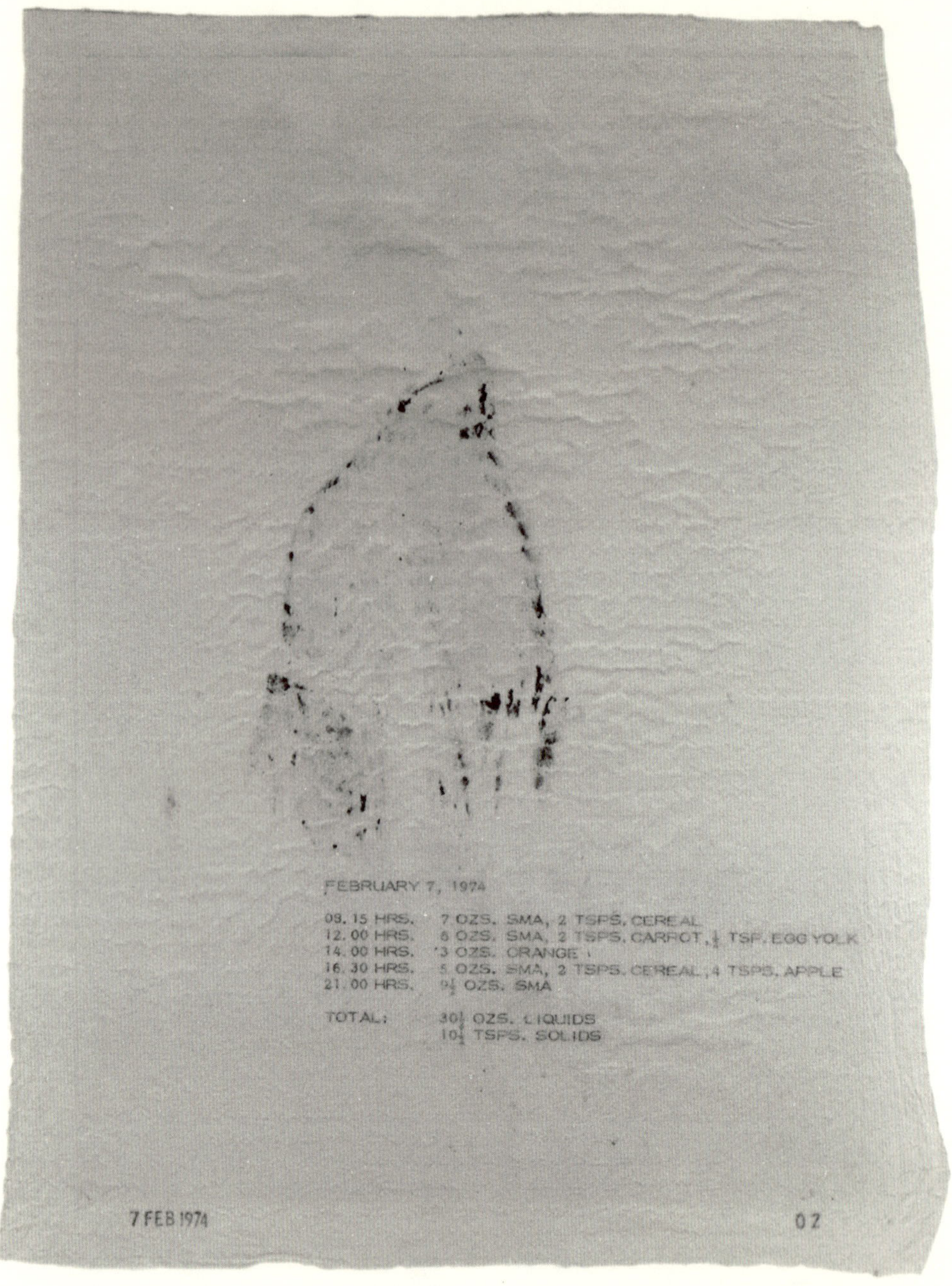
FEBRUARY 7, 1974
08.15 HRS. 7 OZS. SMA, 2 TSPS. CEREAL
12.00 HRS. 6 OZS. SMA, 2 TSPS. CARROT, ½ TSP. EGG YOLK
14.00 HRS. 3 OZS. ORANGE
16.30 HRS. 5 OZS. SMA, 2 TSPS. CEREAL, 4 TSPS. APPLE
21.00 HRS. 9½ OZS. SMA
TOTAL: 30½ OZS. LIQUIDS
10½ TSPS. SOLIDS
7 FEB 1974
O Z

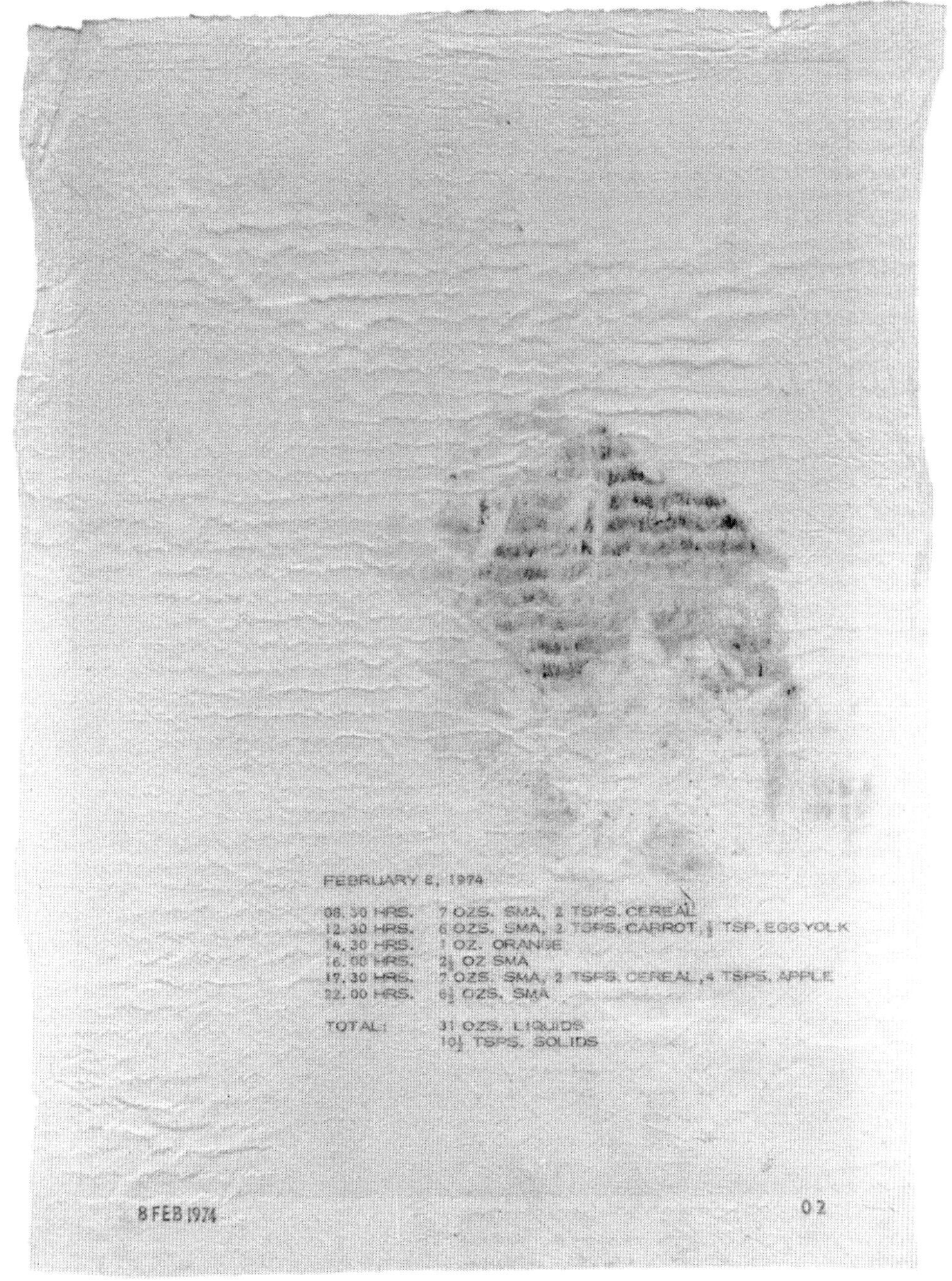

FEBRUARY 8, 1974

08.30 HRS.	7 OZS. SMA, 2 TSPS. CEREAL
12.30 HRS.	6 OZS. SMA, 2 TSPS. CARROT, ½ TSP. EGG YOLK
14.30 HRS.	1 OZ. ORANGE
16.00 HRS.	2½ OZ SMA
17.30 HRS.	7 OZS. SMA, 2 TSPS. CEREAL, 4 TSPS. APPLE
22.00 HRS.	6½ OZS. SMA
TOTAL:	31 OZS. LIQUIDS
	10½ TSPS. SOLIDS

8 FEB 1974

02

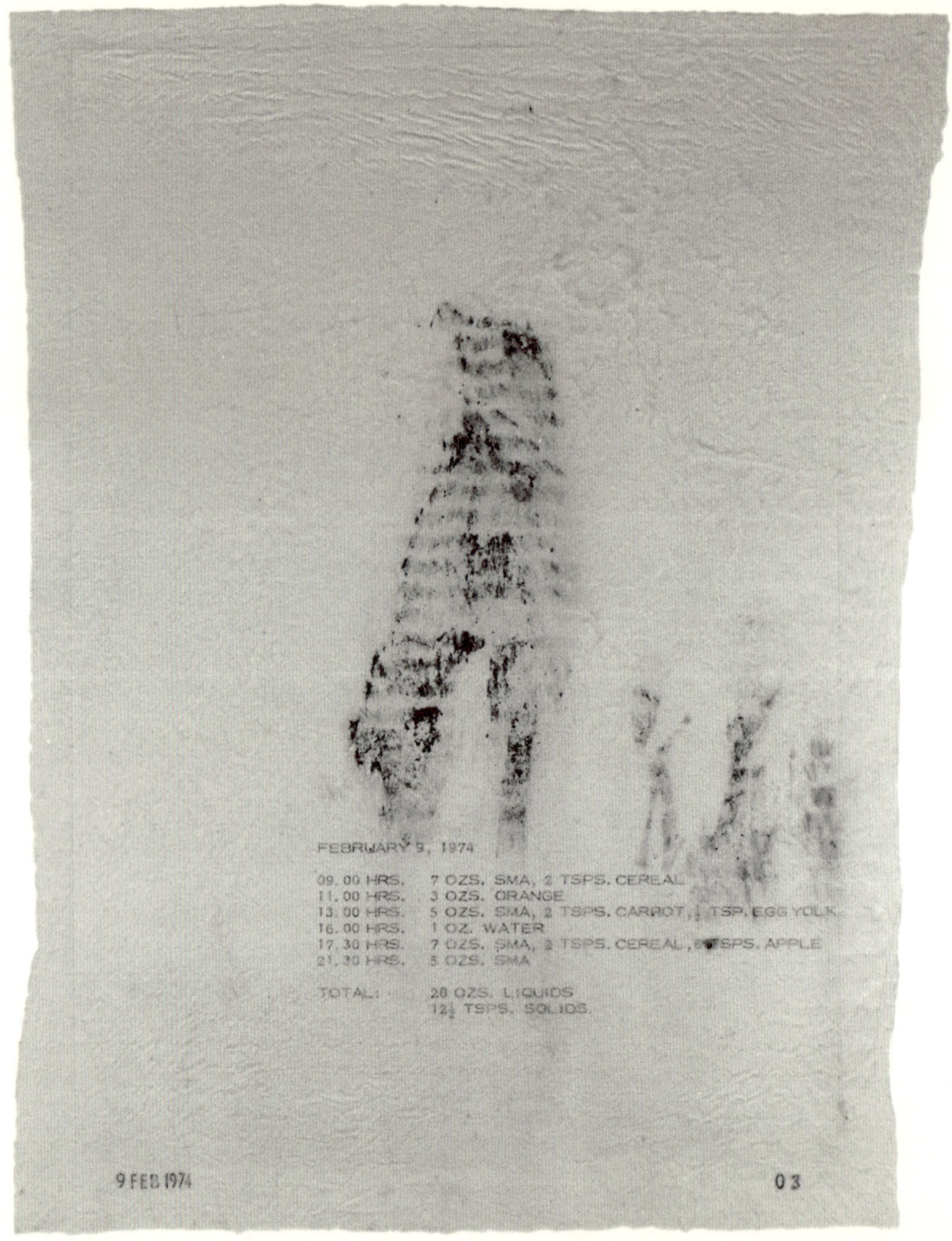
FEBRUARY 9, 1974
09.00 HRS. 7 OZS. SMA, 2 TSPS. CEREAL
11.00 HRS. 3 OZS. ORANGE
13.00 HRS. 5 OZS. SMA, 2 TSPS. CARROT, ½ TSP. EGG YOLK
16.00 HRS. 1 OZ. WATER
17.30 HRS. 7 OZS. SMA, 2 TSPS. CEREAL, 6 TSPS. APPLE
21.30 HRS. 5 OZS. SMA
TOTAL: 28 OZS. LIQUIDS
12½ TSPS. SOLIDS.
9 FEB 1974
03

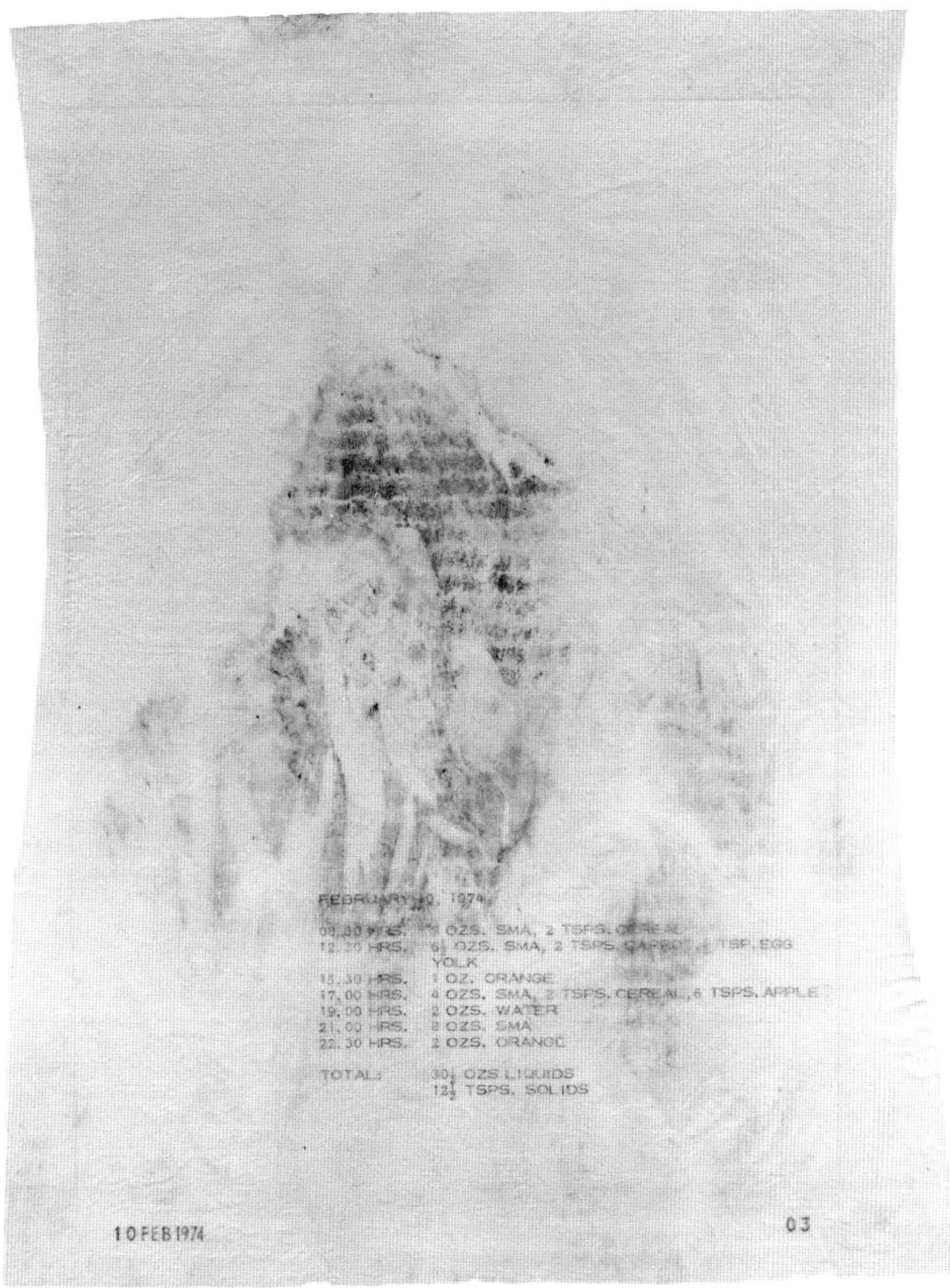
FEBRUARY 10, 1974
OZS. SMA, 2 TSPS.
12.30 HRS. 6½ OZS. SMA, 2 TSPS. TSP. EGG
YOLK
15.30 HRS. 1 OZ. ORANGE
17.00 HRS. 4 OZS. SMA, TSPS. CEREAL, 6 TSPS. APPLE
19.00 HRS. 2 OZS. WATER
21.00 HRS. 8 OZS. SMA
22.30 HRS. 2 OZS. ORANGE
TOTAL: 30½ OZS LIQUIDS
12½ TSPS. SOLIDS
10 FEB 1974
03

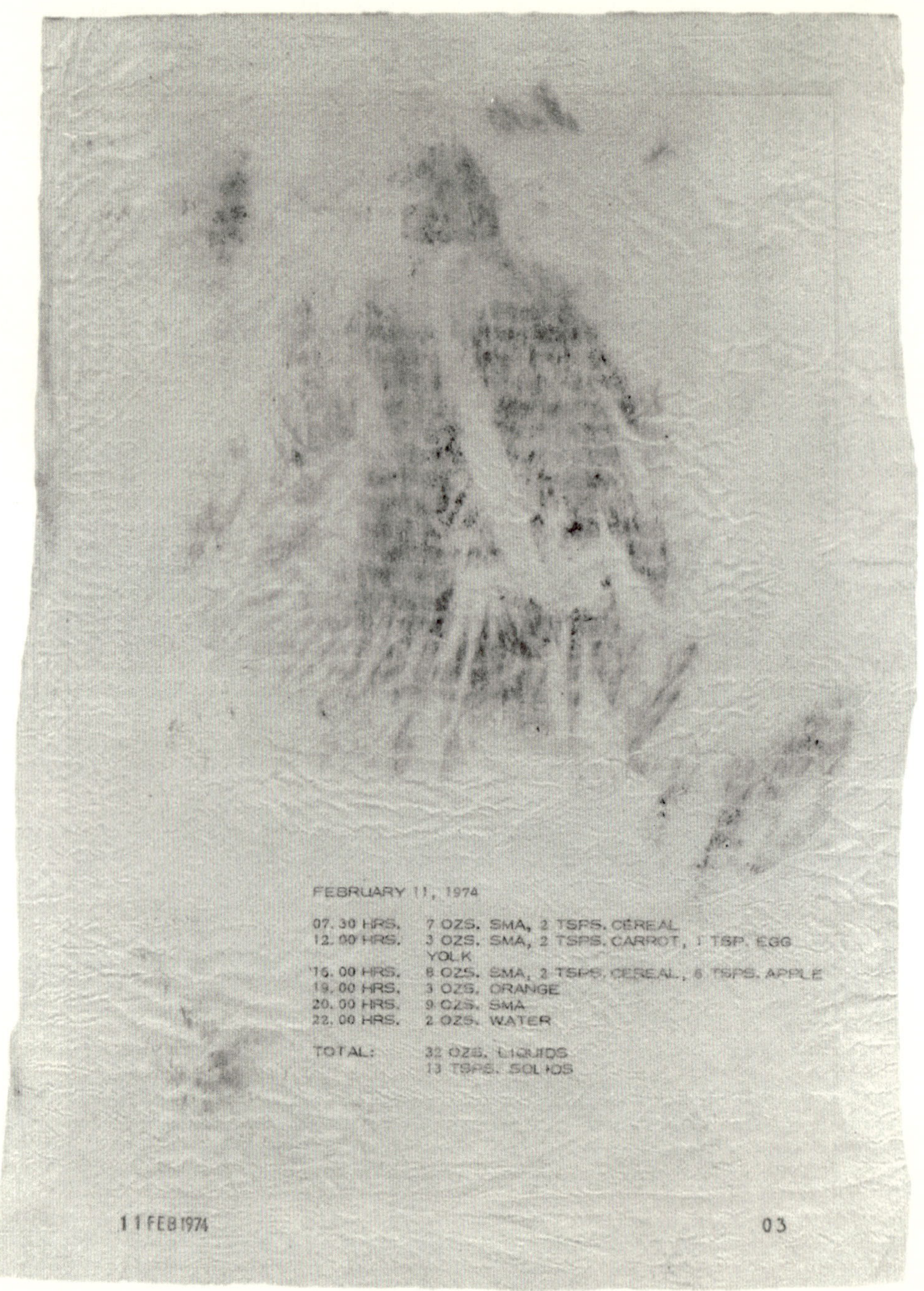
FEBRUARY 11, 1974
07. 30 HRS. 7 OZS. SMA, 2 TSPS. CEREAL
12. 00 HRS. 3 OZS. SMA, 2 TSPS. CARROT, 1 TSP. EGG
YOLK
16. 00 HRS. 8 OZS. SMA, 2 TSPS. CEREAL, 6 TSPS. APPLE
19. 00 HRS. 3 OZS. ORANGE
20. 00 HRS. 9 OZS. SMA
22. 00 HRS. 2 OZS. WATER
TOTAL: 32 OZS. LIQUIDS
13 TSPS. SOLIDS
11 FEB 1974
03

FEBRUARY 12, 1974
07.30 HRS. 5 OZS. SMA, 2 TSPS. CEREAL
09.30 HRS. 3 OZS. ORANGE
12.45 HRS. 4 OZS. SMA, 2 TSPS. CARROT, 1 TSP. EGG YOLK
16.30 HRS. 7 OZS. SMA, 2 TSPS. CEREAL, 6 TSPS. APPLE
20.30 HRS. 9 OZS. SMA
21.30 HRS. 1½ OZS. WATER
TOTAL: 29½ OZS. LIQUIDS
13 TSPS. SOLIDS
12 FEB 1974
04

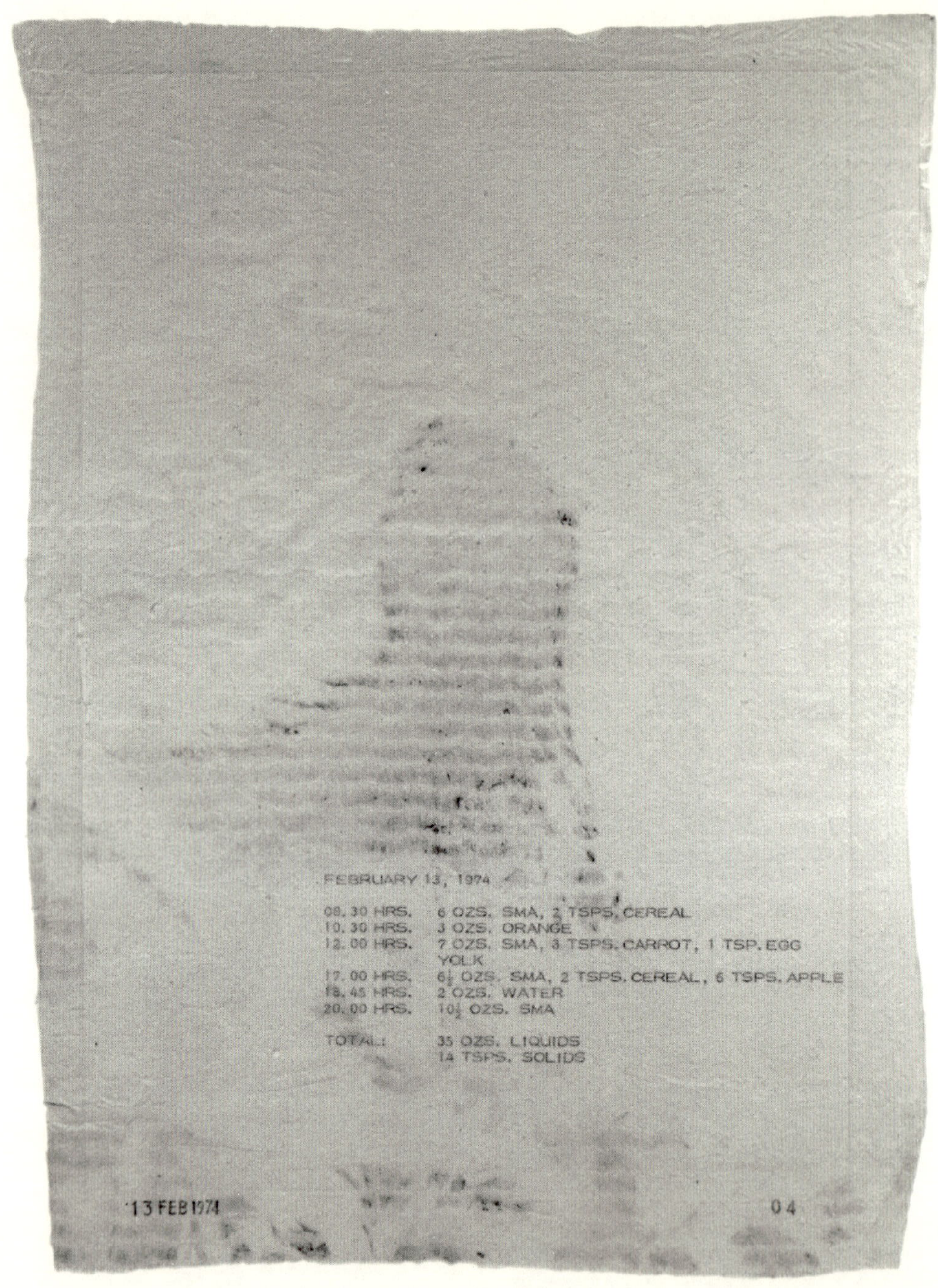

FEBRUARY 13, 1974

08.30 HRS.	6 OZS. SMA, 2 TSPS. CEREAL
10.30 HRS.	3 OZS. ORANGE
12.00 HRS.	7 OZS. SMA, 3 TSPS. CARROT, 1 TSP. EGG YOLK
17.00 HRS.	$6\frac{1}{2}$ OZS. SMA, 2 TSPS. CEREAL, 6 TSPS. APPLE
18.45 HRS.	2 OZS. WATER
20.00 HRS.	$10\frac{1}{2}$ OZS. SMA
TOTAL:	35 OZS. LIQUIDS
	14 TSPS. SOLIDS

13 FEB 1974 04

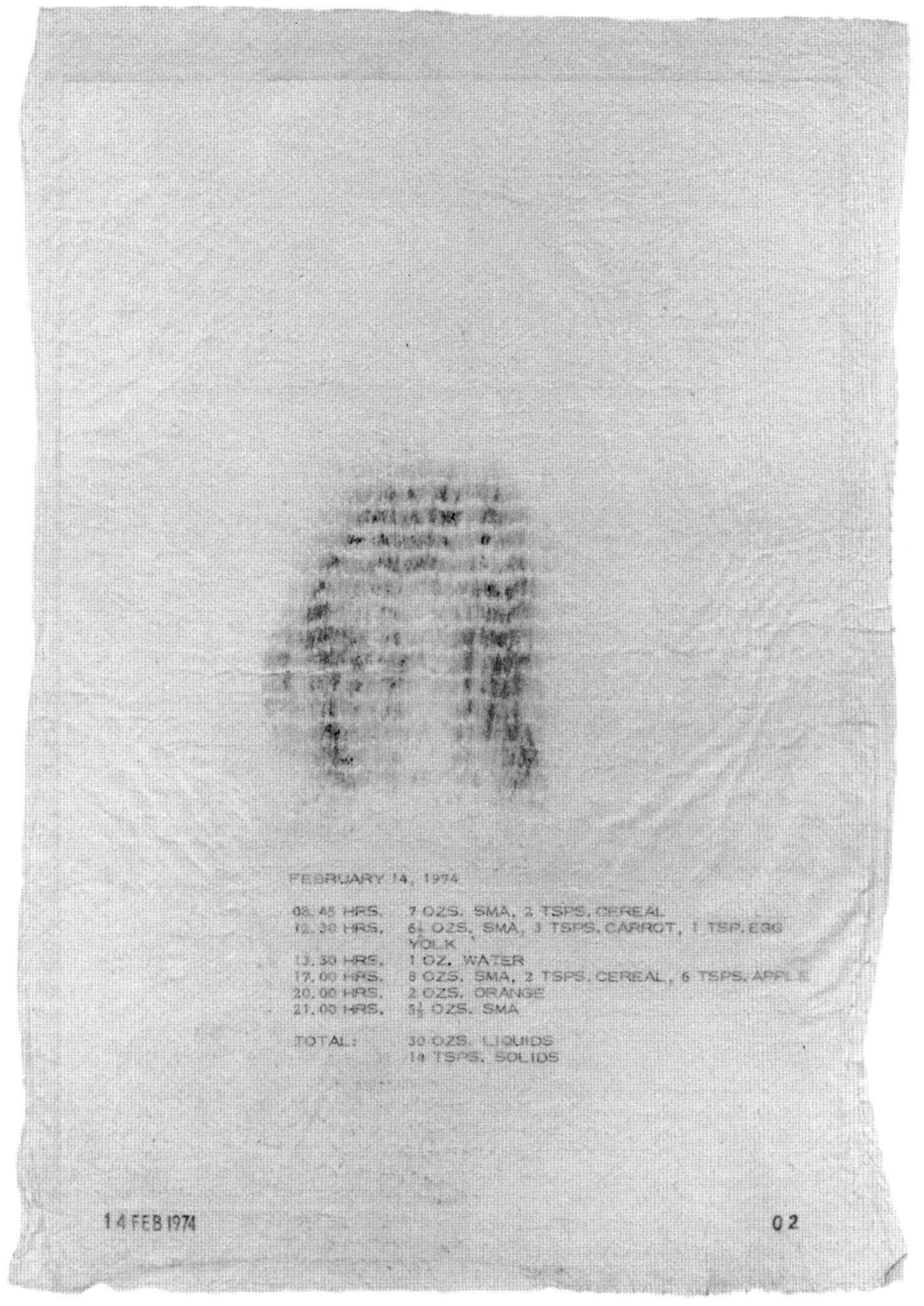
FEBRUARY 14, 1974
08.45 HRS. 7 OZS. SMA, 2 TSPS. CEREAL
12.30 HRS. 6½ OZS. SMA, 3 TSPS. CARROT, 1 TSP. EGG YOLK
13.30 HRS. 1 OZ. WATER
17.00 HRS. 8 OZS. SMA, 2 TSPS. CEREAL, 6 TSPS. APPLE
20.00 HRS. 2 OZS. ORANGE
21.00 HRS. 5½ OZS. SMA
TOTAL: 30 OZS. LIQUIDS
14 TSPS. SOLIDS
14 FEB 1974
02

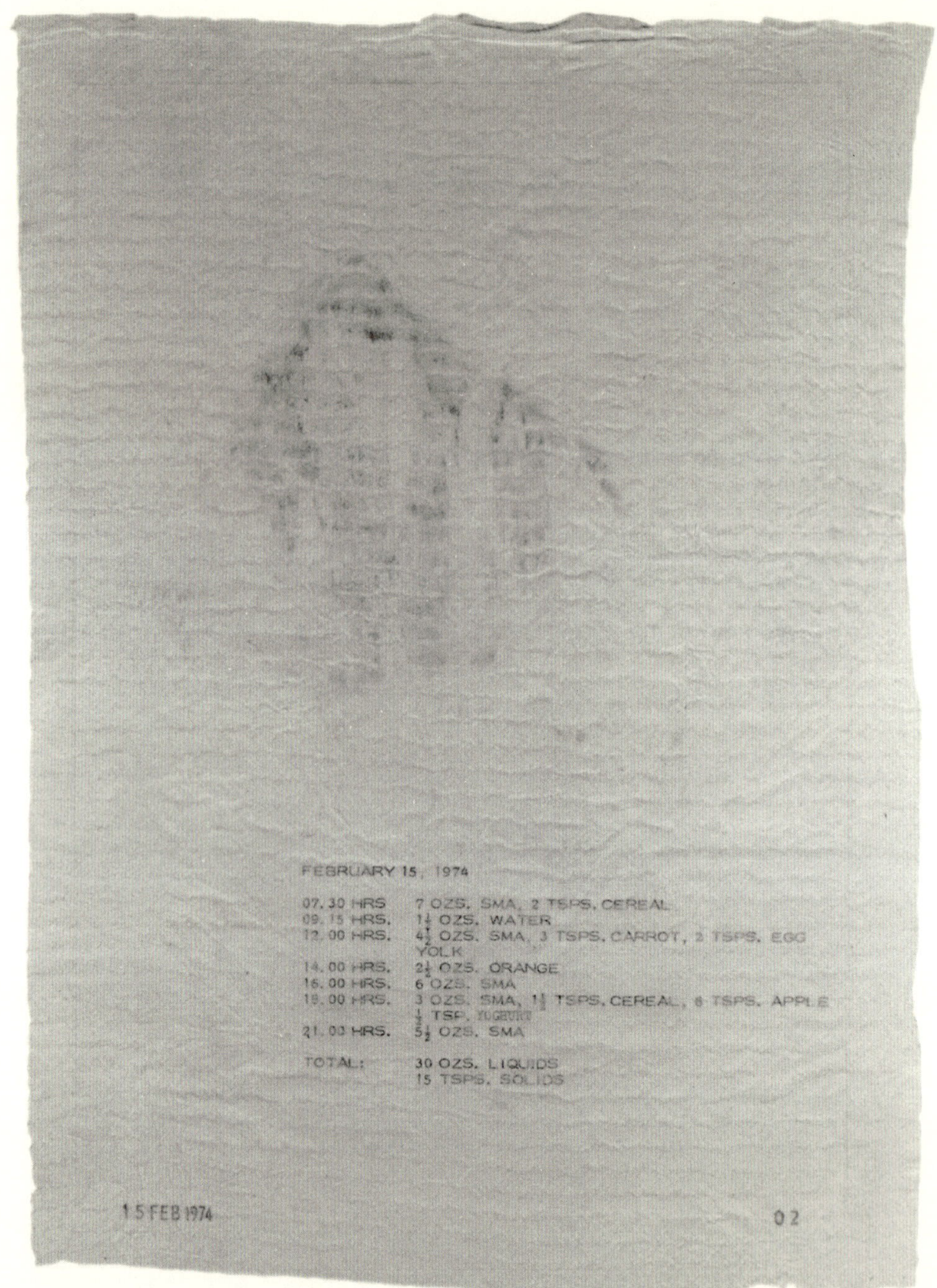

FEBRUARY 15, 1974
07.30 HRS 7 OZS. SMA, 2 TSPS. CEREAL
09.15 HRS. 1½ OZS. WATER
12.00 HRS. 4½ OZS. SMA, 3 TSPS. CARROT, 2 TSPS. EGG YOLK
14.00 HRS. 2½ OZS. ORANGE
16.00 HRS. 6 OZS. SMA
18.00 HRS. 3 OZS. SMA, 1½ TSPS. CEREAL, 6 TSPS. APPLE ½ TSP. YOGHURT
21.00 HRS. 5½ OZS. SMA
TOTAL: 30 OZS. LIQUIDS
15 TSPS. SOLIDS
15 FEB 1974
02

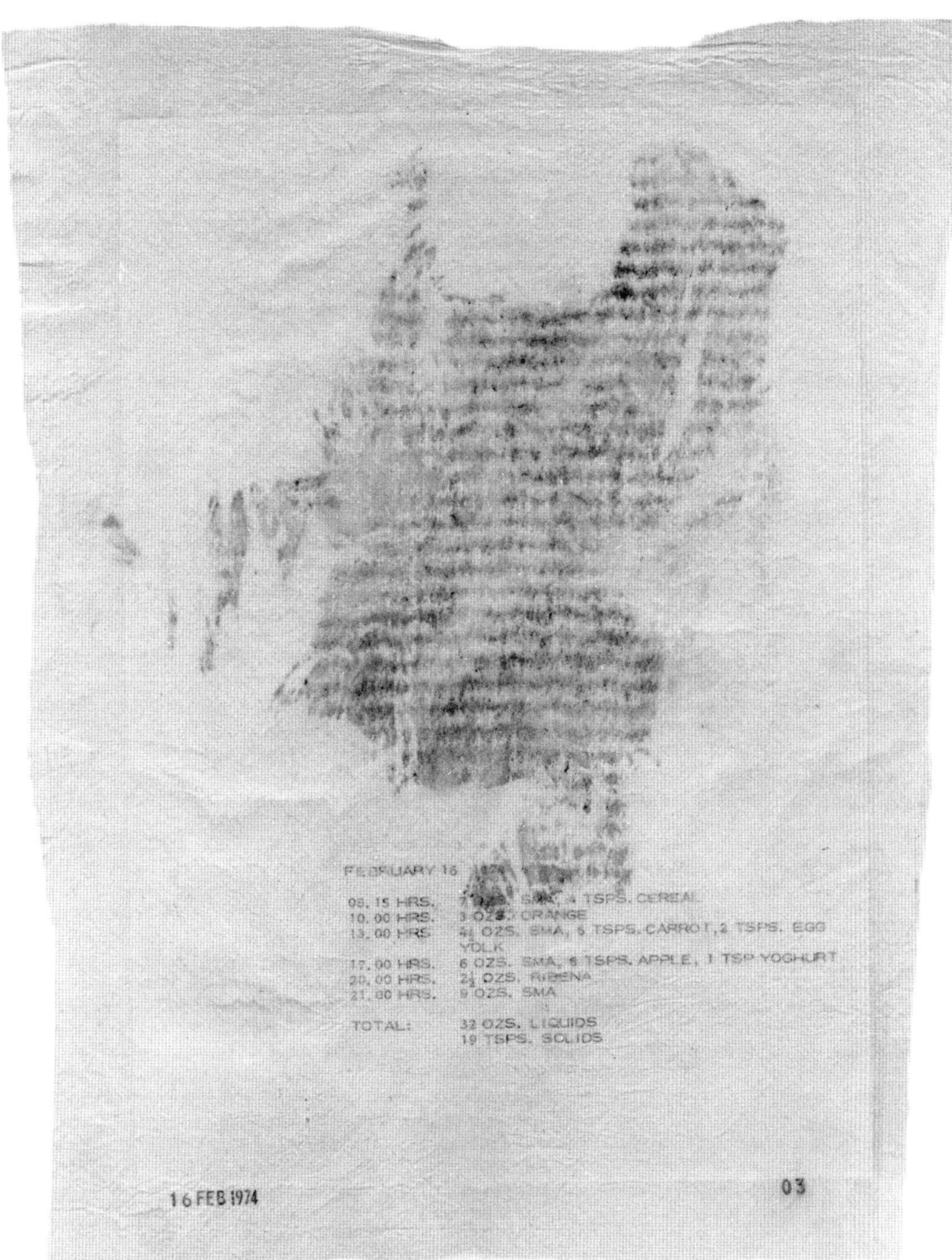
FEBRUARY 16
06. 15 HRS. 7 OZS. SMA, 4 TSPS. CEREAL
10. 00 HRS. 3 OZS. ORANGE
13. 00 HRS. 4½ OZS. SMA, 5 TSPS. CARROT, 2 TSPS. EGG YOLK
17. 00 HRS. 6 OZS. SMA, 6 TSPS. APPLE, 1 TSP YOGHURT
20. 00 HRS. 2½ OZS. RIBENA
21. 00 HRS. 9 OZS. SMA
TOTAL: 32 OZS. LIQUIDS
19 TSPS. SOLIDS
16 FEB 1974
03

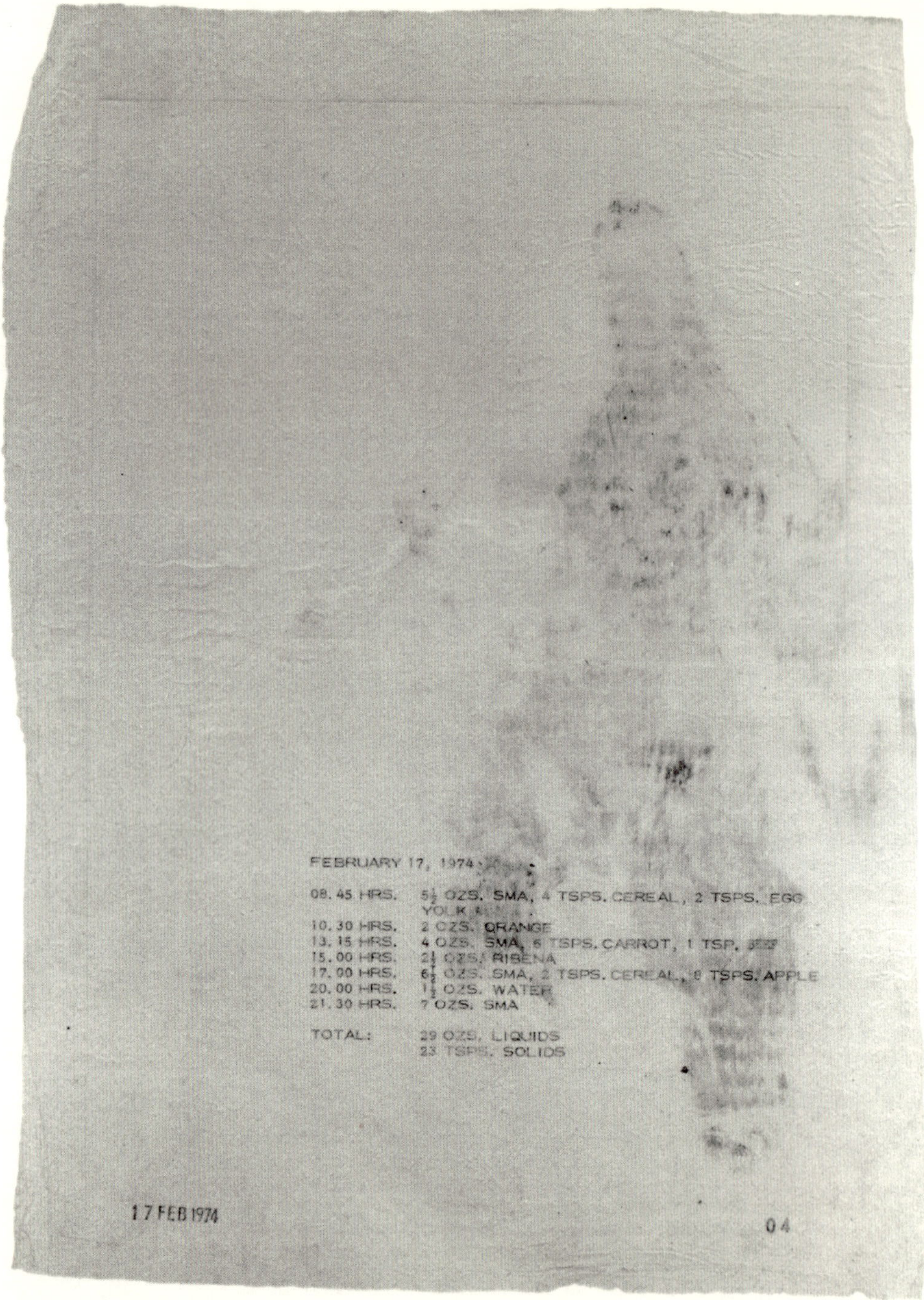

FEBRUARY 17, 1974

08.45 HRS.	$5\frac{1}{2}$ OZS. SMA, 4 TSPS. CEREAL, 2 TSPS. EGG YOLK
10.30 HRS.	2 OZS. ORANGE
13.15 HRS.	4 OZS. SMA, 6 TSPS. CARROT, 1 TSP. BEEF
15.00 HRS.	$2\frac{1}{2}$ OZS. RIBENA
17.00 HRS.	$6\frac{1}{2}$ OZS. SMA, 2 TSPS. CEREAL, 8 TSPS. APPLE
20.00 HRS.	$1\frac{1}{2}$ OZS. WATER
21.30 HRS.	7 OZS. SMA
TOTAL:	29 OZS. LIQUIDS 23 TSPS. SOLIDS

17 FEB 1974

04

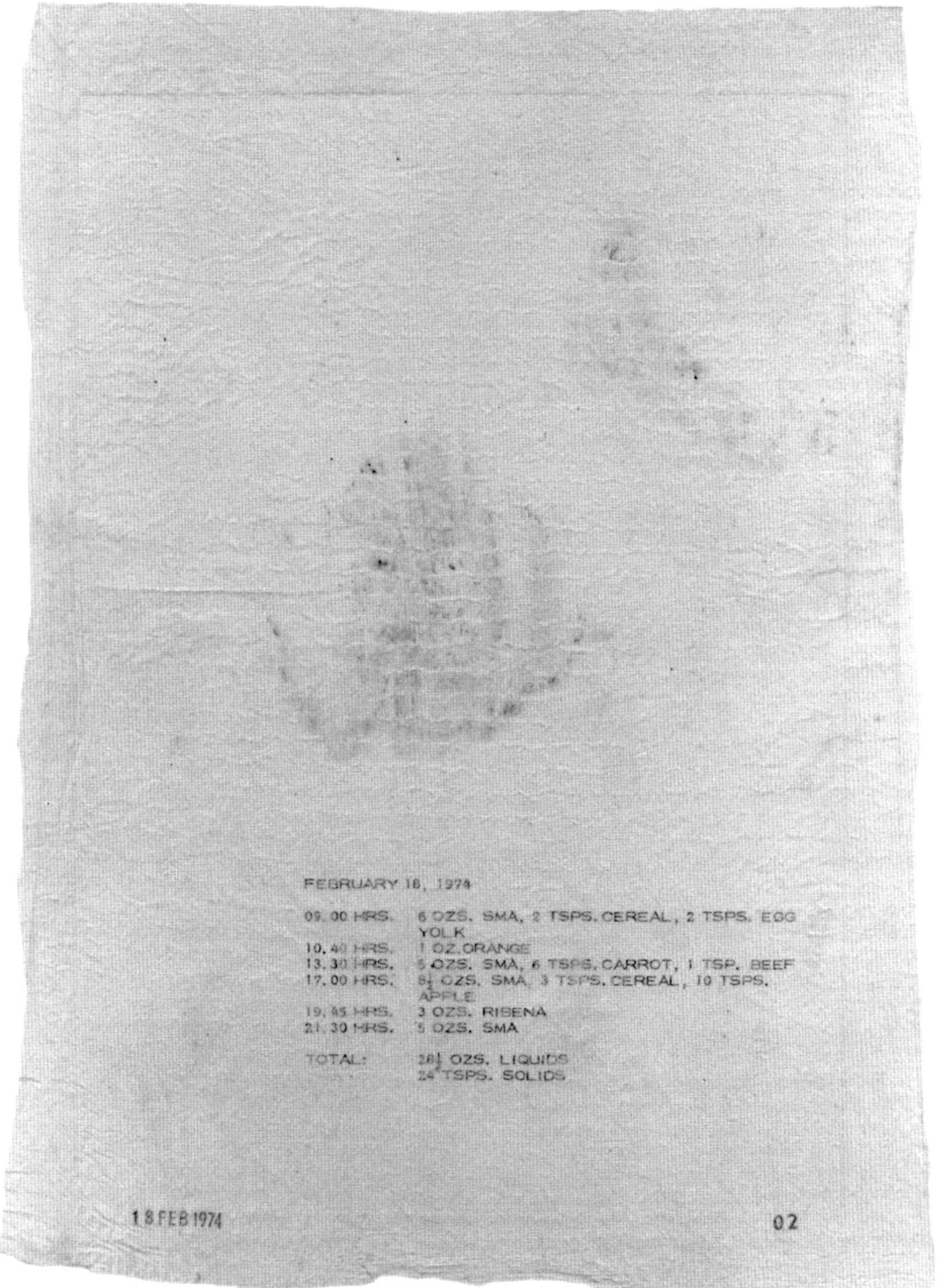
FEBRUARY 18, 1974
09.00 HRS. 6 OZS. SMA, 2 TSPS. CEREAL, 2 TSPS. EGG YOLK
10.40 HRS. 1 OZ. ORANGE
13.30 HRS. 5 OZS. SMA, 6 TSPS. CARROT, 1 TSP. BEEF
17.00 HRS. 8½ OZS. SMA, 3 TSPS. CEREAL, 10 TSPS. APPLE
19.45 HRS. 3 OZS. RIBENA
21.30 HRS. 5 OZS. SMA
TOTAL: 28½ OZS. LIQUIDS
24 TSPS. SOLIDS
18 FEB 1974
02

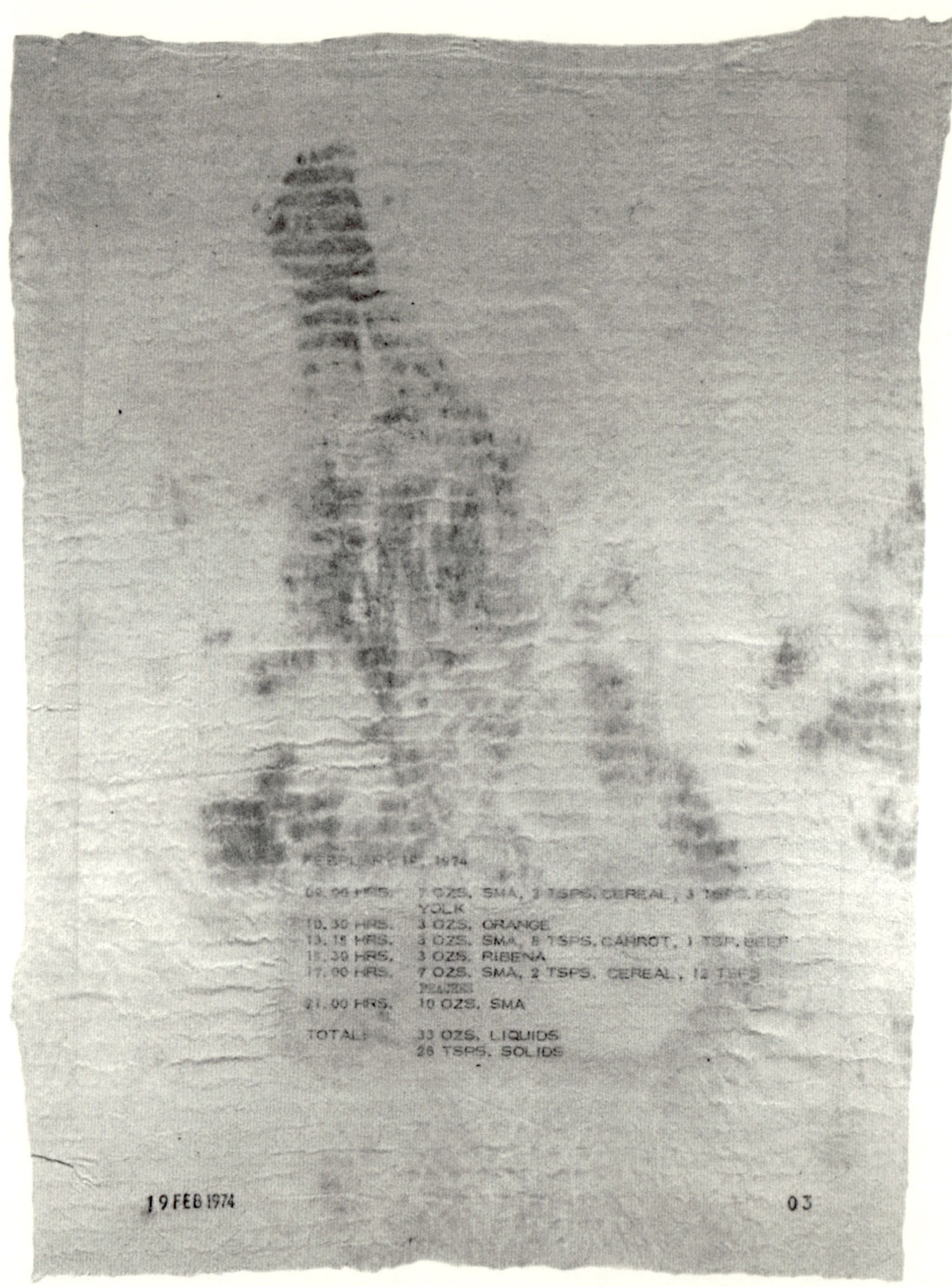
7 OZS. SMA,
YOLK
10.30 HRS. 3 OZS. ORANGE
3 OZS. SMA, TSPS. CARROT, 1 TSP. BEEF
3 OZS. RIBENA
7 OZS. SMA, 2 TSPS. CEREAL,
21.00 HRS. 10 OZS. SMA
TOTAL: 33 OZS. LIQUIDS
26 TSPS. SOLIDS
19 FEB 1974
03

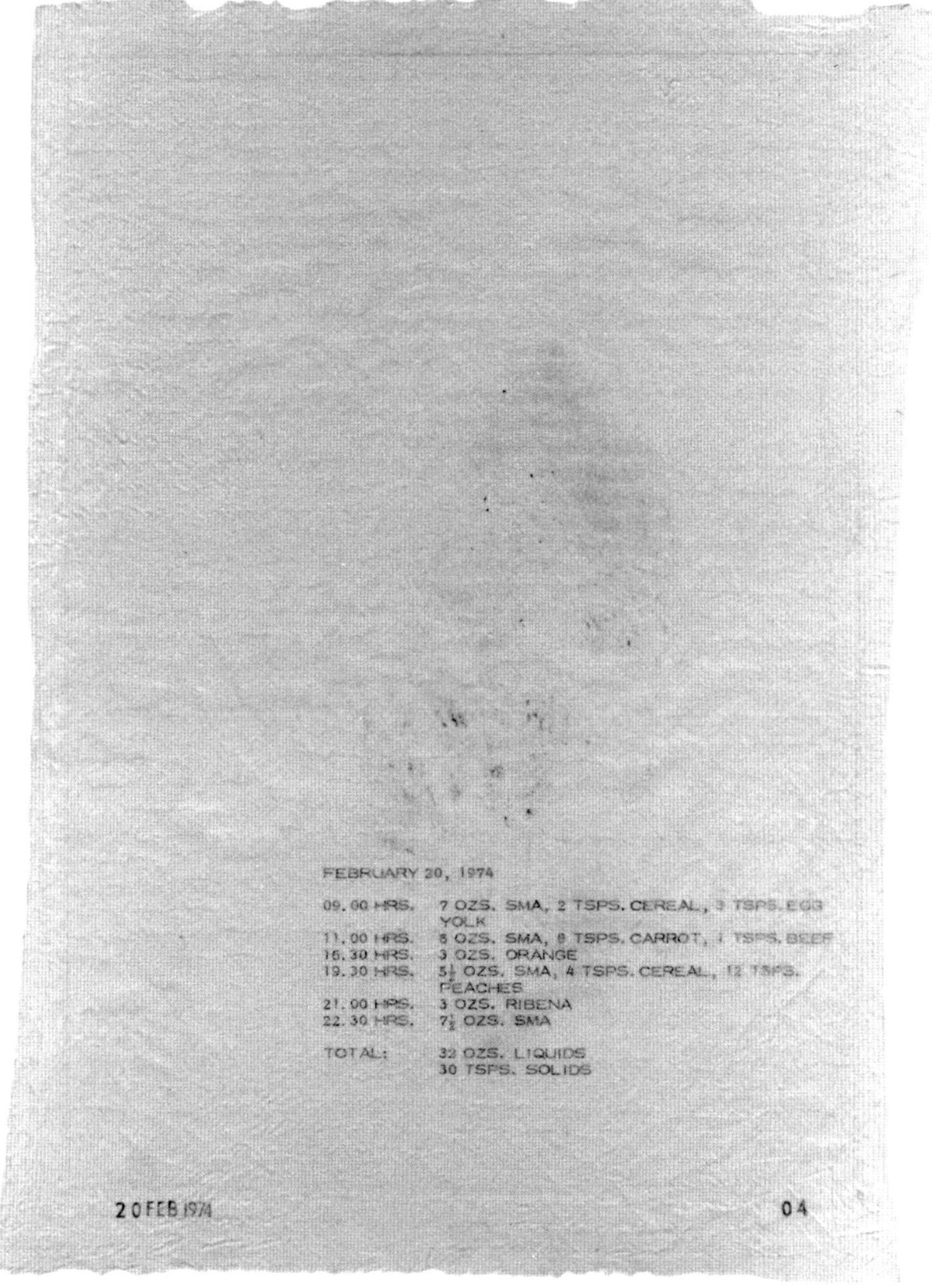

FEBRUARY 20, 1974

09.00 HRS.	7 OZS. SMA, 2 TSPS. CEREAL, 3 TSPS. EGG YOLK
11.00 HRS.	6 OZS. SMA, 8 TSPS. CARROT, 1 TSPS. BEEF
16.30 HRS.	3 OZS. ORANGE
19.30 HRS.	$5\frac{1}{2}$ OZS. SMA, 4 TSPS. CEREAL, 12 TSPS. PEACHES
21.00 HRS.	3 OZS. RIBENA
22.30 HRS.	$7\frac{1}{2}$ OZS. SMA
TOTAL:	32 OZS. LIQUIDS 30 TSPS. SOLIDS

20 FEB 1974

04

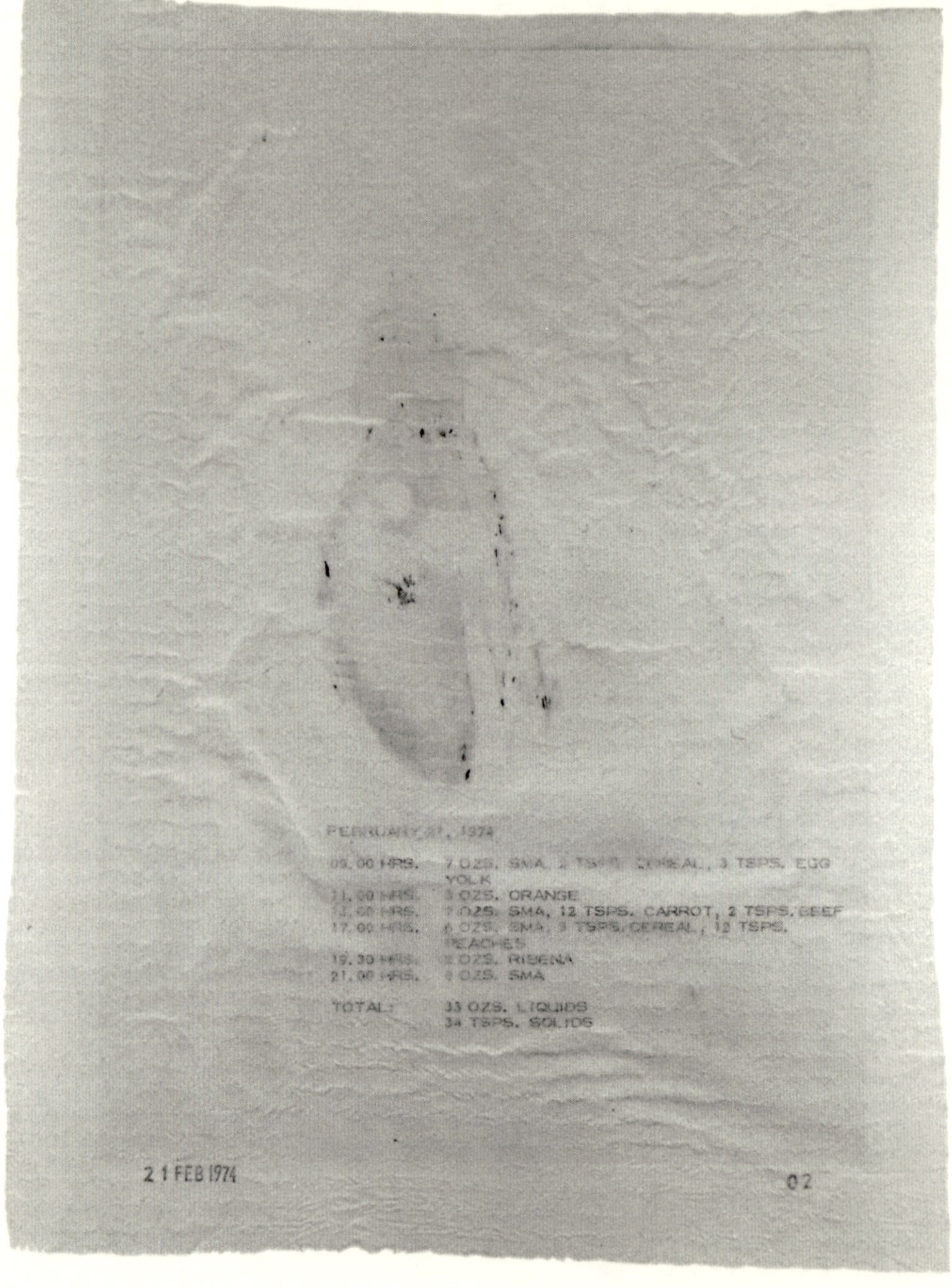

FEBRUARY 21, 1974

09.00 HRS. 7 OZS. SMA, 2 TSPS. CEREAL, 3 TSPS. EGG YOLK
11.00 HRS. 3 OZS. ORANGE
13.00 HRS. 7 OZS. SMA, 12 TSPS. CARROT, 2 TSPS. BEEF
17.00 HRS. 6 OZS. SMA, 3 TSPS. CEREAL, 12 TSPS. PEACHES
19.30 HRS. 2 OZS. RIBENA
21.00 HRS. 8 OZS. SMA

TOTAL: 33 OZS. LIQUIDS
34 TSPS. SOLIDS

2 1 FEB 1974

02

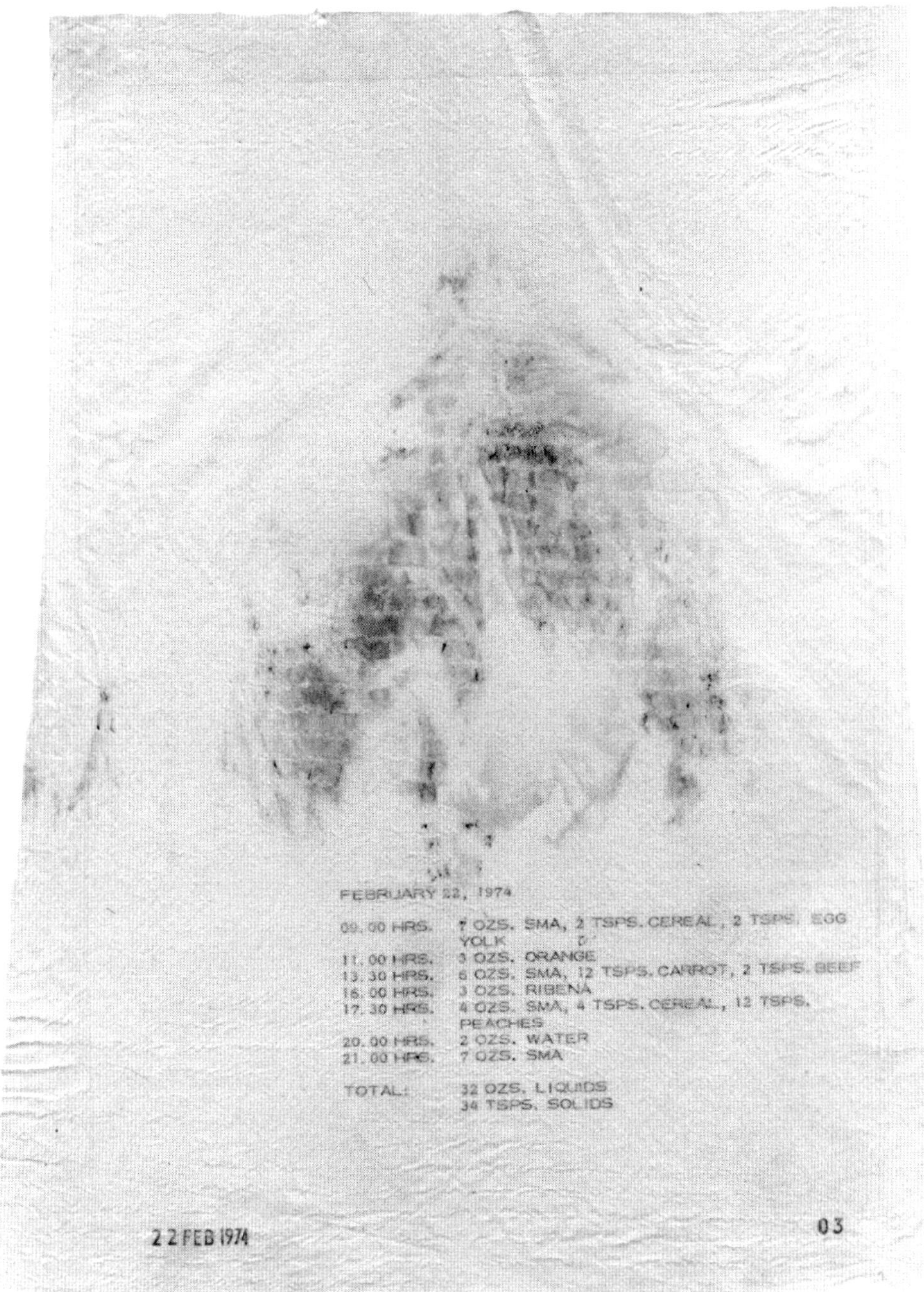
FEBRUARY 22, 1974
09.00 HRS. 7 OZS. SMA, 2 TSPS. CEREAL, 2 TSPS. EGG YOLK
11.00 HRS. 3 OZS. ORANGE
13.30 HRS. 6 OZS. SMA, 12 TSPS. CARROT, 2 TSPS. BEEF
16.00 HRS. 3 OZS. RIBENA
17.30 HRS. 4 OZS. SMA, 4 TSPS. CEREAL, 12 TSPS. PEACHES
20.00 HRS. 2 OZS. WATER
21.00 HRS. 7 OZS. SMA
TOTAL: 32 OZS. LIQUIDS
34 TSPS. SOLIDS
22 FEB 1974
03

FEBRUARY 23, 1974

09.00 HRS.	7 OZS. SMA, 2 TSPS. CEREAL, 3 TSPS. EGG YOLK
11.00 HRS.	1 OZ. ORANGE
14.00 HRS.	4 OZS. SMA, 12 TSPS. CARROT 2 TSPS. BEEF
16.00 HRS.	3 OZS. RIBENA
17.00 HRS.	5 OZS. SMA
20.00 HRS.	2 OZS. ORANGE, 2 TSPS. CEREAL, 12 TSPS. PEACHES
21.30 HRS.	9 OZS. SMA
TOTAL:	30 OZS. LIQUIDS 33 TSPS. SOLIDS

23 FEB 1974

03

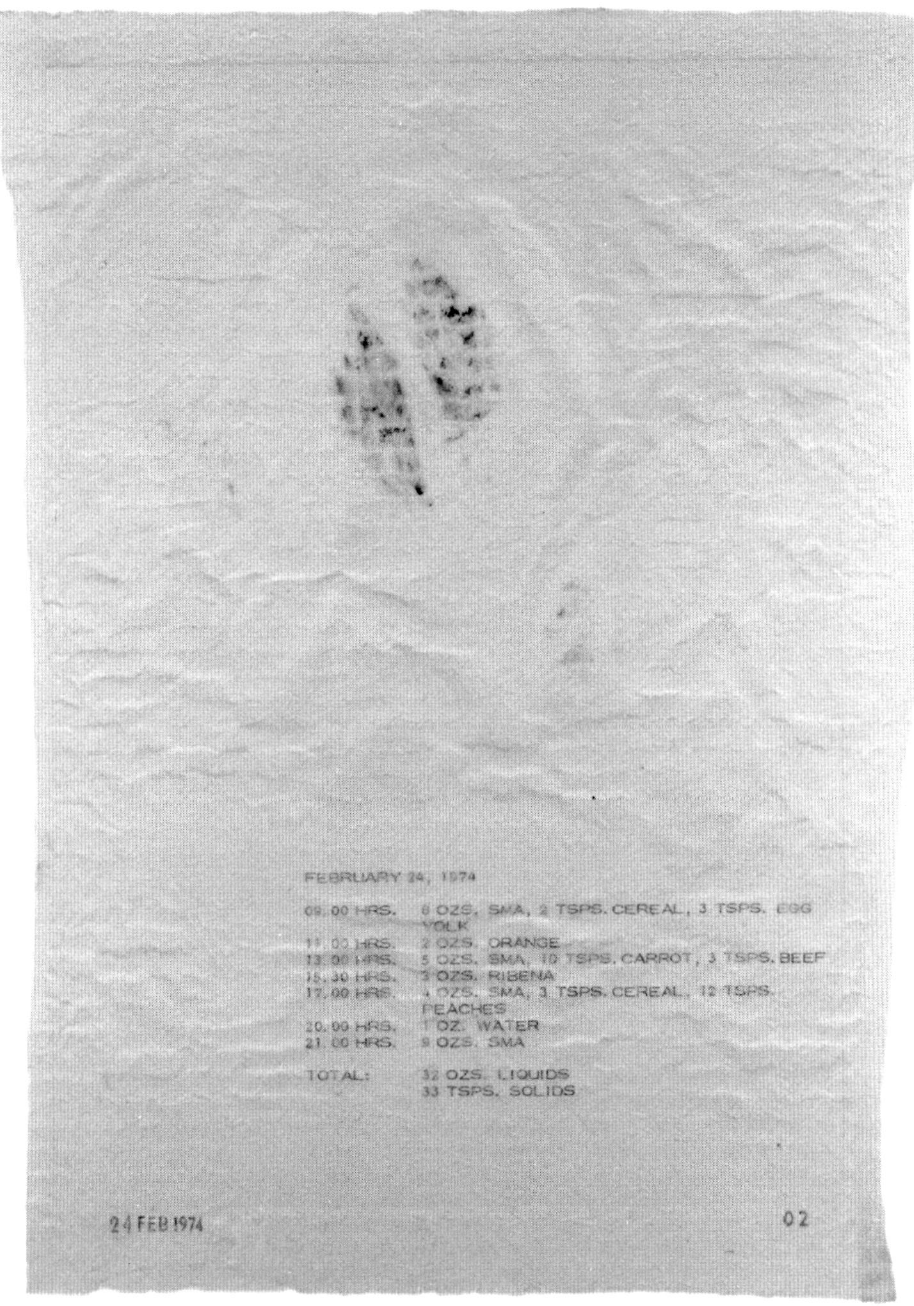

FEBRUARY 24, 1974
09.00 HRS. 8 OZS. SMA, 2 TSPS. CEREAL, 3 TSPS. EGG YOLK
11.00 HRS. 2 OZS. ORANGE
13.00 HRS. 5 OZS. SMA, 10 TSPS. CARROT, 3 TSPS. BEEF
15.30 HRS. 3 OZS. RIBENA
17.00 HRS. 4 OZS. SMA, 3 TSPS. CEREAL, 12 TSPS. PEACHES
20.00 HRS. 1 OZ. WATER
21.00 HRS. 9 OZS. SMA
TOTAL: 32 OZS. LIQUIDS
33 TSPS. SOLIDS
24 FEB 1974
02

FEBRUARY 25, 1974
08.00 HRS. [illegible] OZS. SMA, 2 TSPS. CEREAL, 3 TSPS. EGG YOLK
10.30 HRS. [illegible] OZS. ORANGE
12.00 HRS. [illegible] OZS. SMA, 6 TSPS. CARROT, 6 TSPS. BEEF
15.00 HRS. 3 OZS. RIBENA
16.00 HRS. [illegible] OZS. SMA, 3 TSPS. CEREAL, 12 TSPS. PEACHES
19.00 HRS. 2 OZS. WATER
20.30 HRS. 10 OZS. SMA
TOTAL: [illegible] OZS. LIQUIDS
32 TSPS. SOLIDS
25 FEB 1974
03

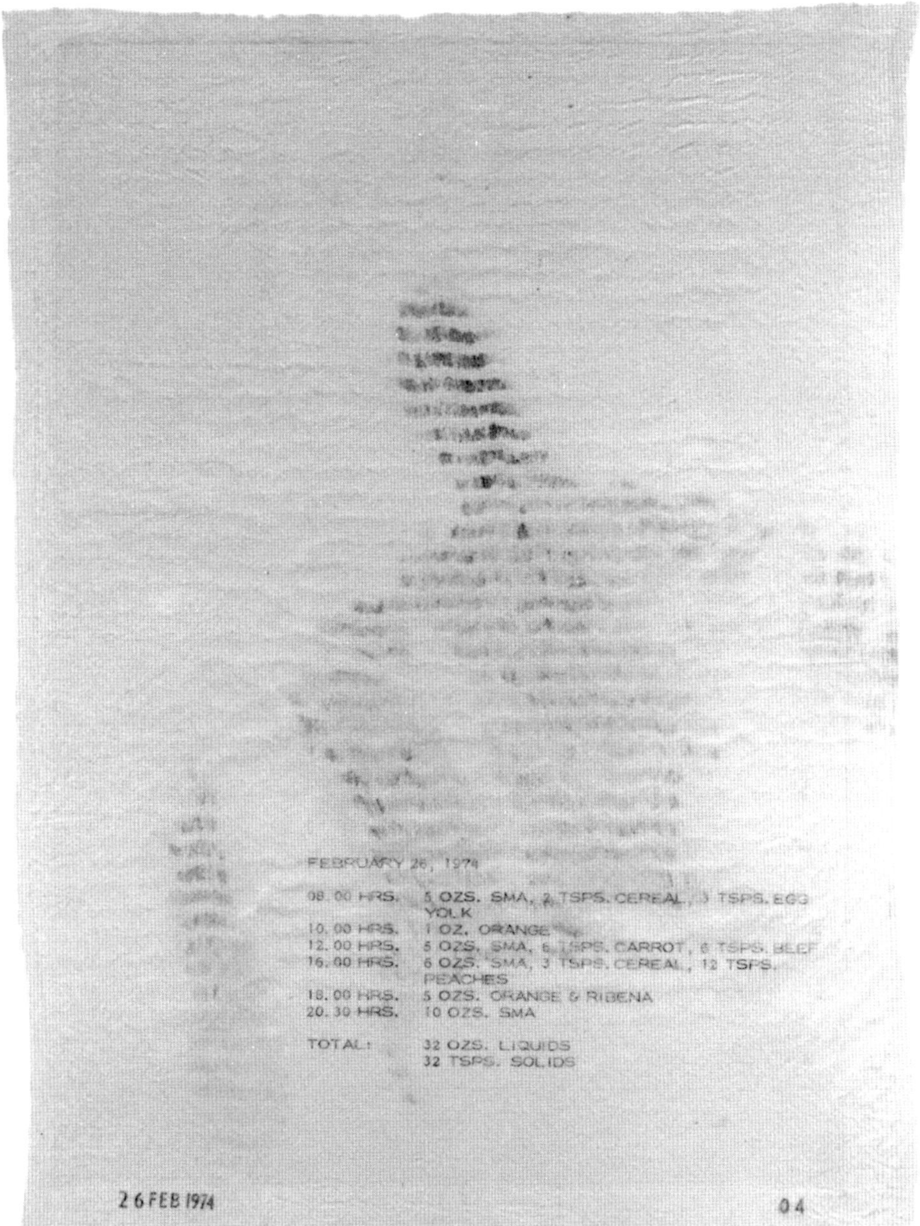

FEBRUARY 26, 1974

08.00 HRS. 5 OZS. SMA, 2 TSPS. CEREAL, 3 TSPS. EGG YOLK
10.00 HRS. 1 OZ. ORANGE
12.00 HRS. 5 OZS. SMA, 6 TSPS. CARROT, 6 TSPS. BEEF
16.00 HRS. 6 OZS. SMA, 3 TSPS. CEREAL, 12 TSPS. PEACHES
18.00 HRS. 5 OZS. ORANGE & RIBENA
20.30 HRS. 10 OZS. SMA

TOTAL: 32 OZS. LIQUIDS
32 TSPS. SOLIDS

26 FEB 1974

04

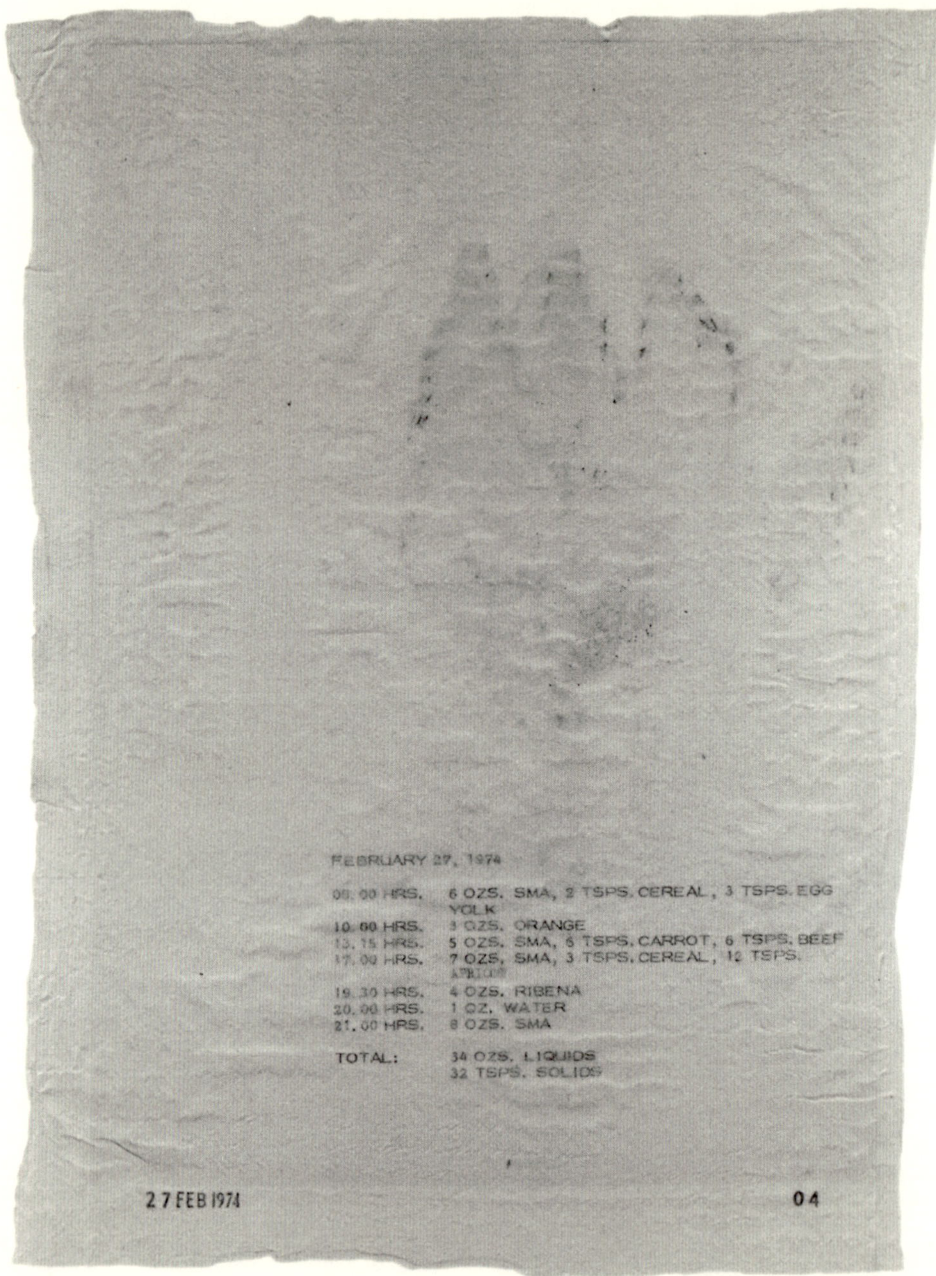

FEBRUARY 27, 1974

06.00 HRS.	6 OZS. SMA, 2 TSPS. CEREAL, 3 TSPS. EGG YOLK
10.00 HRS.	3 OZS. ORANGE
13.15 HRS.	5 OZS. SMA, 6 TSPS. CARROT, 6 TSPS. BEEF
17.00 HRS.	7 OZS. SMA, 3 TSPS. CEREAL, 12 TSPS. APRICOT
19.30 HRS.	4 OZS. RIBENA
20.00 HRS.	1 OZ. WATER
21.00 HRS.	8 OZS. SMA
TOTAL:	34 OZS. LIQUIDS 32 TSPS. SOLIDS

27 FEB 1974 04

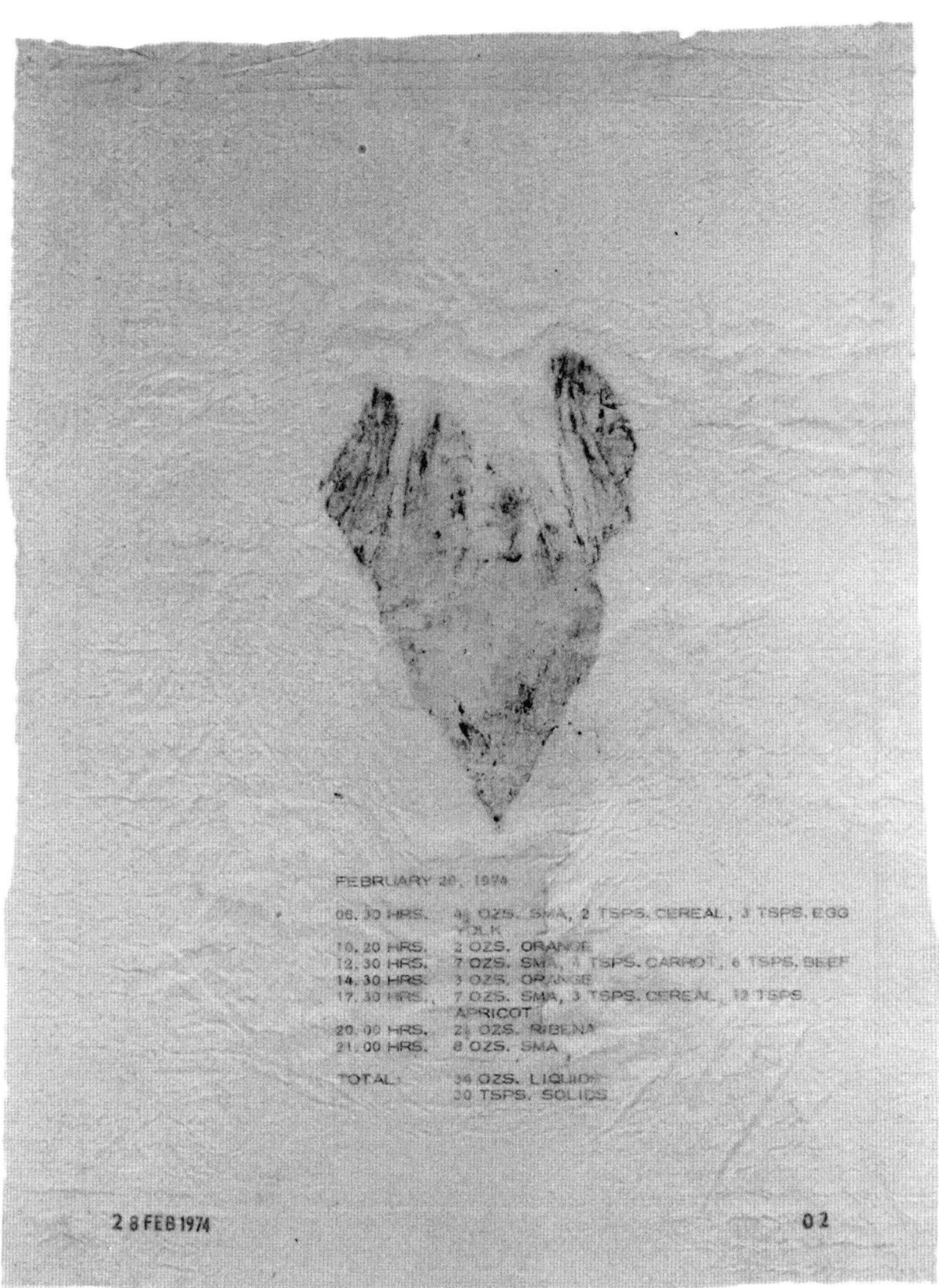
FEBRUARY 28, 1974
06.30 HRS. 4 OZS. SMA, 2 TSPS. CEREAL, 3 TSPS. EGG YOLK
10.20 HRS. 2 OZS. ORANGE
12.30 HRS. 7 OZS. SMA, TSPS. CARROT, 6 TSPS. BEEF
14.30 HRS. 3 OZS. ORANGE
17.30 HRS. 7 OZS. SMA, 3 TSPS. CEREAL, 12 TSPS. APRICOT
20.00 HRS. 2 OZS. RIBENA
21.00 HRS. 8 OZS. SMA
TOTAL: OZS. LIQUIDS
30 TSPS. SOLIDS
2 8 FEB 1974
0 2

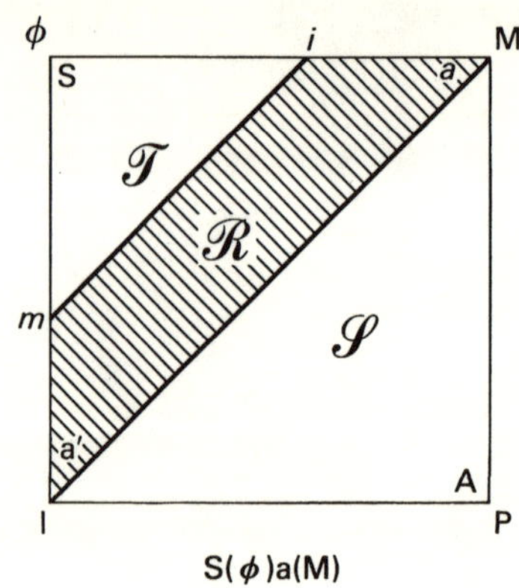

S(ϕ)a(M)

(WHAT HAVE I DONE WRONG?)

S

Experimentum Mentis I
Weaning from the Breast

During the antepartum period (gestation inside the mother's body) and continuing during the breast-feeding phase of early postpartum, the mother's negative place in the patriarchal order—more precisely the Symbolic—can be "misrecognized" because in a sense the child is *the phallus for her. Until birth the child is part of the mother's body, and later comes to her as an object which was once a part of herself. Thus feminine narcissism is reinforced because she can produce complete object love without relinquishing a narcissistic object choice. The mother's "misrecognition" of her negative place at this moment is not necessarily a captation in the Imaginary, as this would indicate psychosis, but rather a confrontation between the Real and the Imaginary which is already grounded within the Symbolic and is ultimately resolved when the primacy of the Symbolic structure is asserted. The specificity of the postpartum confrontation for individual mothers is related to the way in which initial Oedipal conflicts are re-enacted at this moment and as such is the terrain of psychoanalytical therapy. But in general the difficulty of the Symbolic order for women is precisely the difficulty of resolving Oedipal castration when the privileged signifier of that order is the phallus.*

Weaning from the breast is a significant discovery of absence not only for the child but also for the mother. Insofar as it is a real separation (can be specularized), it does not provoke a "recognition" of castration, but it does rupture the symbiosis of the biologically determined mother-child unit.

Weaning from the breast, taken literally, does not only imply the termination of breast-feeding (as this varies) but also the inevitable end of an exclusively liquid diet and the introduction of solid food. This transition has usually taken place by the infant's sixth month. It has a psychical parallel in that around the age of 6 to 8 months the child enters a phase of identification, a transformation takes place in him/her when assuming an image (as in the example of an image in the mirror). It is this identificatory movement of the child towards an ideal which mediates his/her anaclitic and primary relationship to the mother (or a part of her body) and consequently inscribes a sense of lack in her because it threatens her own Imaginary identification with the child as someone who was once a part of her.

There is also at this moment, for the child, a splitting of object love and identification love so that his/her objectal movement towards the mother, that is his/her desire to be what she wants him/her to be, now complements the mother's desire that the child be the phallus for her. In the early postpartum period what the mother wants the child to be is, primarily, "healthy." The normal feces is not only an index of the infant's health but also within the patriarchy it is appropriated as proof of the female's natural capacity for maternity and childcare. But the impending absence of plenitude is expressed in her words, "What have I done wrong?" The child is the mother's symptom insofar as she is judged through him/her. But the child's symptom, as, for example, in the lack of correlation between the nutritional data and the diarrheal stain in Documentation I, F3, undermines the ideological notion of "natural capacity" and queries the expediency of the sexual division of labor through which the mother's secondary social status is confirmed.

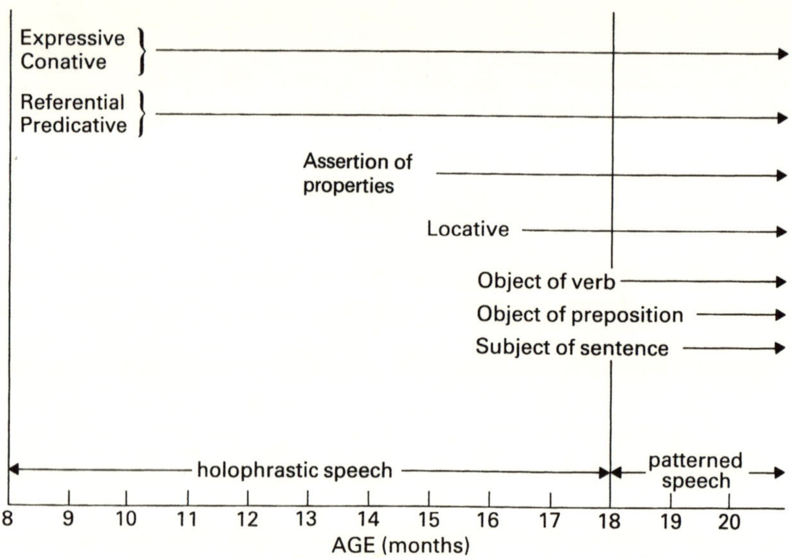
Expressive
Conative
Referential
Predicative
Assertion of properties
Locative
Object of verb
Object of preposition
Subject of sentence
holophrastic speech
patterned speech
8
9
10
11
12
13
14
15
16
17
18
19
20
AGE (months)

Documentation II
Analysed Utterances and Related Speech Events

The transition from single-word utterances to patterned speech (syntax) was recorded in daily 12-minute sessions, over a period of 5 months, January 26 to June 29, 1975. The speech events in this document were selected from the 17th and 18th months because the mean length of utterance by 19 months was 2.38 (consistently two words or more).

The utterances are viewed as holophrastic (i.e., grammatical speech), not primarily to prove that certain factors in the acquisition of language are innate, but rather to suggest that seeing a single word in a grammatical relation ultimately depends upon the observer of that relation and that the mother (or mother substitute) is placed within a specific relation of intersubjectivity with the child whereby she sees single words, and apparently ungrammatical successive utterances, as full sentences conceptually. In the schema on exhibition this relation is analysed as follows:

UTTERANCE	The identifiable phonemic content of the child's utterance.
GLOSS	The grammatical relation in which the mother thinks the utterance.
FUNCTION	The relations of existence, non-existence and recurrence which ground the utterance in an intersubjective discourse.
AGE	The temporal sequence of speech events which shifts the utterance from a paradigmatic axis to a syntagmatic one.

Initially the child's holophrastic utterance as, for example, /ma-ma/R1, is context bound in so far as it is a contradictory cluster of meanings as in /mama/R1 (help me, be there, see this) loosely framed by the functional relation of existence.

The space between assertions of existence and non-existence as in /dere/R2 and /gah/R5 is carved out by successively introducing distinctions on either side. Thus the first splitting on the side of non-existence gives rise to the functional relation of recurrence. It is expressed as the *demand* for the recurrence of that which existed as in /mo/R3 (more milk), /ki-ki/R6 (come back kitty) and finally /weh/ (?) R13-17, which is always uttered in relation to naming a desired object (e.g. R13-17-car, ball, record, baby, picture), precisely in the absence of that object. At this moment the mother is made aware that fulfilling a child's need is not equivalent to meeting his/her demands. In the example of /weh/ she does not even know what it is that is being demanded. A further splitting or non-existence into rejection of that which exists as in /no-no/R11, and of existence into predication as well as simple assertion /see be-be/R23 preposes affirmation and negation. This situates /weh/ as the forerunner of another significant grammatical transformation–the wh-question; the archetypal expression of the unconditional element of demand.

The extra-linguistic context of the utterance, which is crucial in the observer's formulation of it as rudimentary proposition, is set out on index cards below. Transcriptions of the relevant speech events are set out in full and numbered for the purpose of reference. Ongoing behavior is presented in brackets on the same line as the utterance. Utterance boundaries are indicated by a slash, /, and when the pause is somewhat longer the following utterance starts on the line below.

The speech events also identify the particular forms of adult intervention which occur most frequently. They can be summarized as follows:

Mother	Prompting (wh-questions)
	Expansion (repeating child's utterance adding what has been omitted)
Father	Modelling (commenting on what child says), also prompting.
Others	Echoing (repeating without filling in omissions), sometimes modelling.

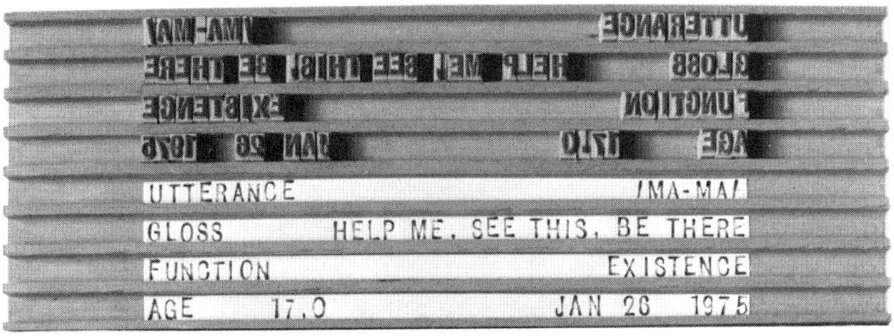

UTTERANCE /MA-MA/
GLOSS HELP ME, SEE THIS, BE THERE
FUNCTION EXISTENCE
AGE 17.0 JAN 26 1975

T1 26.1.75

CONTEXT: M(mother) getting K(son) ready for bed, 21:20 HRS.
SPEECH EVENT(S) /ma-ma/R1
1.1 M. Is that Kelly the baby? (looking in mirror together)
K. /ma-ma/ ma-ma/
M. What, who's the baby? (pointing to K)
K. da/ da/ da-da/ da-da/ (father not there at the time)
M. No, it's Kelly.
1.2 K. /ma-ma/ (looking at object on M's desk)
M. What is it?
1.3 K. /ma/ ma-ma/ ma/ (crying and reaching for desk)
MOST FREQUENT UTTERANCES: /ma-ma/ da-da/ eh/ no/ dere/
MEAN LENGTH OF UTTERANCE: 1.42 17 months

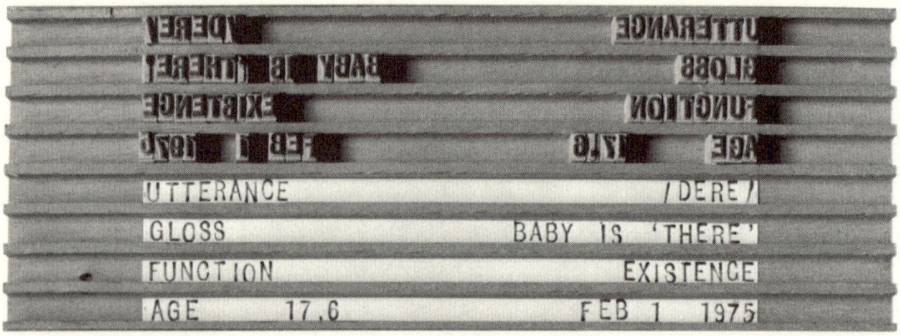

UTTERANCE /DERE/
GLOSS BABY IS 'THERE'
FUNCTION EXISTENCE
AGE 17.6 FEB 1 1975

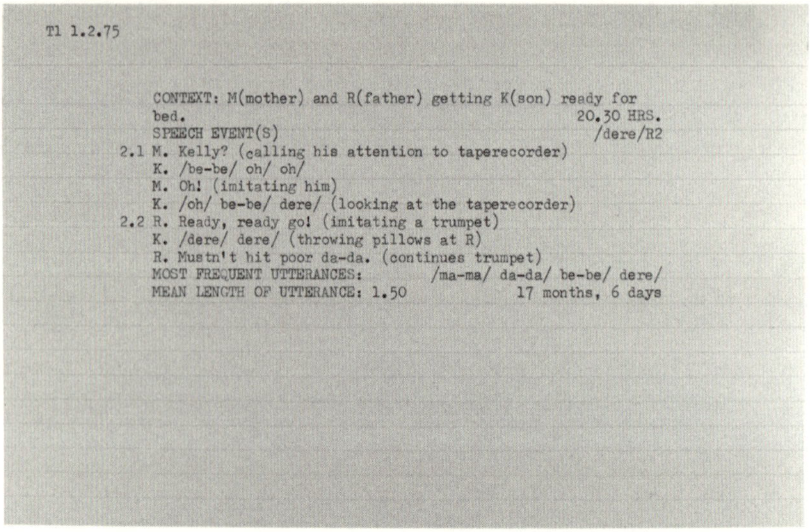

T1 1.2.75

CONTEXT: M(mother) and R(father) getting K(son) ready for bed. 20.30 HRS.
SPEECH EVENT(S) /dere/R2

2.1 M. Kelly? (calling his attention to taperecorder)
K. /be-be/ oh/ oh/
M. Oh! (imitating him)
K. /oh/ be-be/ dere/ (looking at the taperecorder)
2.2 R. Ready, ready go! (imitating a trumpet)
K. /dere/ dere/ (throwing pillows at R)
R. Mustn't hit poor da-da. (continues trumpet)
MOST FREQUENT UTTERANCES: /ma-ma/ da-da/ be-be/ dere/
MEAN LENGTH OF UTTERANCE: 1.50 17 months, 6 days

UTTERANCE /MO/
GLOSS GIVE ME 'MORE' MILK
FUNCTION RECURRENCE
AGE 17.7 FEB 2 1975

T1 2.2.75

CONTEXT: M(mother) and K(son) having tea. 15:30 HRS.
SPEECH EVENT(S) /mo/R3
3.1 K. /ma-ma/ umm/
M. You like that? (referring to drink of milk)
K. /mo/ (M fills cup)
M. I gave you more (pointing to full cup)
K. /mo/ mo/ (drinks it)
/mo/ (M fills cup again)
MOST FREQUENT UTTERANCES: /ma-ma/ mo/ dere/ pe/
MEAN LENGTH OF UTTERANCE: 1.52 17 months, 7 days

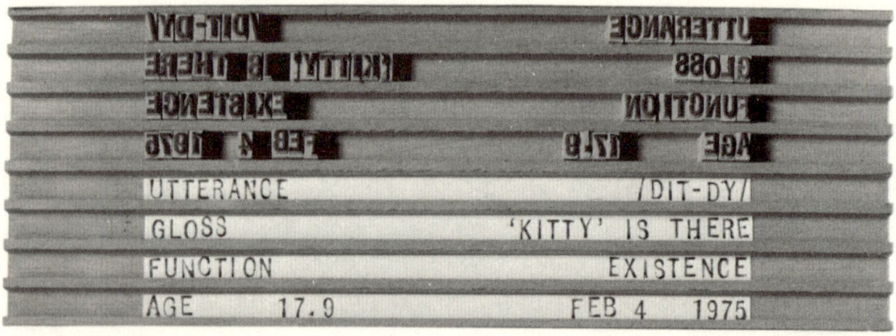

UTTERANCE	/DIT-DY/
GLOSS	'KITTY' IS THERE
FUNCTION	EXISTENCE
AGE 17.9	FEB 4 1975

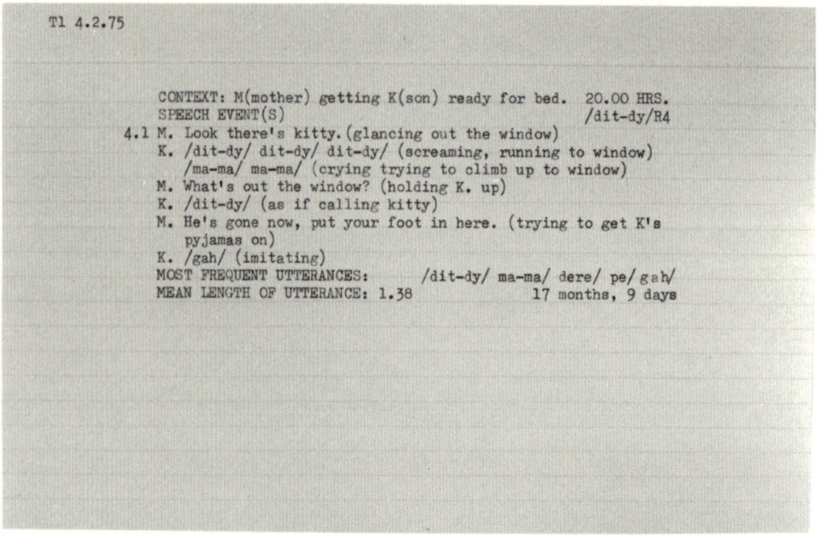

T1 4.2.75

CONTEXT: M(mother) getting K(son) ready for bed. 20.00 HRS.
SPEECH EVENT(S) /dit-dy/R4
4.1 M. Look there's kitty. (glancing out the window)
K. /dit-dy/ dit-dy/ dit-dy/ (screaming, running to window)
/ma-ma/ ma-ma/ (crying trying to climb up to window)
M. What's out the window? (holding K. up)
K. /dit-dy/ (as if calling kitty)
M. He's gone now, put your foot in here. (trying to get K's pyjamas on)
K. /gah/ (imitating)
MOST FREQUENT UTTERANCES: /dit-dy/ ma-ma/ dere/ pe/ gah/
MEAN LENGTH OF UTTERANCE: 1.38 17 months, 9 days

UTTERANCE /GAH/

GLOSS KITTY IS 'GONE'

FUNCTION NON-EXISTENCE

AGE 17.11 FEB 6 1975

T2 6.2.75

CONTEXT: M(mother) putting K(son) to bed. 13.00 HRS.
SPEECH EVENT(S) /gah/R5
5.1 K. /dit-dy/ dit-dy/ e dit-dy/ (seeing kitty out the window)
/gah/ dit-dy gah/ (kitty disappears under a car)
M. Oh! (seeing it come out again)
K. /dere/ dere/ e dere/ e dere/ (excitedly)
MOST FREQUENT UTTERANCES:/dere/ e dere/ gah/ dit-dy/ ah-gah/
MEAN LENGTH OF UTTERANCE: 1.78 17 months, 11 days

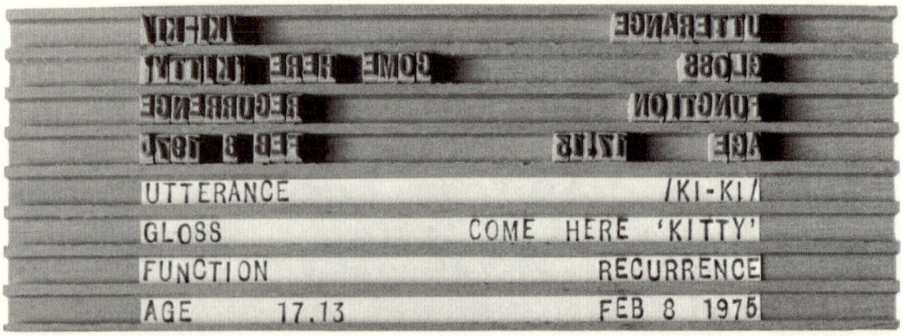

UTTERANCE /KI-KI/
GLOSS COME HERE 'KITTY'
FUNCTION RECURRENCE
AGE 17.13 FEB 8 1975

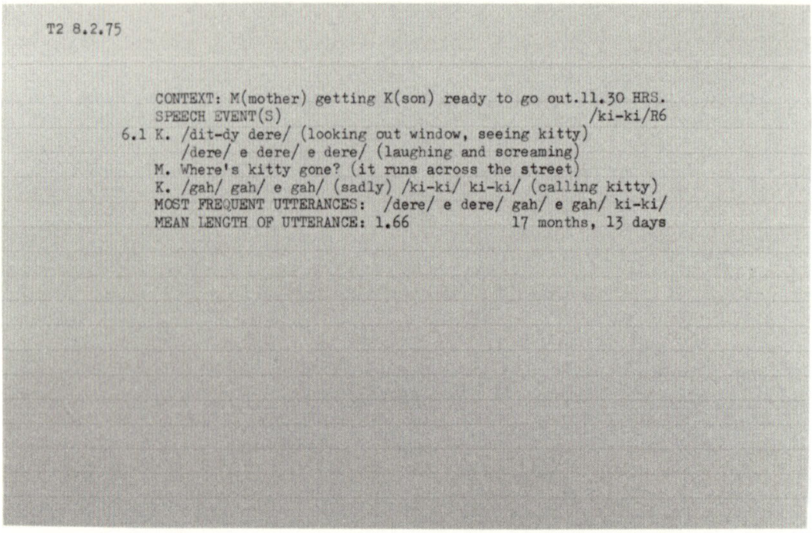

T2 8.2.75

```
    CONTEXT: M(mother) getting K(son) ready to go out.11.30 HRS.
    SPEECH EVENT(S)                                    /ki-ki/R6
6.1 K. /dit-dy dere/ (looking out window, seeing kitty)
       /dere/ e dere/ e dere/ (laughing and screaming)
    M. Where's kitty gone? (it runs across the street)
    K. /gah/ gah/ e gah/ (sadly) /ki-ki/ ki-ki/ (calling kitty)
    MOST FREQUENT UTTERANCES:  /dere/ e dere/ gah/ e gah/ ki-ki/
    MEAN LENGTH OF UTTERANCE: 1.66            17 months, 13 days
```

UTTERANCE /AH-GAH/
GLOSS THE WATER IS 'ALLGONE'
FUNCTION NON-EXISTENCE
AGE 17.14 FEB 9 1975

T2 9.2.75

CONTEXT: M(mother) and R(father) giving K(son) bath before bed. 20.00 HRS.
SPEECH EVENT(S) /ah-gah/R7

7.1 R. Come on Mary, where's the towel? (pulling plug out etc)
K. /ma-ma/ gah/ ah gah/ (seeing water go down the drain)
M. All gone, the water's all gone.
R. Can you see the water going down the little hole?

MOST FREQUENT UTTERANCES: /gah/ ah-gah/ nana/
MEAN LENGTH OF UTTERANCE: 1.52 17 months, 14 days

UTTERANCE /MEH/
GLOSS THAT IS A 'MAN'
FUNCTION EXISTENCE
AGE 17.16 FEB 11 1975

```
T2 2.11.75

      CONTEXT: M(mother) getting K(son) ready for bed.  20.00 HRS.
      SPEECH EVENT(S)                                     /meh/R8
  8.1 M. Where's Kelly going, on Mommy's desk? (climbing up to get
         a screwdriver)
         Look! (taking K from desk to window to distract him)
      K. /ka/ (sees car)
         /mu/ (points out moon)
         /meh/ meh/ e meh/ (referring to both men and women)
      MOST FREQUENT UTTERANCES:    /meh/ e meh/ ka/ e ka/ gah/ bu/
      MEAN LENGTH OF UTTERANCE: 1.38           17 months, 16 days
```

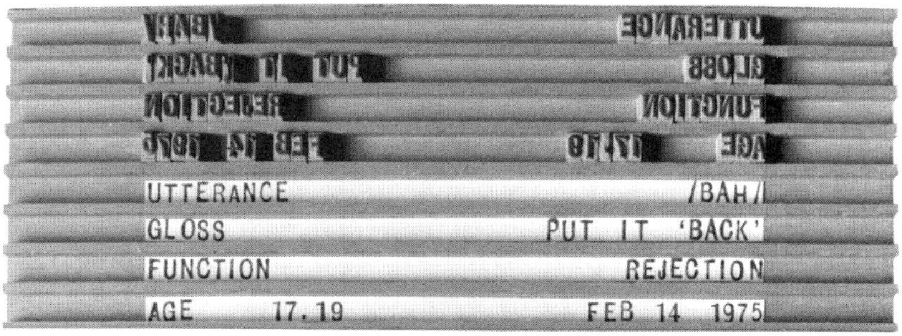

UTTERANCE	/BAH/
GLOSS	PUT IT 'BACK'
FUNCTION	REJECTION
AGE 17.19	FEB 14 1975

T3 14.2.75

CONTEXT: M(mother) getting K(son) dressed. 09.00 HRS.
SPEECH EVENT(S) /bah/R9
9.1 M. Put on your shoes (putting first shoe on)
K. /shu/ shu/ (imitating)
M. Put your little socks on.
One more shoe (looking for second shoe)
K. /shu/ (giving M her own shoe)
M. Kelly's shoe, this one (finding other shoe)
K. /bah/ bah/ (putting M's shoe back)
M. Yes, put it back, very good.
K. /bah e bah/ ah gah/
MOST FREQUENT UTTERANCES: /shu/ e shu/ bah/ gah/
MEAN LENGTH OF UTTERANCE: 1.36 17 months, 19 days

UTTERANCE /SIYEH/
GLOSS 'SEE' THE CAR
FUNCTION EXISTENCE
AGE 17.20 FEB 15 1975

T3 15.2.75

CONTEXT: M(mother) getting K(son) ready for bed. 20.30 HRS.
SPEECH EVENT(S) /siyeh/R10.
10.1 K. /siyeh/ siyeh/ siyeh/ (looking out window)
/ka/ ka/ e ka/ (car passing by)
M. um-hm (struggling to get nappy on)
10.2 K. oh/ siyeh/ siyeh/ (looking up in the sky)
M. You see the moon, way, way up there?
MOST FREQUENT UTTERANCES: /siyeh/ ka/ mu/ gah/
MEAN LENGTH OF UTTERANCE: 1.38 17 months, 20 days

UTTERANCE /NO-NO/
GLOSS 'DON'T TOUCH THAT'
FUNCTION REJECTION
AGE 17.22 FEB 17 1975

T4 17.2.75

CONTEXT: M(mother) and K(son) reading stories. 16.00 HRS.
SPEECH EVENT(S) /no-no/R11
11.1 M. Can I read you a story? (sitting down)
K. /nana/ (looking at tea tray)
M. You've finished the banana now.
K. /no-no/ (seeing slides near tea tray on M's desk)
M. Hey, those are my slides! (getting up)
K. /bah/ bah/ e bah/ (leaving them there)
MOST FREQUENT UTTERANCES: /bah/ no-no/ nana/ dere/
MEAN LENGTH OF UTTERANCE: 1.46 17 months, 22 days

UTTERANCE /MU/
GLOSS SEE THE 'MOON'
FUNCTION EXISTENCE
AGE 17.24 FEB 19 1975

T4 19.2.75

CONTEXT: M(mother) and K(son) reading stories. 20.00 HRS.
SPEECH EVENT(S) /mu/R12
12.1 K. /mu/ mu/ siyeh mu/ (looking out the window, sees moon)
M. Yes, do you want to read about 'Max' now?
K. /e mih/ e mih/ (sitting down with M. on sofa).
12.2 M. Where's the boat? (looking at the pictures).
K. /bo/ (pointing to Max's boat)
/te/ (pointing out the 'Wild Thing's' teeth)
/mu/ mu/ (pointing to the picture of the moon)
MOST FREQUENT UTTERANCES: /mu/ siyeh/ weh ka/ ma ma/
MEAN LENGTH OF UTTERANCE: 1.50 17 months, 24 days

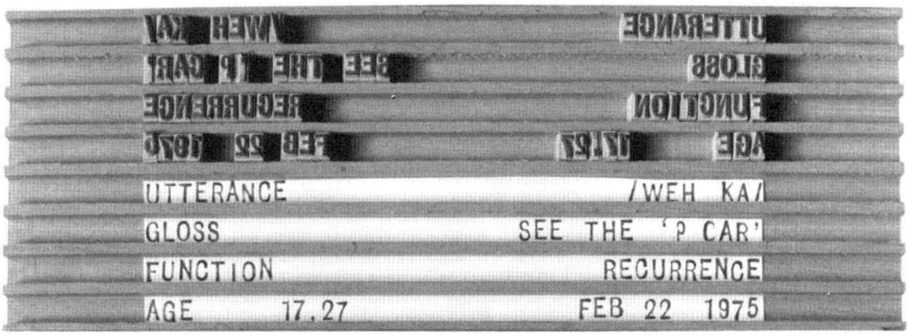

UTTERANCE /WEH KA/
GLOSS SEE THE 'P CAR'
FUNCTION RECURRENCE
AGE 17.27 FEB 22 1975

T4 22.2.75

```
CONTEXT: M(mother) getting K(son) dressed and ready to go out.
                                                   10.40 HRS.
     SPEECH EVENT(S)                                /weh ka/R13
13.1 M. Now we'll get ready to go bye-bye.
     K. /ba-ba/ ka-ka/
        /weh ka/ weh ka/ weh ka/ (excitedly)
     M. Red car? (puzzled as there's no car in sight.)
        There, little climber. (helping K up to window)
     K. /ka/ ka/ weh ka/ e ka/ weh ka/ weh ka/
13.2 M. There's a truck.
     K. /oh/ ka/ ka-ka/ (truck goes away)
        /weh ka/ weh ka/ weh ka/ e gah/ (sadly)
     M. Maybe your friend the rubbish man's coming.
        Can you see him?
     MOST FREQUENT UTTERANCES:      /weh ka/ weh-deh/ no-no/ be-be/
     MEAN LENGTH OF UTTERANCE: 1.60              17 months, 27 days
```

UTTERANCE /WEH DEH WEKO/
GLOSS PUT THE 'P RECORD ON'
FUNCTION RECURRENCE
AGE 18.0 FEB 26 1975

T4 26.2.75

CONTEXT: M(mother) and K(son) playing records. 17.30 HRS.
SPEECH EVENT(S) /weh-deh weko/14R
14.1 K. /weko/ weko/ e weko/ (excitedly)
M. You want to put that record on?
K. /weko/ weh deh weko/ (struggling with M to get record)
M. Okay, let's take that one off (putting another record on.)
K. /weko/ weko/ (anxiously)
M. This is what you do, here, put it on. (trying to keep K from getting into record player)
K. /weko/ (crying)
M. I don't know why you're crying. Here! (giving K a record)
K. /dere /e weko/
MOST FREQUENT UTTERANCES: /weko/ e weko/ weh-deh weko/
MEAN LENGTH OF UTTERANCE: 1.93 18 months

UTTERANCE /WEH BOH/
GLOSS THROW THE 'P BALL'
FUNCTION RECURRENCE
AGE 18.4 MAR 2 1975

T5 2.3.75

CONTEXT: R(father) getting K(son) ready to go out. 11.00 HRS.
SPEECH EVENT(S) /weh boh/15R
15.1 K. /weh boh/ weh boh/ weh boh/ weh boh/
R. All right (looking around for the ball)
15.2 K. /weh-deh/ e weh-deh/ (jumping off sofa).
R. Mind your head.
You want to go out? (trying to get K's coat on)
K. /ba-ba/ ko/ ko/
MOST FREQUENT UTTERANCES: /weh boh/ weh-deh/ ko/ shu/
MEAN LENGTH OF UTTERANCE: 1.70 18 months, 4 days

UTTERANCE /E WEH KA/
GLOSS FIND THE 'P CAR'
FUNCTION RECURRENCE
AGE 18.5 MAR 3 1975

T5 3.3.75

CONTEXT: M(mother) and K(son), having tea. 16.00 HRS.
SPEECH EVENT(S) /e weh ka/R16
16.1 K. /nana/ (crying)
M. There isn't any more, you ate it.
K. /gah/ nana/
M. Banana's gone. Would you like some sugar in your milk?
K. /e weh ka/ e weh ka/
M. Where's your red car gone? (no toy car in sight)
K. /nana/ (looking in bowl)
M. No, that's sugar.
MOST FREQUENT UTTERANCES: /e weh ka/ siyeh/ nana/ no-no/
MEAN LENGTH OF UTTERANCE: 1.86 18 months, 5 days

UTTERANCE /E WEH BOH/
GLOSS WHERE IS THE 'P BALL'
FUNCTION RECURRENCE
AGE 18.8 MAR 6 1975

T5 6.3.75

CONTEXT: S(mother substitute), A (her daughter) and K (M's son, having tea. 16.30 HRS.
SPEECH EVENT(S) /e weh boh/17R
17.1 S. Don't spill it. (K playing with tea cups)
K. /e weh boh/ e weh boh/
S. Go fetch it for me.(no ball in sight)
17.2 A. Where are you? (coming into the room)
Kelly come on let's go outside.
K. /e weh boh/
A. This red ball? (bringing a ball)
MOST FREQUENT UTTERANCES: /e weh boh/ weh ka/ weh gah/
MEAN LENGTH OF UTTERANCE: 1.65 18 months, 8 days

UTTERANCE /E BOH DERE/
GLOSS 'THE BALL IS THERE'
FUNCTION EXISTENCE
AGE 18.9 MAR 7 1975

T6 7.4.75

CONTEXT: R(father) and K(son) playing football. 11.30 HRS.
SPEECH EVENT(S) /e boh dere/R18
18.1 K. /e weh boh/ (excitedly)
R. Okay, ready! (getting the ball)
K. /e boh dere/ 'ere's a boh/
MOST FREQUENT UTTERANCES: /e weh boh/ e boh dere/ e bo-bo/
MEAN LENGTH OF UTTERANCE: 2.08 18 months, 9 days

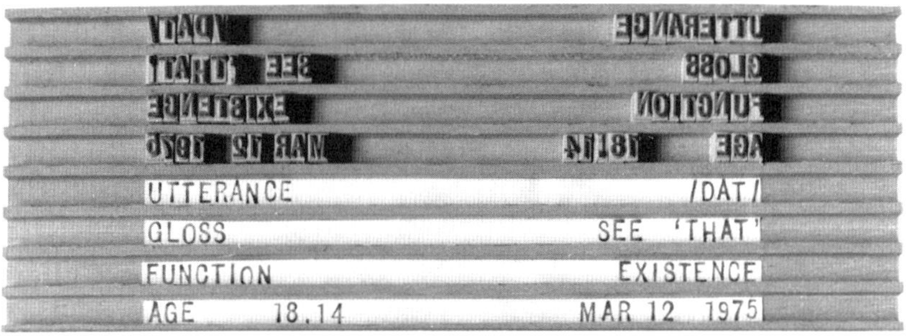

UTTERANCE /DAT/
GLOSS SEE 'THAT'
FUNCTION EXISTENCE
AGE 18.14 MAR 12 1975

T6 12.4.75

```
        CONTEXT: M(mother) and K(son), bedtime.            19.00 HRS.
        SPEECH EVENT(S)                                       /dat/19R
19.1    K. /dah/ dah/ dah/ dah/ dat/ (sees wood carving tools)
        M. What are you doing, be careful!
        K. /no-no/ no-no/ (looking at a gouge.
        M. Are you finished, put them back in the box.
        K. /dere/ (giving them to M).
           /dat/ dat/ ma-ma/
        M. Thank you. (hiding tools).
        MOST FREQUENT UTTERANCES:          /dat/ no-no/ siyeh/ dere/
        MEAN LENGTH OF UTTERANCE: 1.40          18 months, 14 days
```

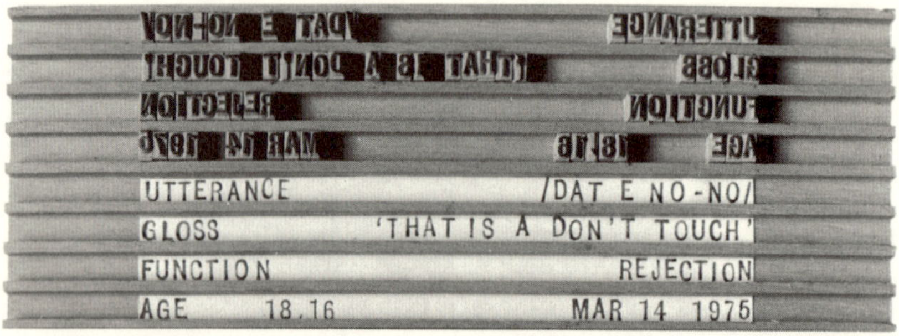

UTTERANCE /DAT E NO-NO/
GLOSS 'THAT IS A DON'T TOUCH'
FUNCTION REJECTION
AGE 18.16 MAR 14 1975

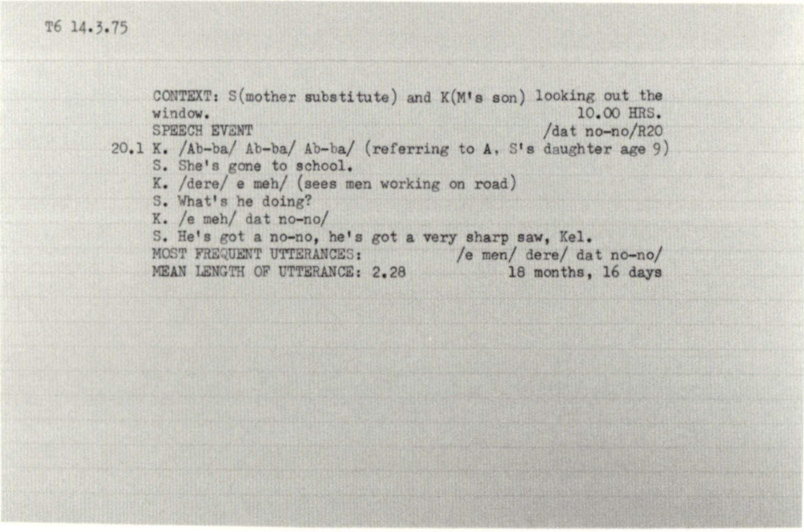

T6 14.3.75

CONTEXT: S(mother substitute) and K(M's son) looking out the window. 10.00 HRS.
SPEECH EVENT /dat no-no/R20
20.1 K. /Ab-ba/ Ab-ba/ Ab-ba/ (referring to A. S's daughter age 9)
S. She's gone to school.
K. /dere/ e meh/ (sees men working on road)
S. What's he doing?
K. /e meh/ dat no-no/
S. He's got a no-no, he's got a very sharp saw, Kel.
MOST FREQUENT UTTERANCES: /e men/ dere/ dat no-no/
MEAN LENGTH OF UTTERANCE: 2.28 18 months, 16 days

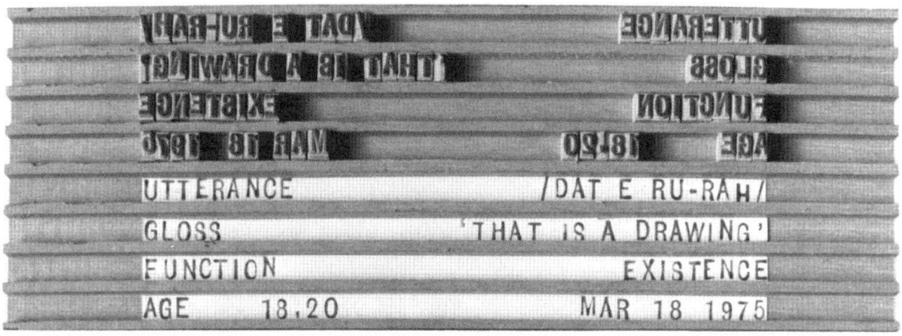

UTTERANCE /DAT E RU-RAH/
GLOSS 'THAT IS A DRAWING'
FUNCTION EXISTENCE
AGE 18.20 MAR 18 1975

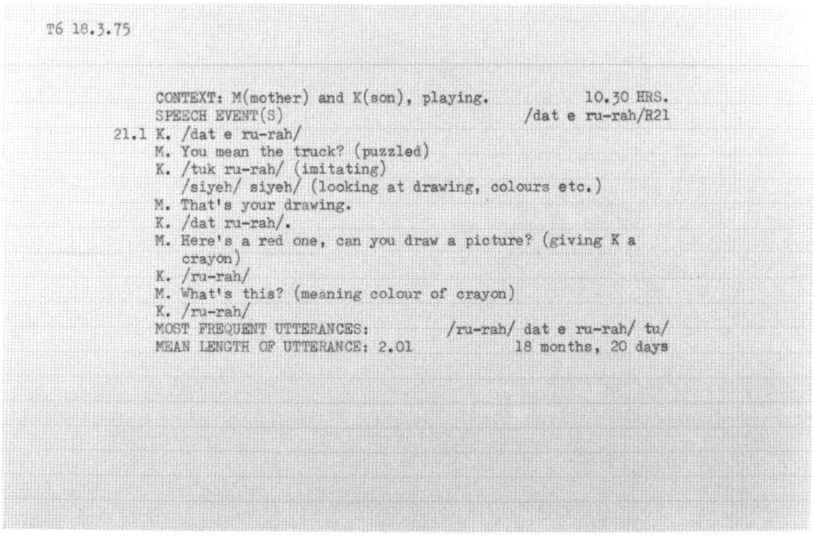

T6 18.3.75

CONTEXT: M(mother) and K(son), playing. 10.30 HRS.
SPEECH EVENT(S) /dat e ru-rah/R21

21.1 K. /dat e ru-rah/
M. You mean the truck? (puzzled)
K. /tuk ru-rah/ (imitating)
/siyeh/ siyeh/ (looking at drawing, colours etc.)
M. That's your drawing.
K. /dat ru-rah/.
M. Here's a red one, can you draw a picture? (giving K a crayon)
K. /ru-rah/
M. What's this? (meaning colour of crayon)
K. /ru-rah/

MOST FREQUENT UTTERANCES: /ru-rah/ dat e ru-rah/ tu/
MEAN LENGTH OF UTTERANCE: 2.01 18 months, 20 days

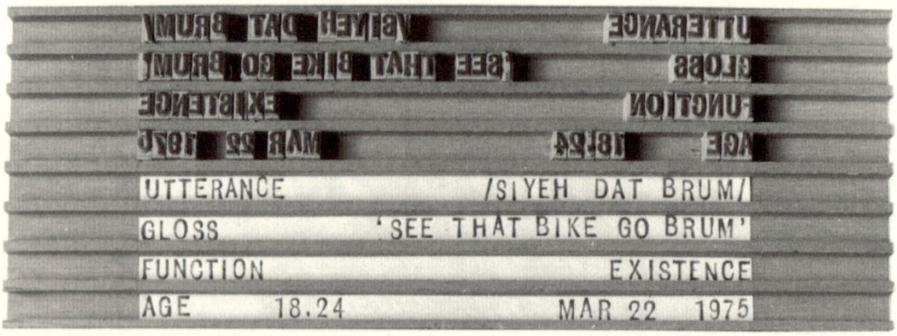

UTTERANCE /SIYEH DAT BRUM/
GLOSS 'SEE THAT BIKE GO BRUM'
FUNCTION EXISTENCE
AGE 18.24 MAR 22 1975

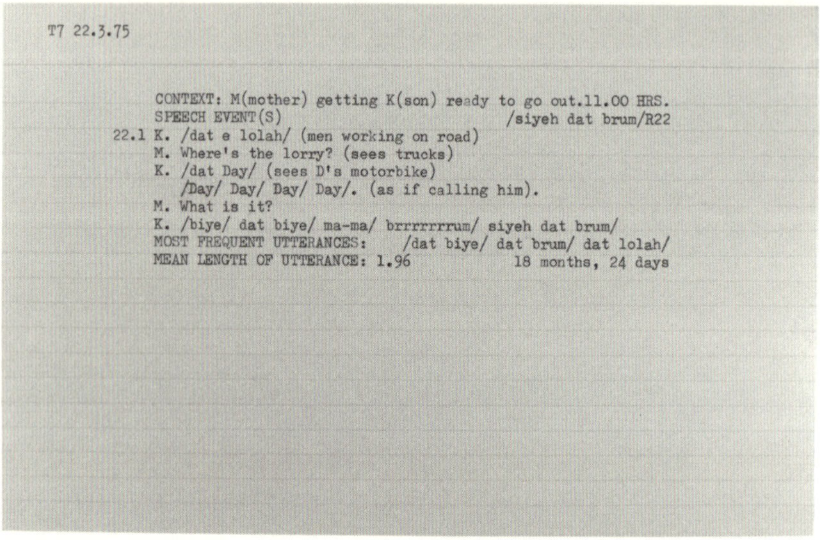

T7 22.3.75

CONTEXT: M(mother) getting K(son) ready to go out.11.00 HRS.
SPEECH EVENT(S) /siyeh dat brum/R22
22.1 K. /dat e lolah/ (men working on road)
M. Where's the lorry? (sees trucks)
K. /dat Day/ (sees D's motorbike)
/Day/ Day/ Day/ Day/. (as if calling him).
M. What is it?
K. /biye/ dat biye/ ma-ma/ brrrrrrrum/ siyeh dat brum/
MOST FREQUENT UTTERANCES: /dat biye/ dat brum/ dat lolah/
MEAN LENGTH OF UTTERANCE: 1.96 18 months, 24 days

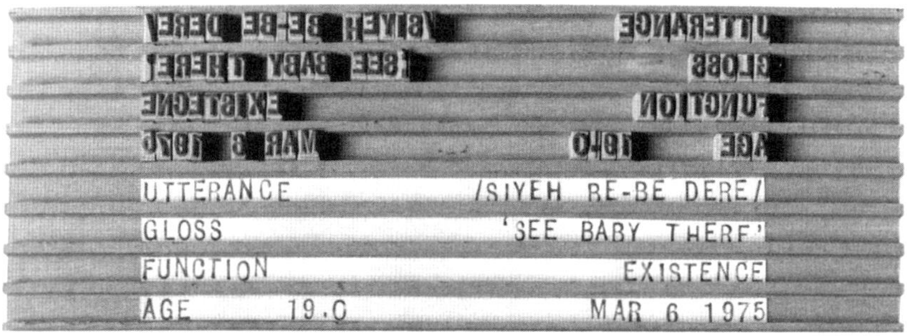

UTTERANCE /SIYEH BE-BE DERE/
GLOSS 'SEE BABY THERE'
FUNCTION EXISTENCE
AGE 19.0 MAR 6 1975

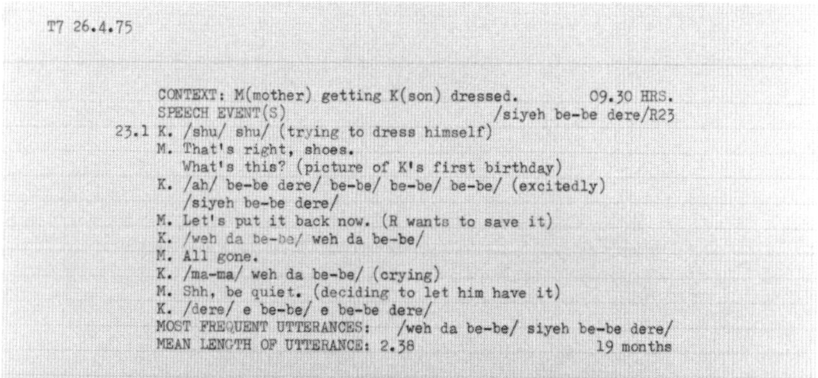

T7 26.4.75

CONTEXT: M(mother) getting K(son) dressed. 09.30 HRS.
SPEECH EVENT(S) /siyeh be-be dere/R23
23.1 K. /shu/ shu/ (trying to dress himself)
M. That's right, shoes.
What's this? (picture of K's first birthday)
K. /ah/ be-be dere/ be-be/ be-be/ be-be/ (excitedly)
/siyeh be-be dere/
M. Let's put it back now. (R wants to save it)
K. /weh da be-be/ weh da be-be/
M. All gone.
K. /ma-ma/ weh da be-be/ (crying)
M. Shh, be quiet. (deciding to let him have it)
K. /dere/ e be-be/ e be-be dere/
MOST FREQUENT UTTERANCES: /weh da be-be/ siyeh be-be dere/
MEAN LENGTH OF UTTERANCE: 2.38 19 months

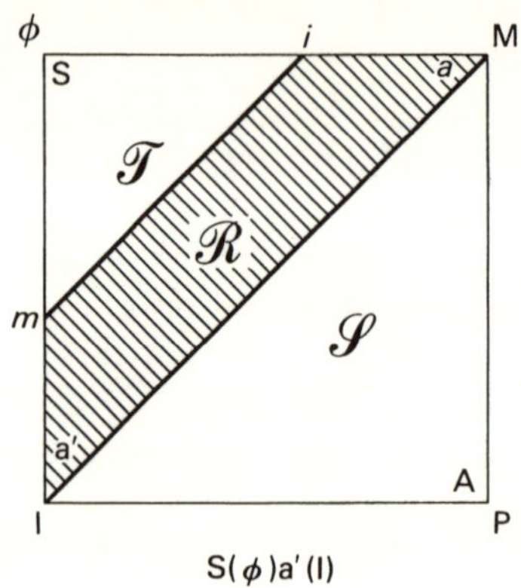

S(ϕ)a′(I)

(WHY DON'T I UNDERSTAND?)

s

Experimentum Mentis II
Weaning from the Holophrase

Because the acquisition of language is founded on a discovery of absence which is Imaginary, not Real, it is not only the constitutive instance in the formation of the child's castration complex but also the pivotal moment in the mother's "rerecognition" of castration and of her own negative entry into language and culture. During the period of prepatterned speech (i.e., prior to syntax) a unique process of signification develops within the specific relation of intersubjectivity between mother and child. The child's single-word utterance is thought by the mother as a holophrase, that is a conceptually complete sentence. Consequently it is the moment of the child's emerging syntax (i.e., patterned speech) of "weaning" from the holophrase, which reiterates the lack of object (i.e. child as phallus) for the mother. Specifically, it is the enigmatic pivot, as, for example, /weh/ in Documentation II, R3-17, which provokes the maternal utterance "Why don't I understand?" and once again demonstrates the contingency of the "natural capacity" for maternity. Insofar as the pivot is always combined with another utterance it anticipates the child's capacity for expressing him/herself grammatically and eventually being understood without the mediation of the maternal signified.

Significantly, the moment of emerging syntax coincides with the termination of the mirror phase, around 18 months. By then the child's projected image of him/herself can be returned and internalized allowing him/her to situate an Imaginary and libidinal relation to the mother "in the world." This ultimately "weans" the mother from the Other who was once part of her in so far as she is no longer identified as the child's mirror, returning his/her image in her own look or returning his/her word with her own meaning. Thus the mother must reconstitute her narcissistic object choice along the lines of an identification with the child as what she would like to be.

For the child, the Imaginary Other of the mirror phase also includes an Imaginary identification with the "imago" of the father. This initiates an ambivalent rivalry whereby the child desires to be in the father's place as the Other of the mother's desire and simultaneously in the mother's place as signifier of the father's desire. The former is complemented by the father's desire to be in the child's place insofar as the child is the signifier of the mother's desire, and in the latter by the mother's desire to be in the father's place because he is the Other of the child's desire. The conflicts which characterize the formation of the Oedipus complex are only resolved, if ever, when the child takes up a masculine or feminine position in language.

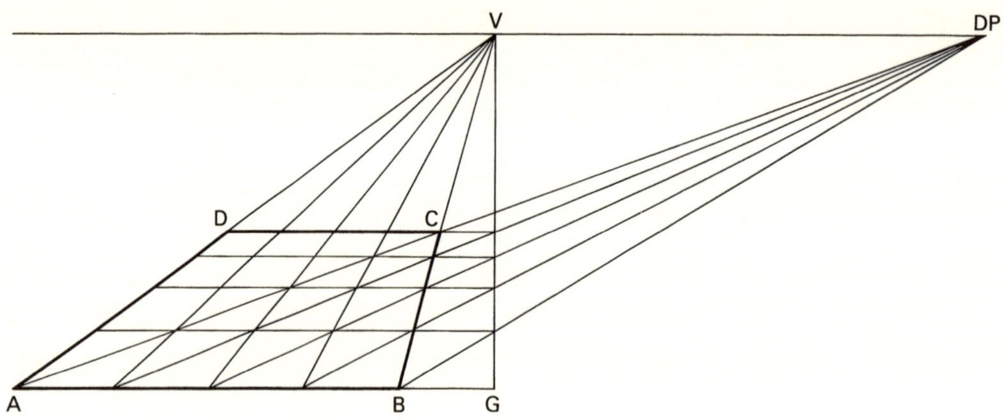
V
DP
D
C
A
B
G

Documentation III
Analysed Markings and Diary-perspective Schema

The diaries in this document were based on recorded conversations between mother and child during the crucial moment of the child's entry into an extrafamilial process of socialization, i.e. nursery school. The conversations took place at weekly intervals between September 7 and November 26, 1975. They came to an end with his/her "adjustment" to school. At this moment a kind of splitting of the dyadic mother-child unit occurred. This was evidenced in the mother's references, in the diaries, to the father's presence and by the child's use of pronouns (significantly "I" 9S), in his conversations and by the implied diagrams (concentric markings and circles 5–10S) in his drawings. The marking process was regulated by the nursery routine, so that almost daily finished works were presented by the children to their mothers. In retrospect, these markings became the logical terrain on which to map out the signification of the maternal discourse. The diary schema reads as follows:

R1 A condensed transcription of the child's conversation, playing it back immediately following the recording session.

R2 A transcription of the mother's *inner speech* in relation to R1, recalling it during a playback later the same day.

R3 A secondary revision of R2, one week later, locating the conversation (as object) within a specific time interval (as spatial metaphor) and rendering it "in perspective" (as a mnemic system).

The diary schema above is articulated within a revised presentation of the traditional artificial perspective system, which reads, metaphorically, as follows:

ABCD The object to be drawn or the "real" in the sense of what is real for the subject.

V	The vanishing point or the vanishing reality which defines the subject in terms of a lost object.
DP	The distance point or the distancing function of the Symbolic father which inserts the lack of object into the dialectic of the Oedipus complex.

Most children follow the same graphic evolution in discovering a mode of visual symbolization. By the age of 2 years, they place scribbling so that the total configuration implies a shape, and by 3 years, children make the kind of diagrammatic marks (i.e., crosses, circles, squares, triangles, and "odd shape" aggregates) which will become, on the one hand, the signifying system of written language, and on the other, the signifying practice of art. In this document, the figuration of the diary-perspective schema is superimposed on the child's drawings, which are also analyzed according to the specific placement of markings and his age at the time of making them (25–28 mos.).

S1	overall
S2	centered
S3	spaced border
S4	vertical half
S5	horizontal half
S6	two-sided balance
S7	diagonal half
S8	extended diagonal half
S9	diagonal axis
S10	two-thirds division
S11	quarter page
S12	two-corner arch
S13	three-corner arch
S14	across the paper

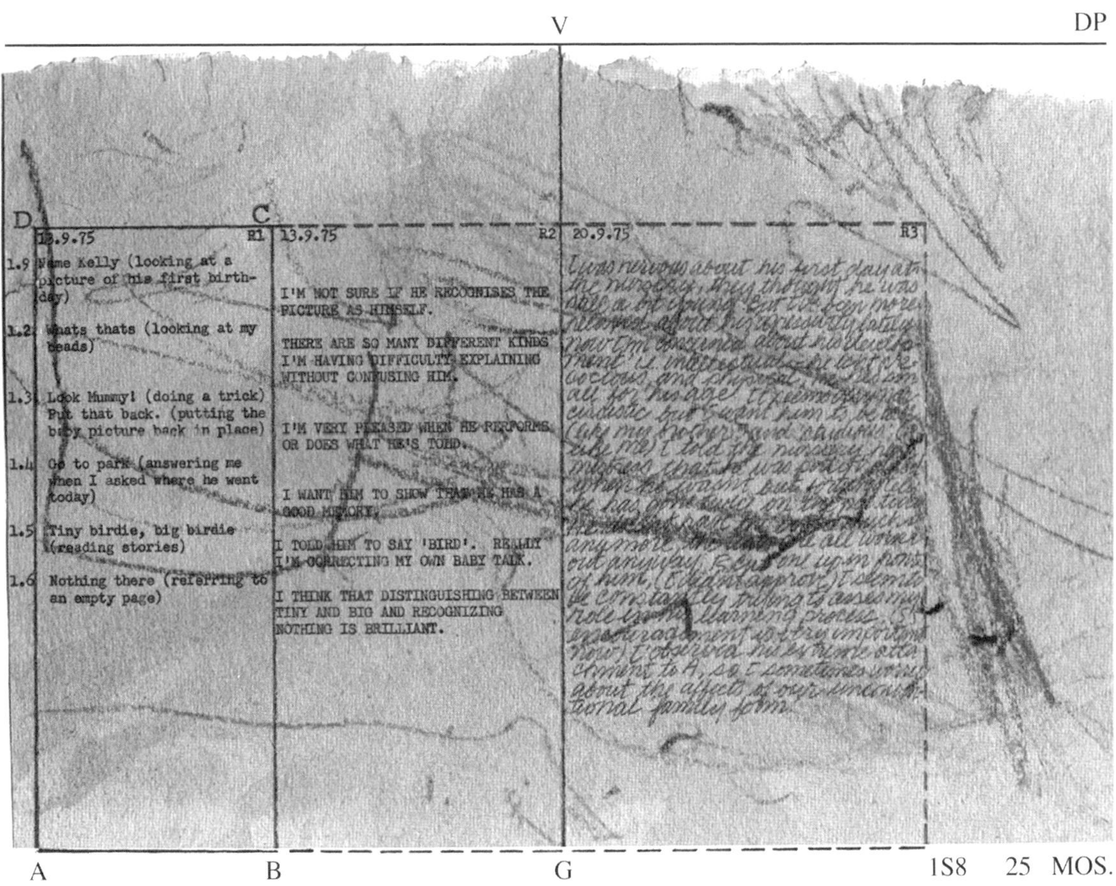
V
DP
D
C
13.9.75
R1
1.9 Name Kelly (looking at a picture of his first birthday)
1.2 Whats thats (looking at my beads)
1.3 Look Mummy! (doing a trick) Put that back. (putting the baby picture back in place)
1.4 Go to park (answering me when I asked where he went today)
1.5 Tiny birdie, big birdie (reading stories)
1.6 Nothing there (referring to an empty page)
13.9.75
R2
I'M NOT SURE IF HE RECOGNISES THE PICTURE AS HIMSELF.
THERE ARE SO MANY DIFFERENT KINDS I'M HAVING DIFFICULTY EXPLAINING WITHOUT CONFUSING HIM.
I'M VERY PLEASED WHEN HE PERFORMS OR DOES WHAT HE'S TOLD.
I WANT HIM TO SHOW THAT HE HAS A GOOD MEMORY.
I TOLD HIM TO SAY 'BIRD'. REALLY I'M CORRECTING MY OWN BABY TALK.
I THINK THAT DISTINGUISHING BETWEEN TINY AND BIG AND RECOGNIZING NOTHING IS BRILLIANT.
20.9.75
R3
A
B
G
1S8
25 MOS.

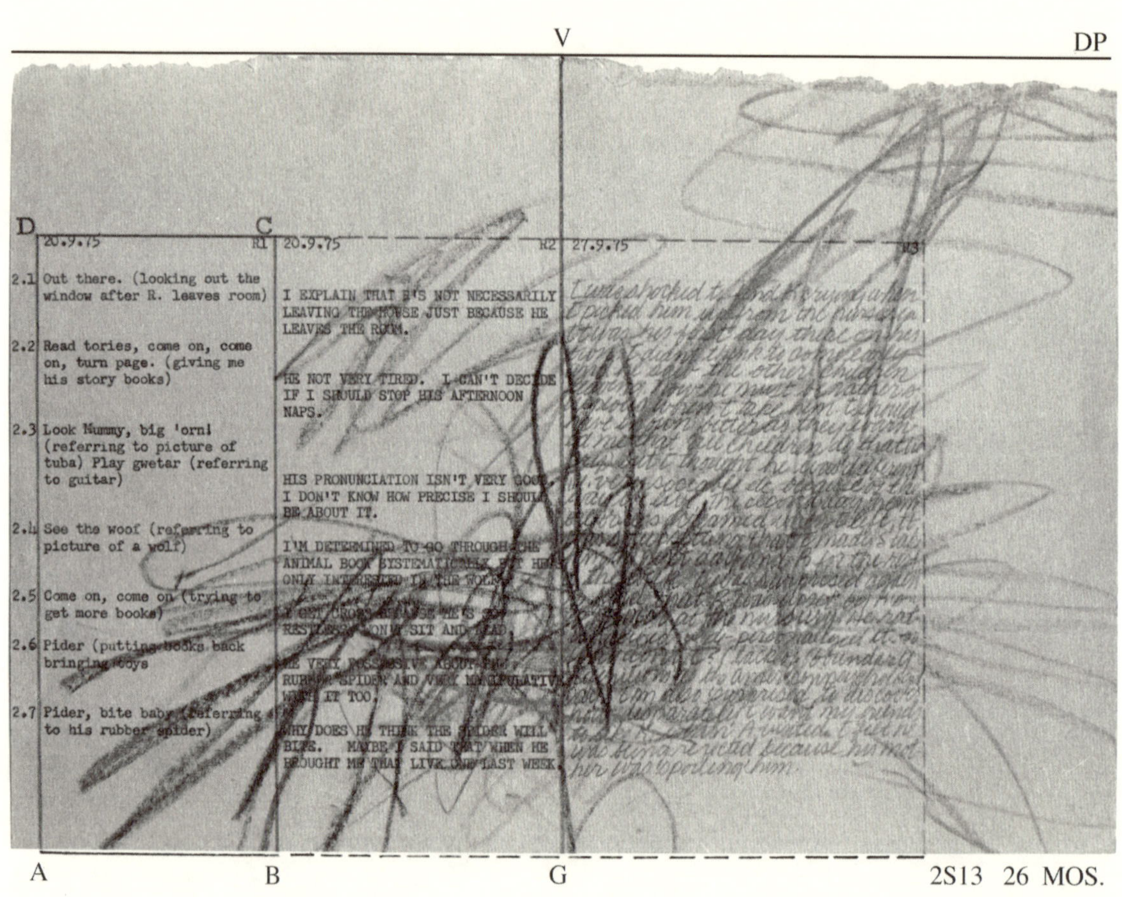

V
DP
D
C
20.9.75 R1
2.1 Out there. (looking out the window after R. leaves room)
2.2 Read tories, come on, come on, turn page. (giving me his story books)
2.3 Look Mummy, big 'orn! (referring to picture of tuba) Play gwetar (referring to guitar)
2.4 See the woof (referring to picture of a wolf)
2.5 Come on, come on (trying to get more books)
2.6 Pider (putting books back
2.7 Pider, bite baby (referring to his rubber spider)
20.9.75 R2
I EXPLAIN THAT H'S NOT NECESSARILY LEAVING THE HOUSE JUST BECAUSE HE LEAVES THE ROOM.
HE NOT VERY TIRED. I CAN'T DECIDE IF I SHOULD STOP HIS AFTERNOON NAPS.
HIS PRONUNCIATION ISN'T VERY GOOD. I DON'T KNOW HOW PRECISE I SHOULD BE ABOUT IT.
I'M DETERMINED TO GO THROUGH THE ANIMAL BOOK
27.9.75 R3
A
B
G
2S13 26 MOS.

V DP

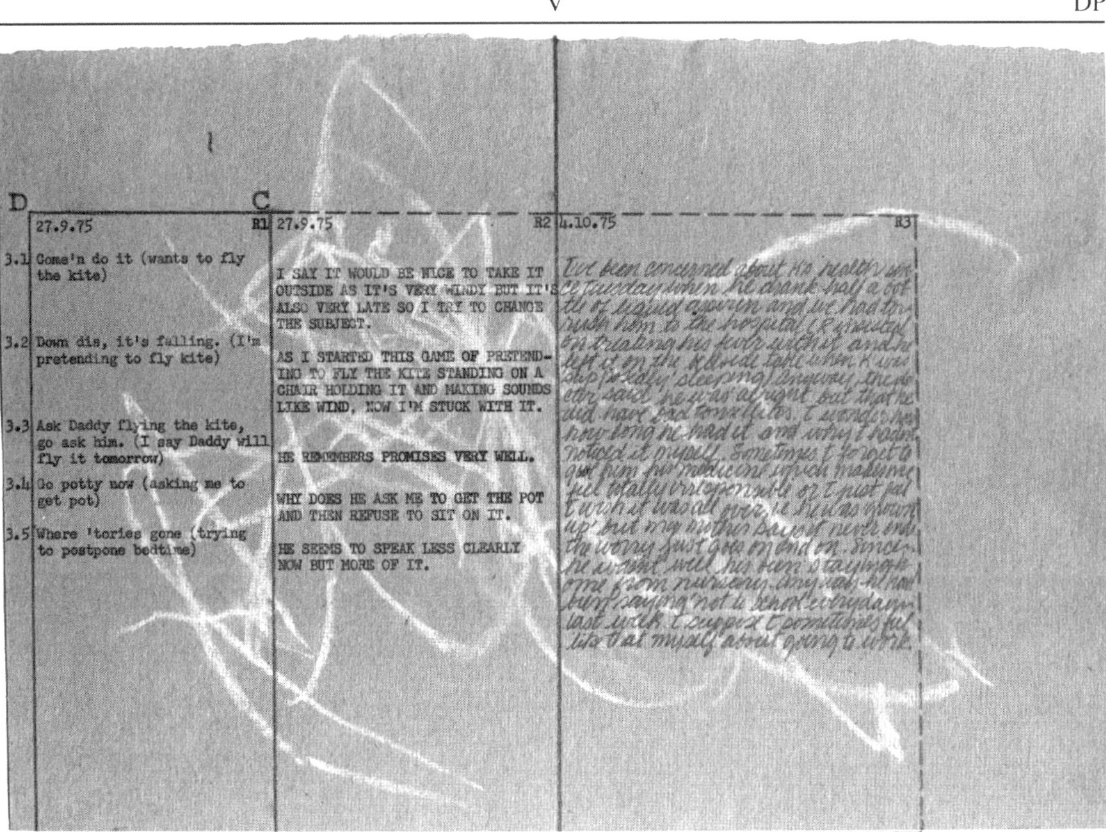

D C

27.9.75 R1	27.9.75 R2	4.10.75 R3
3.1 Come'n do it (wants to fly the kite)	I SAY IT WOULD BE NICE TO TAKE IT OUTSIDE AS IT'S VERY WINDY BUT IT'S ALSO VERY LATE SO I TRY TO CHANGE THE SUBJECT.	I've been concerned about his health since Tuesday when he drank half a bottle of liquid aspirin and we had to rush him to the hospital. (R insisted on treating his fever with it and he left it on the bedside table when K was supposedly sleeping.) Anyway, the doctor said he was alright but that he did have bad tonsillitis. I wonder how long he had it and why I hadn't noticed it myself. Sometimes I forget to give him his medicine which makes me feel totally irresponsible or I just feel I wish it was all over, i.e. he was 'grown up' but my mother says it never ends, the worry just goes on and on. Since he wasn't well he's been staying home from nursery. Anyway, he has been saying 'not to school' every day last week. I suppose I sometimes feel like that myself about going to work.
3.2 Down dis, it's falling. (I'm pretending to fly kite)	AS I STARTED THIS GAME OF PRETENDING TO FLY THE KITE STANDING ON A CHAIR HOLDING IT AND MAKING SOUNDS LIKE WIND, NOW I'M STUCK WITH IT.	
3.3 Ask Daddy flying the kite, go ask him. (I say Daddy will fly it tomorrow)	HE REMEMBERS PROMISES VERY WELL.	
3.4 Go potty now (asking me to get pot)	WHY DOES HE ASK ME TO GET THE POT AND THEN REFUSE TO SIT ON IT.	
3.5 Where 'tories gone (trying to postpone bedtime)	HE SEEMS TO SPEAK LESS CLEARLY NOW BUT MORE OF IT.	

A B G 3S9 26 MOS.

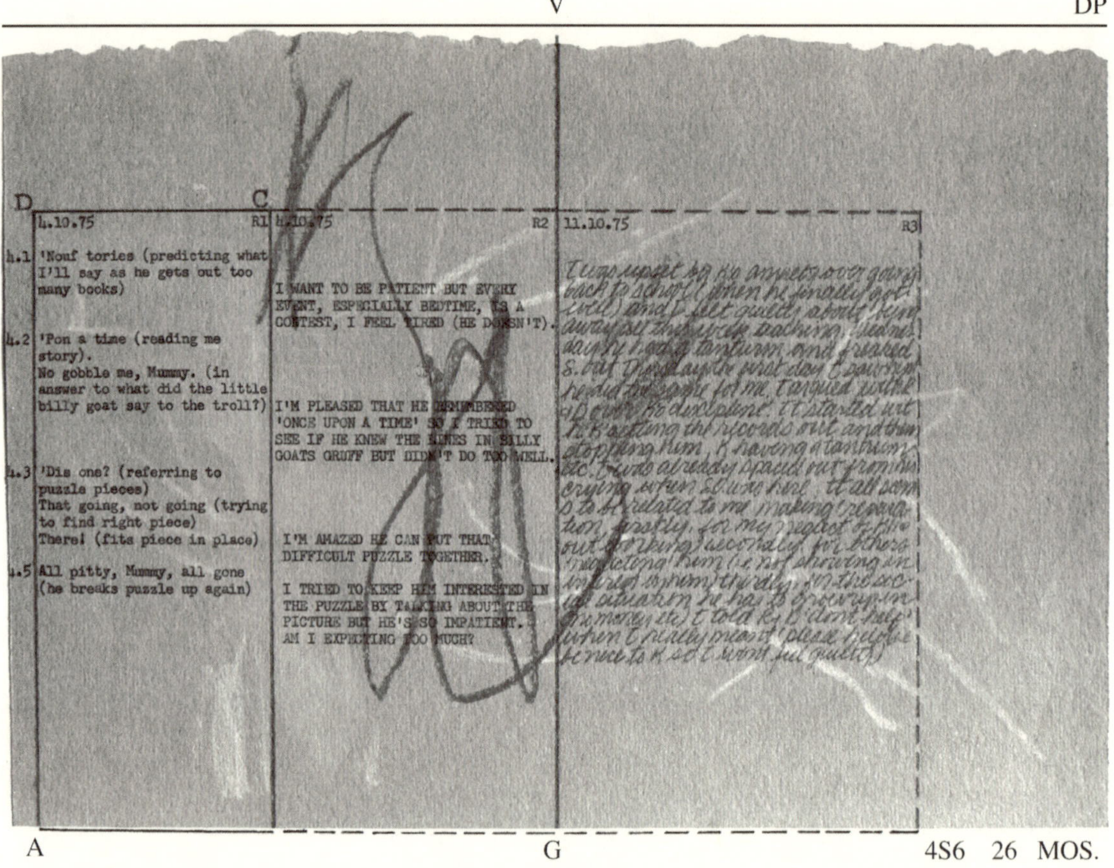
V
DP
D
C
4.10.75
R1
4.1 'Nouf tories (predicting what I'll say as he gets out too many books)
4.2 'Pon a time (reading me story).
No gobble me, Mummy. (in answer to what did the little billy goat say to the troll?)
4.3 'Dis one? (referring to puzzle pieces)
That going, not going (trying to find right piece)
There! (fits piece in place)
4.5 All pitty, Mummy, all gone (he breaks puzzle up again)
4.10.75
R2
I WANT TO BE PATIENT BUT EVERY EVENT, ESPECIALLY BEDTIME, IS A CONTEST, I FEEL TIRED (HE DOESN'T).
I'M PLEASED THAT HE REMEMBERED 'ONCE UPON A TIME' SO I TRIED TO SEE IF HE KNEW THE LINES IN BILLY GOATS GRUFF BUT DIDN'T DO TOO WELL.
I'M AMAZED HE CAN PUT THAT DIFFICULT PUZZLE TOGETHER.
I TRIED TO KEEP HIM INTERESTED IN THE PUZZLE BY TALKING ABOUT THE PICTURE BUT HE'S SO IMPATIENT. AM I EXPECTING TOO MUCH?
11.10.75
R3
A
G
4S6 26 MOS.

V DP

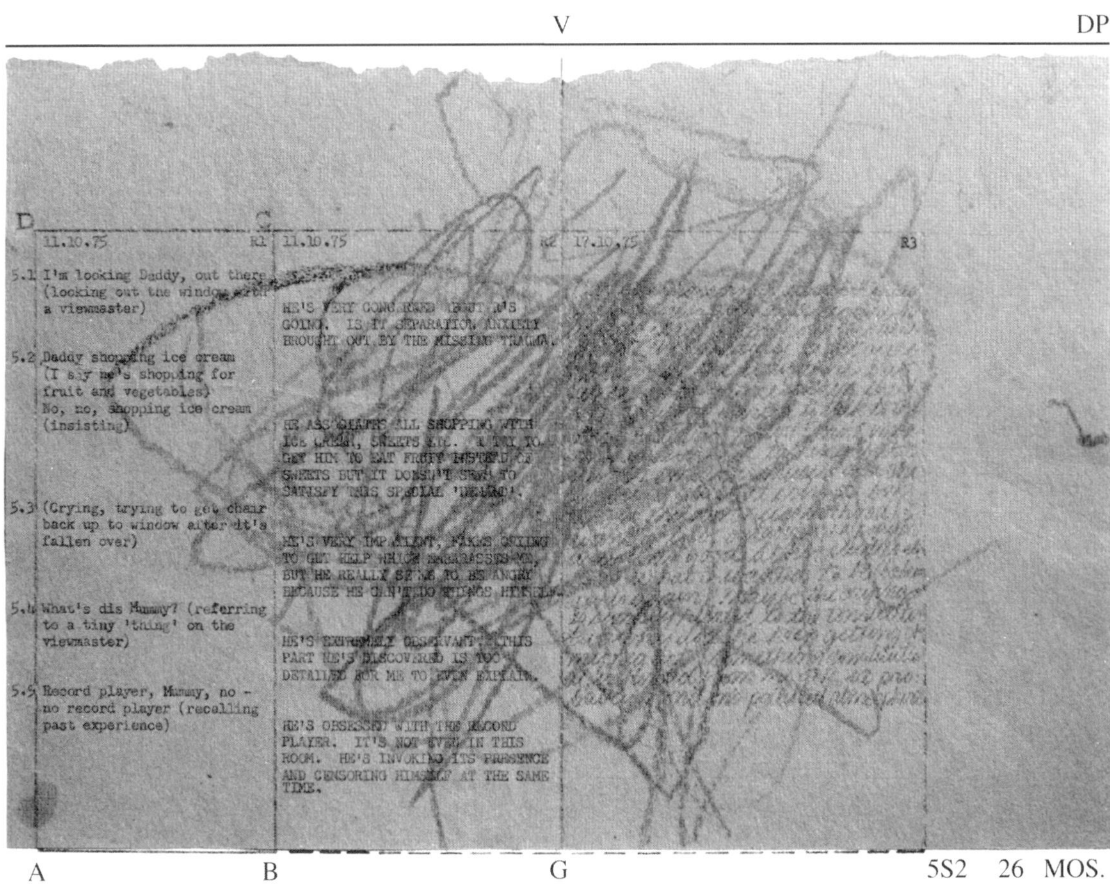
D C

11.10.75 R1	11.10.75 R2	17.10.75 R3
5.1 I'm looking Daddy, out there (looking out the window with a viewmaster)	HE'S VERY CONCERNED ABOUT IT'S GOING. IS IT SEPARATION ANXIETY BROUGHT OUT BY THE MISSING TRAUMA.	
5.2 Daddy shopping ice cream (I say he's shopping for fruit and vegetables) No, no, shopping ice cream (insisting)	HE ASSOCIATES ALL SHOPPING WITH ICE CREAM, SWEETS ETC. I TRY TO GET HIM TO EAT FRUIT INSTEAD OF SWEETS BUT IT DOESN'T SEEM TO SATISFY THIS SPECIAL 'DEMAND'.	
5.3 (Crying, trying to get chair back up to window after it's fallen over)	HE'S VERY IMPATIENT, FAKES CRYING TO GET HELP WHICH EMBARASSES ME, BUT HE REALLY SEEMS TO BE ANGRY BECAUSE HE CAN'T DO THINGS HIMSELF.	
5.4 What's dis Mummy? (referring to a tiny 'thing' on the viewmaster)	HE'S EXTREMELY OBSERVANT. THIS PART HE'S DISCOVERED IS TOO DETAILED FOR ME TO EVEN EXPLAIN.	
5.5 Record player, Mummy, no - no record player (recalling past experience)	HE'S OBSESSED WITH THE RECORD PLAYER. IT'S NOT EVEN IN THIS ROOM. HE'S INVOKING ITS PRESENCE AND CENSORING HIMSELF AT THE SAME TIME.	

A B G 5S2 26 MOS.

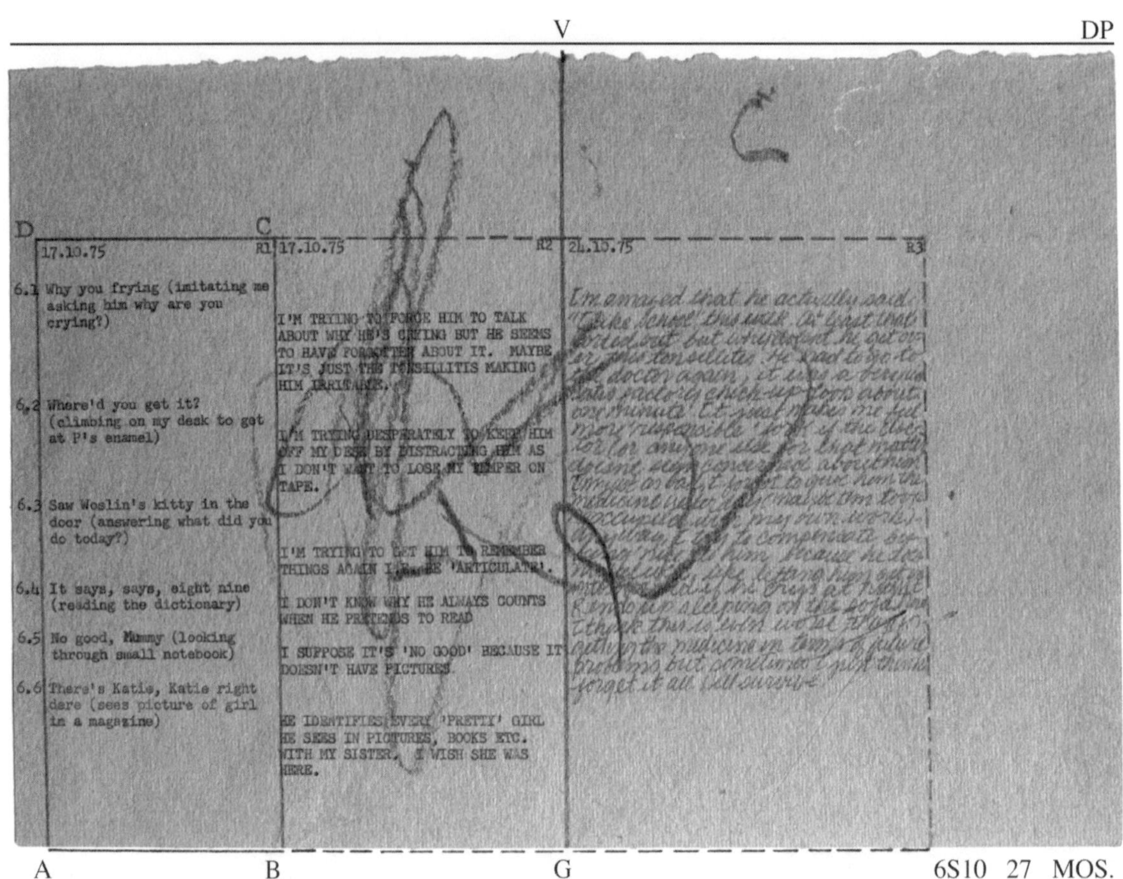

17.10.75 R1

6.1 Why you frying (imitating me asking him why are you crying?)

6.2 Where'd you get it? (climbing on my desk to get at P's enamel)

6.3 Saw Woslin's kitty in the door (answering what did you do today?)

6.4 It says, says, eight nine (reading the dictionary)

6.5 No good, Mummy (looking through small notebook)

6.6 There's Katie, Katie right dere (sees picture of girl in a magazine)

17.10.75 R2

I'M TRYING TO FORCE HIM TO TALK ABOUT WHY HE'S CRYING BUT HE SEEMS TO HAVE FORGOTTEN ABOUT IT. MAYBE IT'S JUST THE TONSILLITIS MAKING HIM IRRITABLE.

I'M TRYING DESPERATELY TO KEEP HIM OFF MY DESK BY DISTRACTING HIM AS I DON'T WANT TO LOSE MY TEMPER ON TAPE.

I'M TRYING TO GET HIM TO REMEMBER THINGS AGAIN LIKE HE 'ARTICULATE'.

I DON'T KNOW WHY HE ALWAYS COUNTS WHEN HE PRETENDS TO READ

I SUPPOSE IT'S 'NO GOOD' BECAUSE IT DOESN'T HAVE PICTURES.

HE IDENTIFIES EVERY 'PRETTY' GIRL HE SEES IN PICTURES, BOOKS ETC. WITH MY SISTER. I WISH SHE WAS HERE.

24.10.75 R3

I'm amazed that he actually said "[illegible] school" this week. At least that [illegible] but [illegible] he out [illegible] tonsilitis. He had to go to the doctor again, it was a [illegible] check-up took about one minute. [illegible] makes me feel more 'responsible' [illegible] of the doctor (or anyone else [illegible]) [illegible] to give him the medicine [illegible] occupied with my own work [illegible] to compensate [illegible] him because he [illegible] sleeping on the sofa. I think this is [illegible] getting the medicine in terms of future problems but sometimes I just think forget it all. [illegible]

V DP

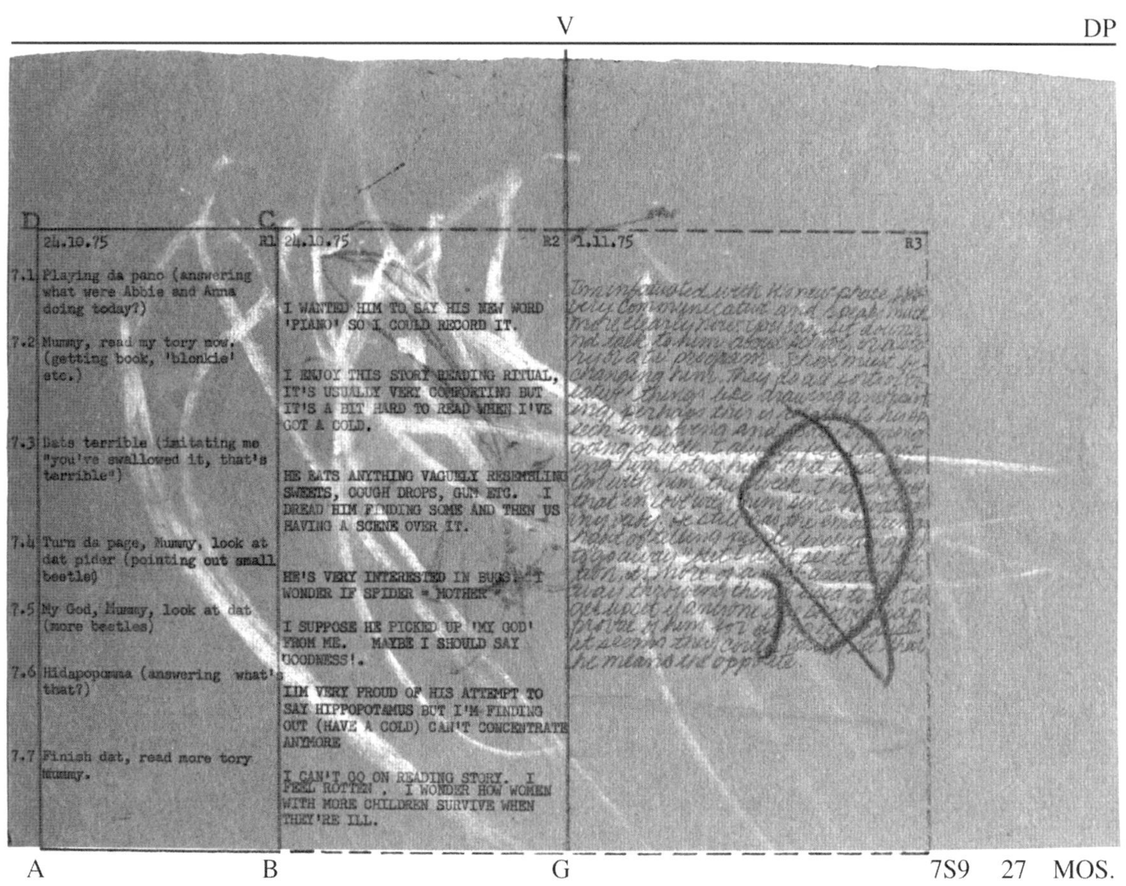

A B G 7S9 27 MOS.

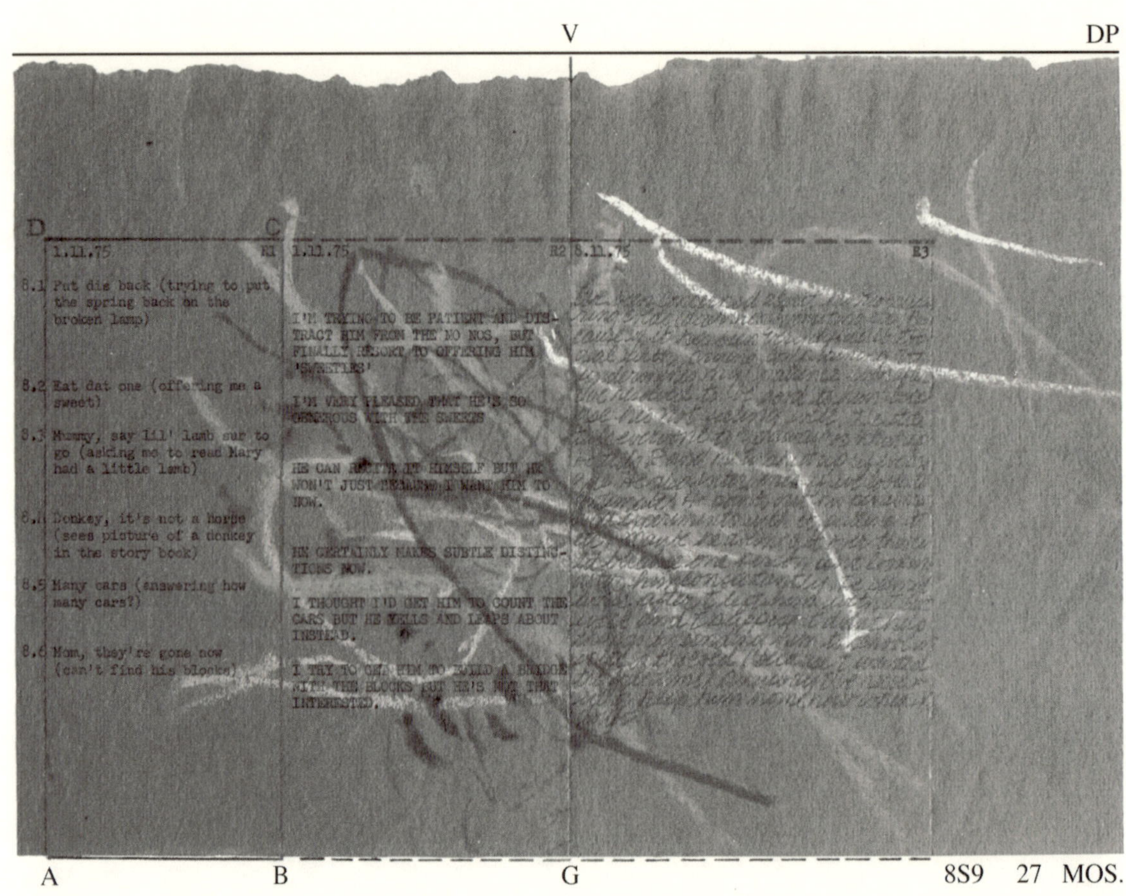
V
DP
D
C
1.11.75 R1
8.1 Put dis back (trying to put the spring back on the broken lamp)
8.2 Eat dat one (offering me a sweet)
8.3 Mummy, say lil' lamb sur to go (asking me to read Mary had a little lamb)
8.4 Donkey, it's not a horse (sees picture of a donkey in the story book)
8.5 Many cars (answering how many cars?)
8.6 Mom, they're gone now (can't find his blocks)
1.11.75 R2
I'M TRYING TO BE PATIENT AND DISTRACT HIM FROM THE NO NOS, BUT FINALLY RESORT TO OFFERING HIM 'SWEETIES'
I'M VERY PLEASED THAT HE'S SO GENEROUS WITH THE SWEETS
HE CAN RECITE IT HIMSELF BUT HE WON'T JUST BECAUSE I WANT HIM TO NOW.
HE CERTAINLY MAKES SUBTLE DISTINCTIONS NOW.
I THOUGHT I'D GET HIM TO COUNT THE CARS BUT HE YELLS AND LEAPS ABOUT INSTEAD.
I TRY TO GET HIM TO BUILD A BRIDGE WITH THE BLOCKS BUT HE'S NOT THAT INTERESTED.
8.11.75 R3
A
B
G
8S9 27 MOS.

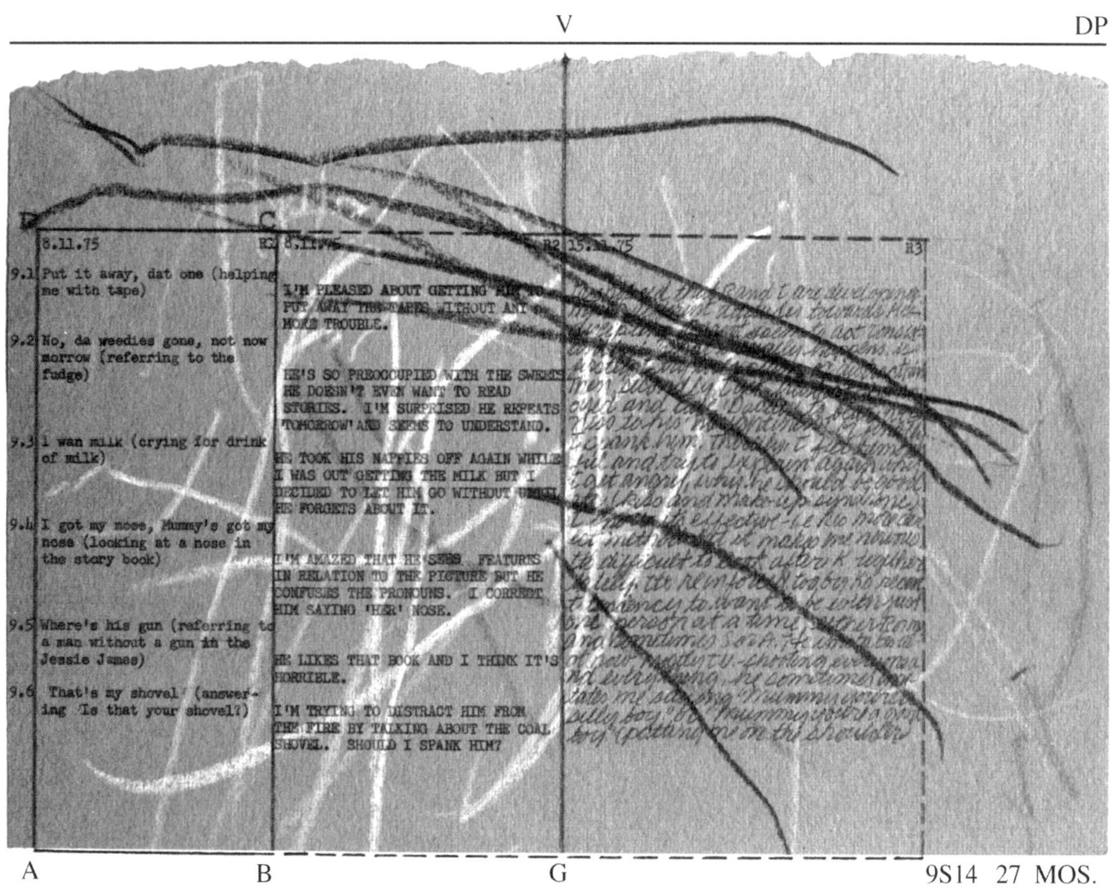

V
DP
D
C
8.11.75
R2
9.1 Put it away, dat one (helping me with tape)
9.2 No, da weedies gone, not now morrow (referring to the fudge)
9.3 I wan milk (crying for drink of milk)
9.4 I got my nose, Mummy's got my nose (looking at a nose in the story book)
9.5 Where's his gun (referring to a man without a gun in the Jessie James)
9.6 That's my shovel (answering 'Is that your shovel?)
R2
MORE TROUBLE.
HE'S SO PREOCCUPIED WITH THE SWEETS HE DOESN'T EVEN WANT TO READ STORIES. I'M SURPRISED HE REPEATS 'TOMORROW' AND SEEMS TO UNDERSTAND.
HE TOOK HIS NAPPIES OFF AGAIN WHILE I WAS OUT GETTING THE MILK BUT I DECIDED TO LET HIM GO WITHOUT
HE FORGETS ABOUT IT.
I'M AMAZED THAT HE SEES FEATURES IN RELATION TO THE PICTURE BUT HE CONFUSES THE PRONOUNS. I CORRECT HIM SAYING 'HER' NOSE.
HE LIKES THAT BOOK AND I THINK IT'S HORRIBLE.
I'M TRYING TO DISTRACT HIM FROM THE FIRE BY TALKING ABOUT THE COAL SHOVEL. SHOULD I SPANK HIM?
R3
A
B
G
9S14 27 MOS.

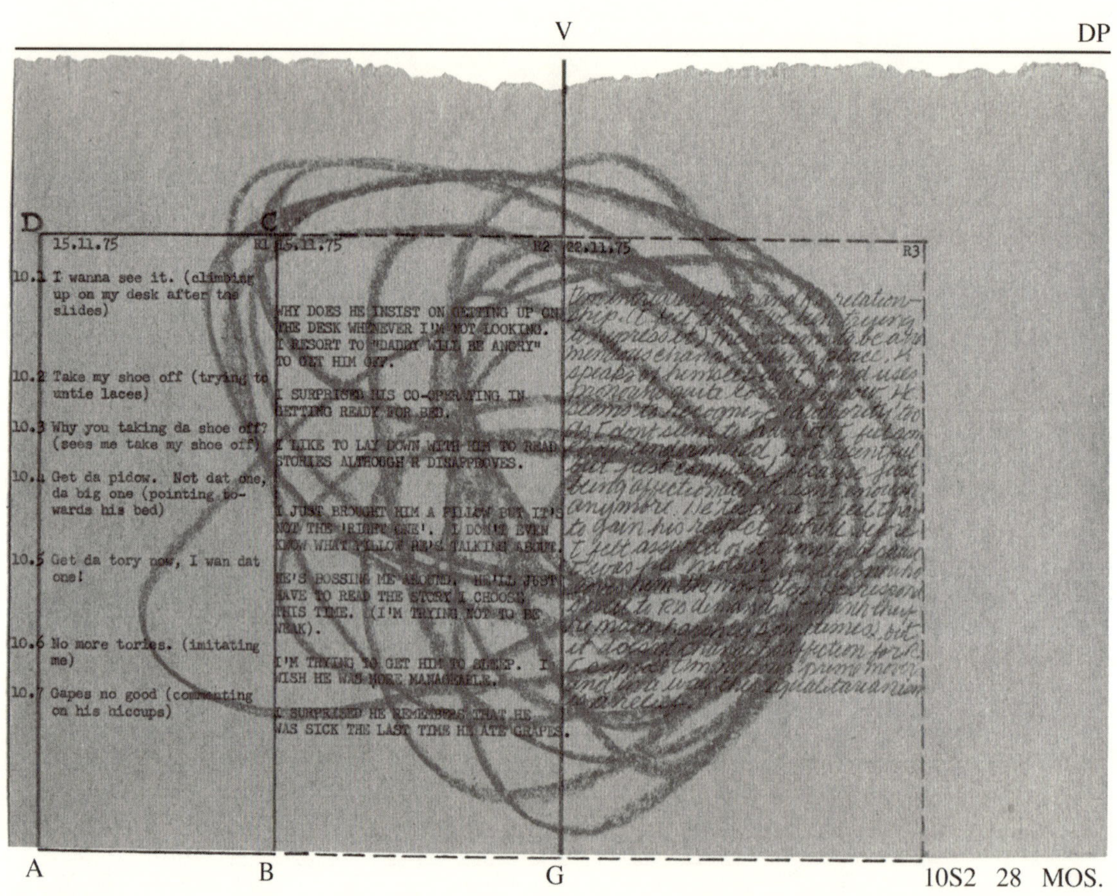
V
DP
D
C
15.11.75
R1
10.1 I wanna see it. (climbing up on my desk after the slides)
10.2 Take my shoe off (trying to untie laces)
10.3 Why you taking da shoe off? (sees me take my shoe off)
10.4 Get da pidow. Not dat one, da big one (pointing towards his bed)
10.5 Get da tory now, I wan dat one!
10.6 No more tories. (imitating me)
10.7 Gapes no good (commenting on his hiccups)
15.11.75
R2
WHY DOES HE INSIST ON GETTING UP ON THE DESK WHENEVER I'M NOT LOOKING. I RESORT TO "DADDY WILL BE ANGRY" TO GET HIM OFF.
I SURPRISED HIS CO-OPERATING IN GETTING READY FOR BED.
I LIKE TO LAY DOWN WITH HIM TO READ STORIES ALTHOUGH R DISAPPROVES.
I JUST BROUGHT HIM A PILLOW BUT IT'S NOT THE 'RIGHT ONE'. I DON'T EVEN KNOW WHAT PILLOW HE'S TALKING ABOUT.
HE'S BOSSING ME AROUND. HE'LL JUST HAVE TO READ THE STORY I CHOOSE THIS TIME. (I'M TRYING NOT TO BE WEAK).
I'M TRYING TO GET HIM TO SLEEP. I WISH HE WAS MORE MANAGEABLE.
I SURPRISED HE REMEMBERS THAT HE WAS SICK THE LAST TIME HE ATE GRAPES.
22.11.75
R3
A
B
G
10S2 28 MOS.

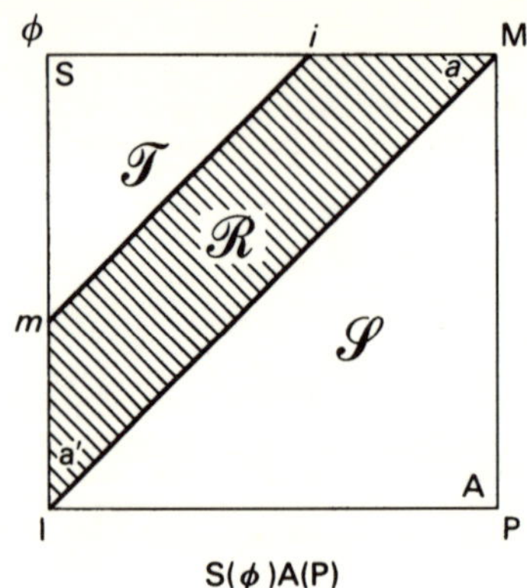
ϕ
i
M
S
a
𝒯
ℛ
m
𝒮
a'
A
I
P
S(ϕ)A(P)

(WHY IS HE/SHE LIKE THAT?)

S

Experimentum Mentis III
Weaning from the Dyad

For both the mother and the child, the crucial moment of "weaning" is constituted by the intervention of a third term (i.e., the father), thus consolidating the Oedipal triad and undermining the Imaginary dyad which determined the intersubjectivity of the pre-Oedipal instance. This intervention situates the Imaginary third term of the primordial triangle (the child as phallus) and the paternal "imago" of the mirror phase within the dominance of the Symbolic structure through the Word of the father. That is, the mother's words referring to the authority of the "father" to which the real father may or may not conform. When she calls upon him to bear witness to the child's indiscretions, as for example in Documentation III, 10S, she is conclusively reinstated in her negative place precisely because, in order to be what she herself would like to be, the child must be handed over to the Symbolic father, the figure of the Law. In this way the "cutting out" of the child's ego leaves what is lacking in the mother's ego, that is, her lack of the privileged signifier of the Symbolic. The consequent denigration of the mother for this lack posits her insufficiency as an ego-ideal for the child and this reinforces the initial depletion of her own ego.

This critical moment is overdetermined by the child's entry into an extra-familial process of socialization (the school). It is ultimately here that the child masters the finite system of language and sublimates the absence on which it is founded through the infinite fabrications (marks, songs, rhymes) of his/her autonomous desire. The Oedipal child learns that being what the mother wants him/her to be is what he/she wants to be but cannot be. Consequently, the mother's sense of lack is lived through as the repetitious transgressing, by the child, of her narcissistic aim. This provokes her question "Why is he/she like that?" For the boy it is because he is like his father, a projection which reinforces the maternal separation; but for the girl, inevitably, it is because she is like her mother, an introjection which recapitulates the ambivalence of the Oedipal moment for the female subject.

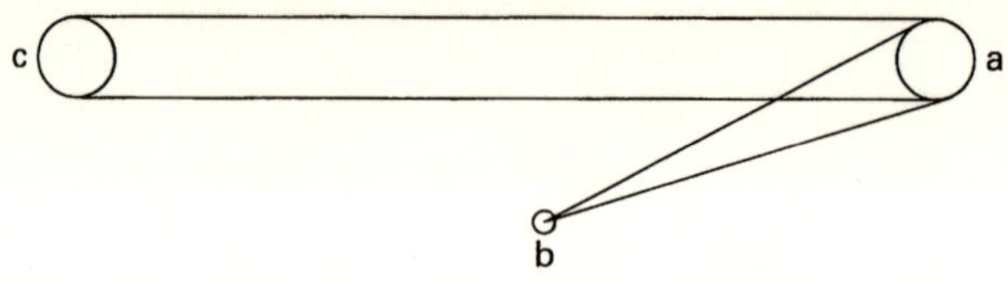
c
a
b

Documentation IV
Transitional Objects, Diary and Diagram

In this document, "transitional objects" refer to the child's comforter ("blankie") and to the plaster "hand plaques" which constitute part of the mother's "memorabilia" (reminiscent of baby's first photos, shoes, lock of hair, etc.). The clay imprints were initiated as an extension of the child's play activities at nursery school between the age of 2.5–2.9.

The diary texts, inscribed on the comforter fragments, were recorded at irregular intervals between January and May 1976. They functioned on the one hand as a confessional, expressing the mother's ambivalence about "working outside the home," and on the other, as a polemic, interrogating the familiar theme of "separation anxiety" by placing emphasis on the consequences for the mother rather than the child.

The inclusion of Schema R within the discourse of "Documentation IV" summarizes and, to a certain extent, subverts its use in "Experimentum Mentis I–III." The diagram, which is stamped on the hand imprints, does not correspond literally to the diary texts in the sense of illustrating the subject's history. It unfolds as a representation of the static states of the subjects (S) within the fields of the Imaginary, the Symbolic and the Real.

(I) the Imaginary; including (a) the figure of the Imaginary other of the mirror stage, (a′) the paternal imago (ø) the Imaginary object, i.e., the phallus.

(S) the Symbolic; including (M) the signifier of the primordial object (I) the Ideal of the ego (P) the Name-of-the-Father in the locus of the Other (A).

(R) the Real; framed and maintained by the relations of the Imaginary and the Symbolic (the Real cannot be articulated but remains as a kind of residue of articulation, foreclosed to representation as such).

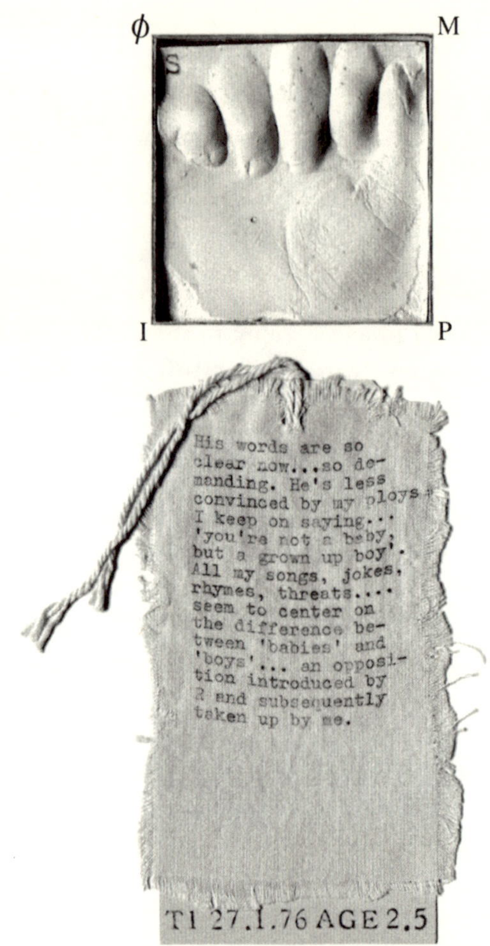
ϕ
M
S
I
P
His words are so
clear now...so de-
manding. He's less
convinced by my ploys.
I keep on saying...
'you're not a baby,
but a grown up boy'.
All my songs, jokes,
rhymes, threats....
seem to center on
the difference be-
tween 'babies' and
'boys'... an opposi-
tion introduced by
R and subsequently
taken up by me.
TI 27.1.76 AGE 2.5

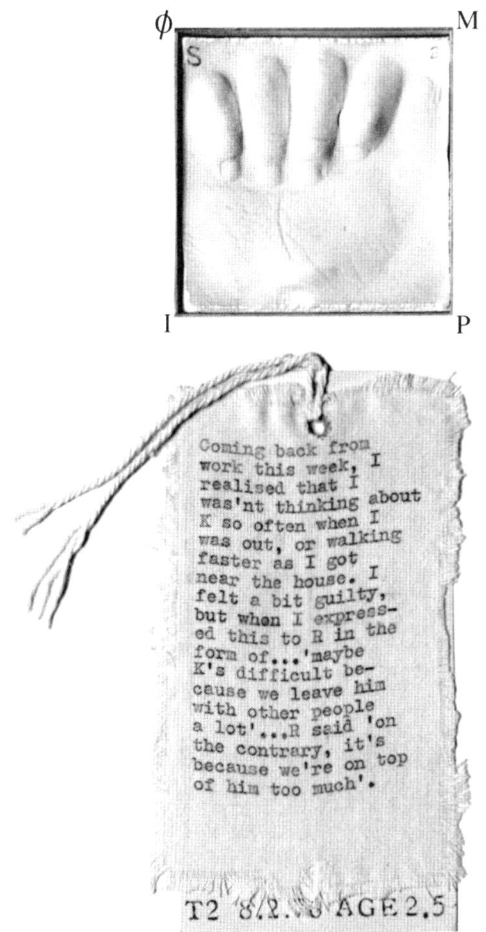
φ
M
S
I
P
Coming back from
work this week, I
realised that I
was'nt thinking about
K so often when I
was out, or walking
faster as I got
near the house. I
felt a bit guilty,
but when I express-
ed this to R in the
form of...'maybe
K's difficult be-
cause we leave him
with other people
a lot'...R said 'on
the contrary, it's
because we're on top
of him too much'.
T2 8.2. AGE 2.5

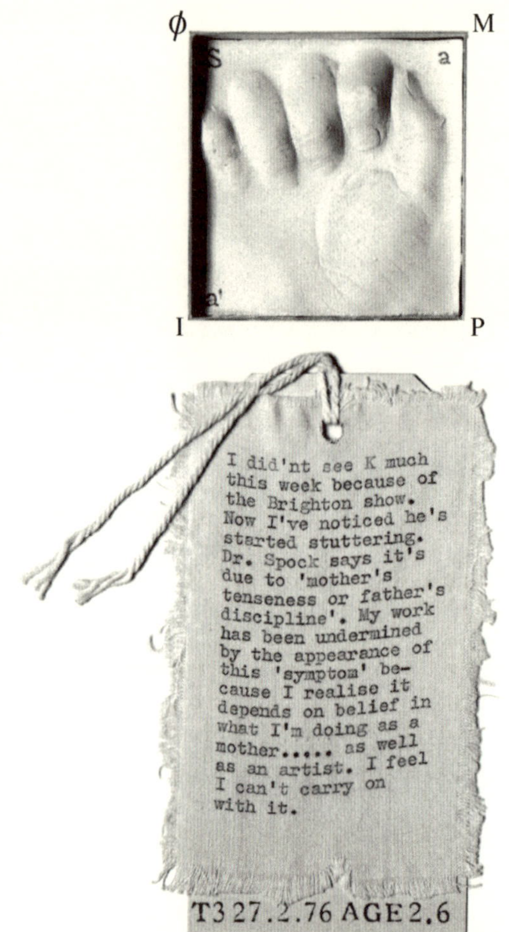
ϕ
M
S
a
a'
I
P
I did'nt see K much this week because of the Brighton show. Now I've noticed he's started stuttering. Dr. Spock says it's due to 'mother's tenseness or father's discipline'. My work has been undermined by the appearance of this 'symptom' because I realise it depends on belief in what I'm doing as a mother..... as well as an artist. I feel I can't carry on with it.
T3 27.2.76 AGE 2.6

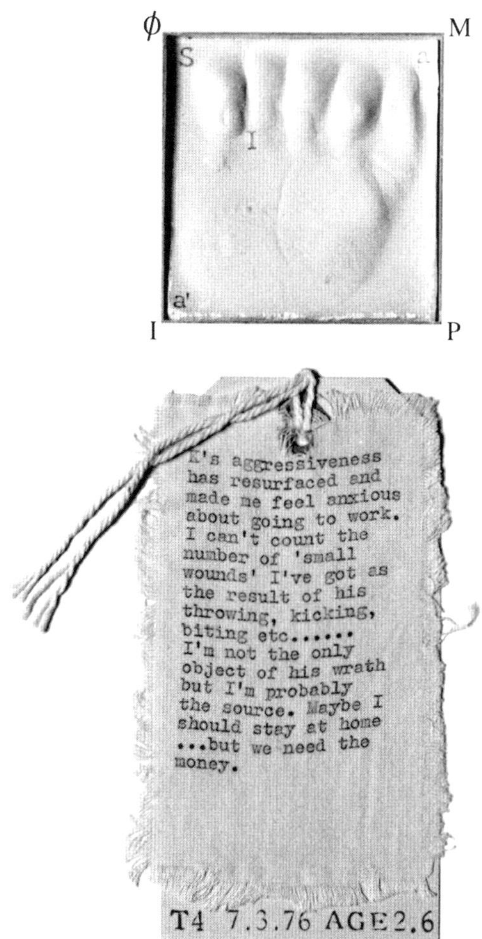
ϕ
M
S
a
I
a'
I
P
K's aggressiveness
has resurfaced and
made me feel anxious
about going to work.
I can't count the
number of 'small
wounds' I've got as
the result of his
throwing, kicking,
biting etc......
I'm not the only
object of his wrath
but I'm probably
the source. Maybe I
should stay at home
...but we need the
money.
T4 7.3.76 AGE2.6

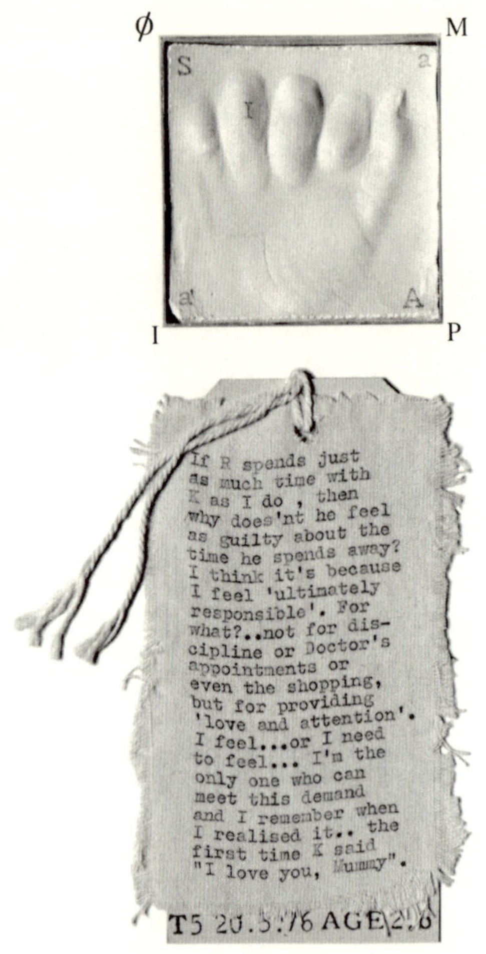
Ø
M
S
a
a
A
I
P
If R spends just
as much time with
K as I do , then
why does'nt he feel
as guilty about the
time he spends away?
I think it's because
I feel 'ultimately
responsible'. For
what?..not for dis-
cipline or Doctor's
appointments or
even the shopping,
but for providing
'love and attention'.
I feel...or I need
to feel... I'm the
only one who can
meet this demand
and I remember when
I realised it.. the
first time K said
"I love you, Mummy".
T5 20.5.76 AGE 2.6

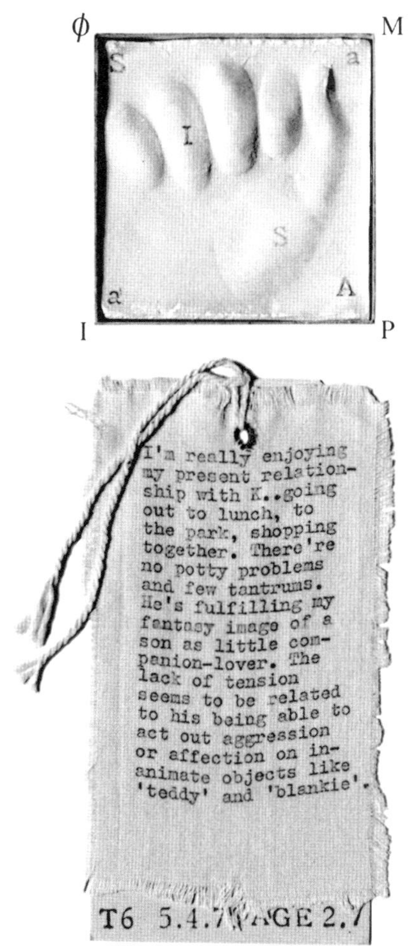
ϕ
M
S
a
I
S
a
A
I
P
I'm really enjoying my present relationship with K..going out to lunch, to the park, shopping together. There're no potty problems and few tantrums. He's fulfilling my fantasy image of a son as little companion-lover. The lack of tension seems to be related to his being able to act out aggression or affection on inanimate objects like 'teddy' and 'blankie'.
T6 5.4.7
AGE 2.7

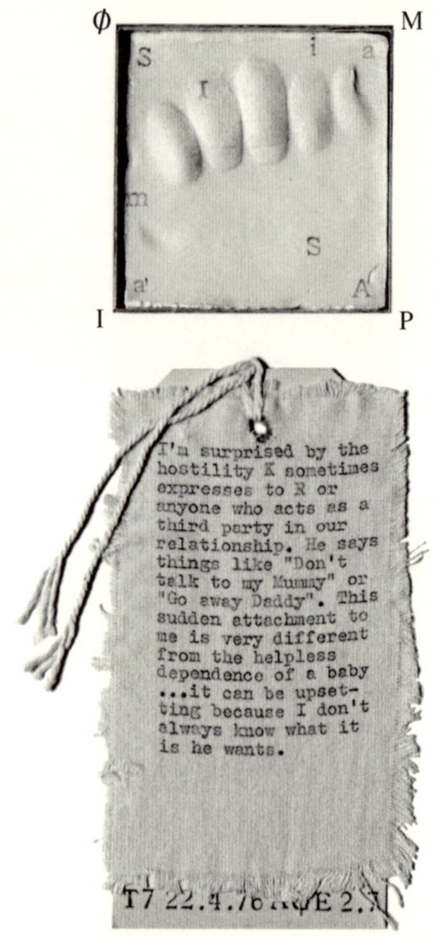
Ø
M
I
P
I'm surprised by the hostility K sometimes expresses to R or anyone who acts as a third party in our relationship. He says things like "Don't talk to my Mummy" or "Go away Daddy". This sudden attachment to me is very different from the helpless dependence of a baby ...it can be upsetting because I don't always know what it is he wants.
T7 22.4.76

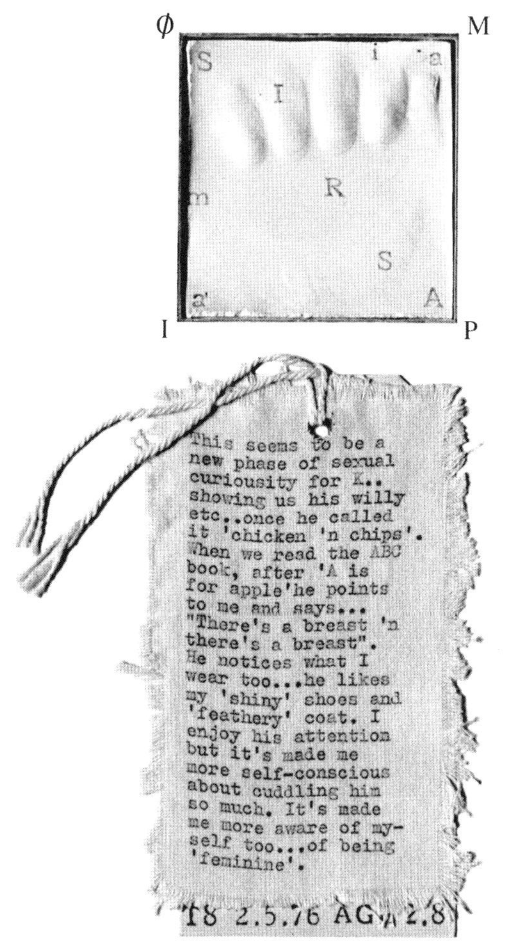
Ø
M
I
P
This seems to be a new phase of sexual curiousity for K.. showing us his willy etc..once he called it 'chicken 'n chips'. When we read the ABC book, after 'A is for apple'he points to me and says... "There's a breast 'n there's a breast". He notices what I wear too...he likes my 'shiny' shoes and 'feathery' coat. I enjoy his attention but it's made me more self-conscious about cuddling him so much. It's made me more aware of my-self too...of being 'feminine'.
T8 2.5.76 AG.A 2.8

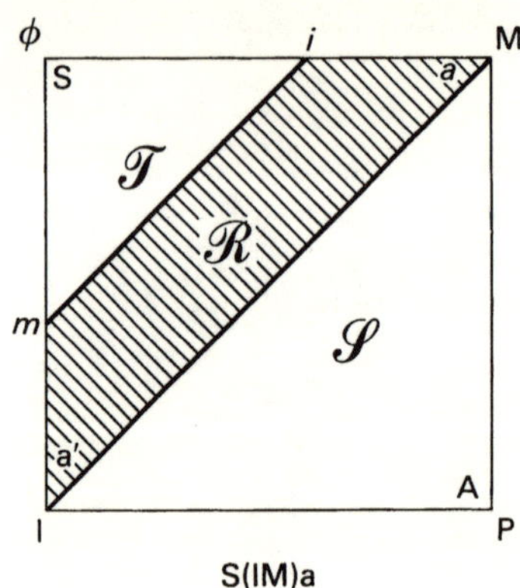

S(IM)a

(WHAT DO YOU WANT?)

S

Experimentum Mentis IV
On Femininity

At the Oedipal moment, the mother, father and child inhabit a closed field of desire. But for the mother, the distancing function of the father uncovers the source of narcissistic satisfaction which is sustained by her Imaginary object, the child as phallus. This is the pleasure of maternal femininity. The site of this excavation is precisely the corporeal reality of the child's body (the soft, round, perfectly formed body of her baby), because the pleasure she derives from it must be relinquished. This loss is preordained, on the one hand, by the natural process of maturation, and, on the other, by the prohibitions of the Father and the Law. The Oedipal melodrama is staged as a maternal version of the Fort/Da game, "How grown up you are"/"You're still my baby," or elided as in Documentation IV, T1, "You're not a baby, but a grown-up boy" (i.e., "I wish you were still my baby but ...").

This moment is decisive if her child is a boy since the prohibition to incest is insured by the threat of castration. However, the mother-daughter relationship is more ambivalent because the girl enters the Oedipal situation in retreat rather than in confrontation, in hope of receiving the phallus from her father, eventually in the form of a child. To achieve this end, she must identify herself with her own mother and take up a position of lack. This process of identification with the ideal type of her sex makes it possible for a woman to see herself as desirable, to enter into a sexual relationship with a man and to satisfy the needs of the child produced by this relationship; but it also introduces her to the pleasure of having the mother's body, cathecting her own body as that of her mother (or of another woman). Beyond the pleasure of the real of the child's body lies the pleasure of the maternal body experienced as real through it; the loss of this pleasure constitutes the ultimate threat to the mother's narcissism. Her "memorabilia" and the child's "transitional objects" are emblems which testify to the threatened loss of mutual enjoyment, but the desire in which they are grounded can only be caused in the unconscious by the specific structure of fantasy.

When the mother anxiously poses the question "What do you want? (!)" in response to her child's whining, aggressive or clinging complaints, she is essentially asking herself "What does he/she want of me?" The child's demand constitutes the mother as the Other who has the privilege of satisfying his/her needs and at the same time, the whimsical power of depriving him/her of this satisfaction. To a certain extent the mother recognizes the unconditional element of demand as a demand for love. It is this recognition which underlies her feeling of "ultimate responsibility" for the child even when the sexual division of labor in childcare is radically altered to include the father.

But there is another cause for this asymmetry which is not necessarily given at the level of consciousness. This is the mother's desire to remain the privileged Other of the pre-Oedipal instance, insofar as the child's demands are the guarantee of her maternal femininity. Thus, she transforms the child's gifts into proofs of love and his/her indiscretions into denials. In this situation it is difficult for the child to locate his/her desire. Finally, it is the Law, of which the Father is the original representative, that intervenes to insure the autonomous status of desire, i.e. to substitute for the unconditional element in the demand for love, the absolute condition of desire. Paradoxically this implies a detachment which is the minimum condition for the Oedipal child's unsolicited expression, as in Documentation IV, T5, "I love you, Mummy." Through the child's words, "the real" of the mother's body is represented as signifier of the Real Other in the register of the Symbolic.

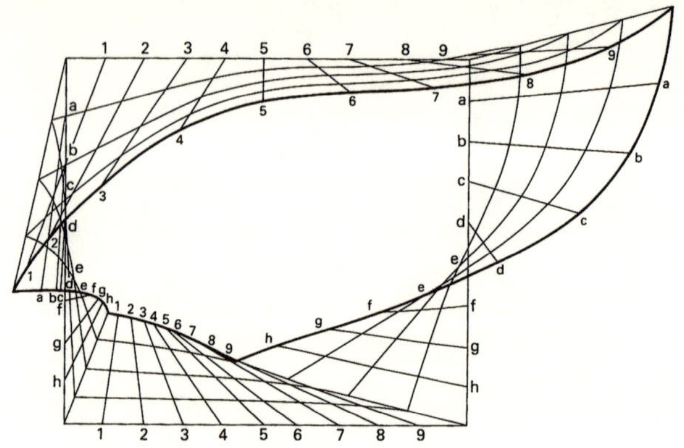

1 2 3 4 5 6 7 8 9
a b c d e f g h
1 2 3 4 5 6 7 8 9

Documentation V Classified Specimens, Proportional Diagrams, Statistical Tables, Research and Index

The specimens in this document were collected between July 1976 and September 1977. They were not selected according to a scientific procedure, but were determined by the child's spontaneous investigations of things in his everyday life (age 2.9–4.1). The items in the collection were not rare or valuable, except for the mother. In so far as they were gifts from the child, and more importantly because they coincided with his questions about sexuality, the specimens constituted a set of discursive events. Each event was documented in three sections as follows:

(1) L1–11: Mounted Specimens and Labels

The specimens are mounted on entomological pinning blocks (i.e., improvised variations) and stamped with the date and place of collection. The labels give taxonomic information: common name and scientific name including species, with author's name in brackets, genus and family. Field data is limited to habitat. All the botanical specimens are in the Angiospermae group (flowering plants). Most of the zoological samples are from the class Insecta (orders Coleoptera and Lepidoptera) with the exception of one example which is Gastropoda. However, classification, in this document, is used to construct a metaphorical space in which the mother's body is *named* through the researches of her child.

(2) Figs. 1–11a: Proportional Diagrams and Research

Photocopied reproductions of the specimens are set out as archaeological fragments within the "frame of reference" of a proportional diagram. The diagram is also intended to refer to the Method of Co-ordinates on which the theory of transformations is based. It was first used to study related forms and later applied to the analysis of plant and animal morphology. For instance, by inscribing the outline of an organism (e.g. a snail, Helix aspersa, L4) within a grid of rectangular, equidistant co-ordinates, it is possible to alter this network (i.e., to extend it along one or other axis), thus deforming the original figure and arriving at the related structure of another organism within the same zoological class (e.g., Gastropoda). The system of co-ordinates is also used to describe hypothetical structures (i.e., reconstructions of transitional stages). Although the evolutionist projects of natural history have been superseded in modern science by biology (bio-chemistry, bio-energetics, etc.), they survive at the level of social mythology, particularly with regard to the derivative nature of female anatomy.

Thus, by juxtaposing the diagram with the child's research, the Method of Co-ordinates is also used to suggest the operations of the unconscious, that place where the eccentricity and extravagance of anatomical transformation is not bounded by logic or by the specular image but by the discourse of the Other.

(3) Figs. 1–11b: Statistical Tables and Index

The photocopied fragments in this section were taken from a single diagram of a full-term pregnancy. They plot the hypothetical curves of familiar statistical tables (infant mortality, fetal growth, intra-uterine temperature, etc.). The mother's body is systematically scanned in response to the child's questions, but it is viewed through the functionalist grid of current medical practice (including the self-help manuals which appropriate this "knowledge" for women in the form of a cookery book/map/dictionary). The Index attempts to speak to/through the lacunae in the mother's answers, but it is circumscribed by a system of representation which outlines an inherent pathology of the female body. In addition, "patriarchal" taxonomy designates the common name (species) by means of the selected elements which determine the proper name (genus). Homo sapiens is a genus with only one living species—man. In so far as sexual difference is designated (M/F), then the "female" is defined by elements related to reproduction; any elements not related to these are irrelevant or derivative. This ultimately endorses a repression of the heterogeneity of feminine sexuality. But in moving away from the visible space of nomenclature towards the invisible space of organic structure, experimental science leaves a space of *possibility* for the subversion of biological determinism.

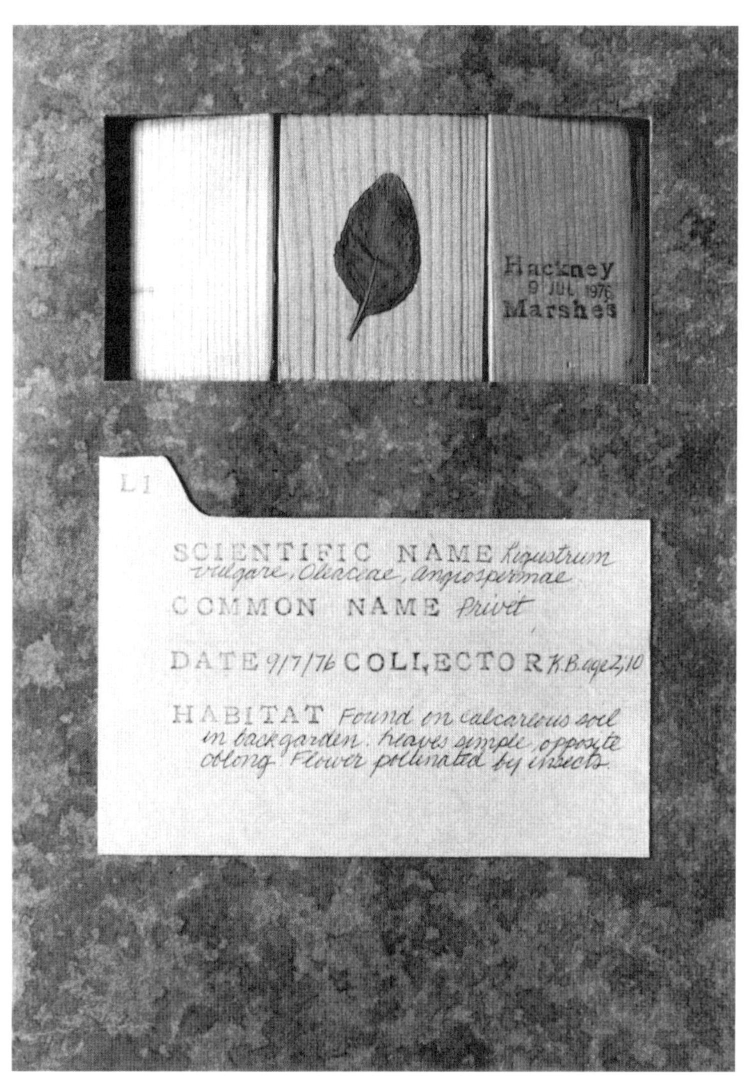
Hackney
9 JUL 1976
Marshes
L1
SCIENTIFIC NAME Ligustrum vulgare, Oleaceae, Angiospermae
COMMON NAME Privet
DATE 9/7/76 COLLECTOR K.B. age 2,10
HABITAT Found on calcareous soil in backgarden. Leaves simple, opposite oblong. Flower pollinated by insects.

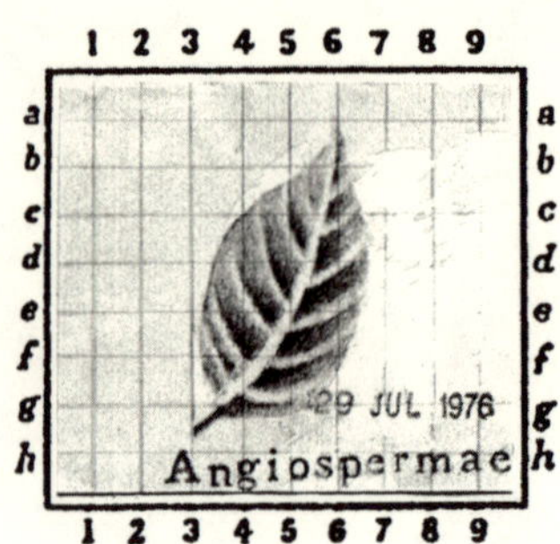

Fig. 1a

L1. RESEARCH I Homo sapiens (F)

Age 2;11, July 29, 1976
(7:30 A.M., getting into our bed)

K. Mummy, where's your willy?
M. I haven't got one. I'm a girl and you're a boy. You're like Daddy. You two have got one and I don't.
K. Show me.
M. Oh Kel...

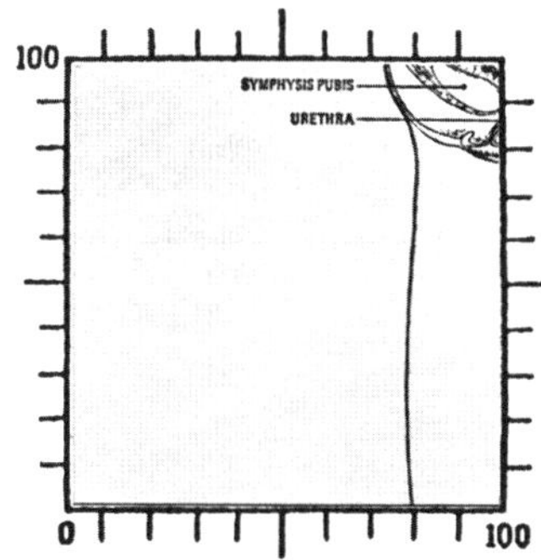

Fig. 1b

L1. INDEX A Homo sapiens (F)

ABDOMEN-abdominal cavity, abdominal delivery, abdominal muscles, abdominal pregnancy, AB-NORMAL PREGNANCY, ABORTION-incomplete abortion, septic abortion, spontaneous abortion, therapeutic abortion, AFTERBIRTH, AFTERPAINS, AMNIOCENTESIS, AMNION, AMNIOTIC FLUID, ANAEMIA, ANAESTHESIA, ANAESTHETIC, ANAL FISSURE, ANKLES SWELLING, ANTE-NATAL, ANTE-PARTUM, ANUS, AREOLA, ARTIFICIAL INSEMINATION.

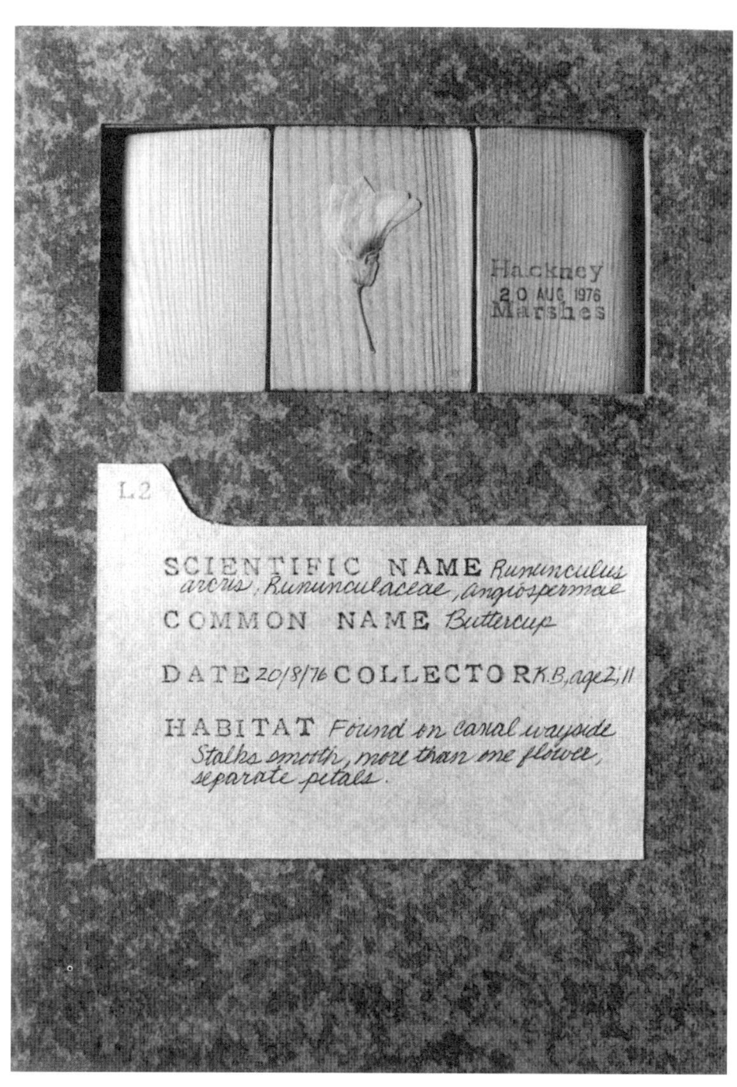
Hackney
20 AUG 1976
Marshes
L2
SCIENTIFIC NAME Rununculus arcris, Rununculaceae, Angiospermae
COMMON NAME Buttercup
DATE 20/8/76 COLLECTOR K.B, age 2;11
HABITAT Found on canal wayside
Stalks smooth, more than one flower, separate petals.

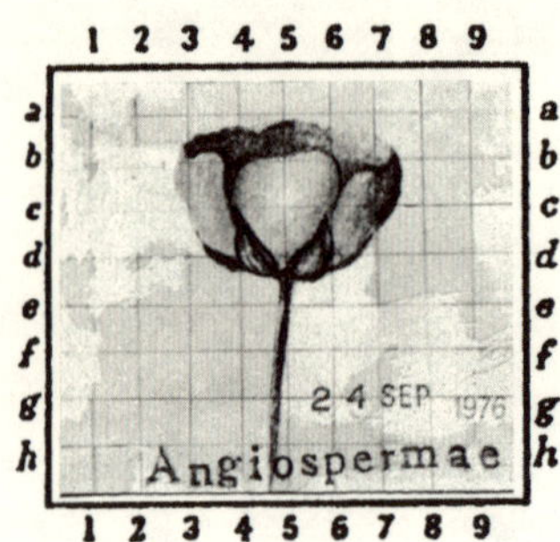

Fig. 2a

L2. RESEARCH II Homo sapiens (F)

Age 3;0, September 24, 1976
(11:30 A.M. coming into the bathroom)

K. Where does your wee come from? Show me.
M. There.

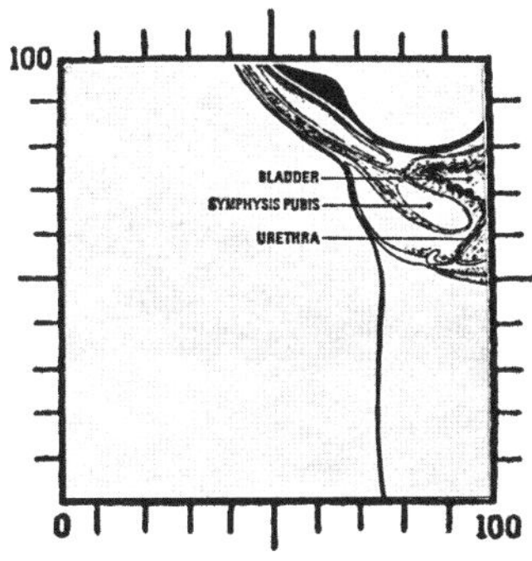

Fig. 2b

L2. INDEX B Homo sapiens (F)

BABY, BACKACHE, BEARING DOWN, BIRTH CANAL, BIRTHMARKS, BLADDER, BLEEDING-after intercourse, in pregnancy, in labour, intermenstrual, post-menstrual, BLOCKED DUCT, BLOCKED TUBE, BLOOD GROUP, BLOOD PRESSURE, BLOOD TEST, BOTTLE FEEDING, BREASTS-breast abscess, breast cancer, breast feeding, breast fluid, breast milk, breast swelling, BREATHLESSNESS, BREATHING TECHNIQUES, BREECH DELIVERY, BREECH LABOUR, BROW PRESENTATION, BUCCAL PITOCIN.

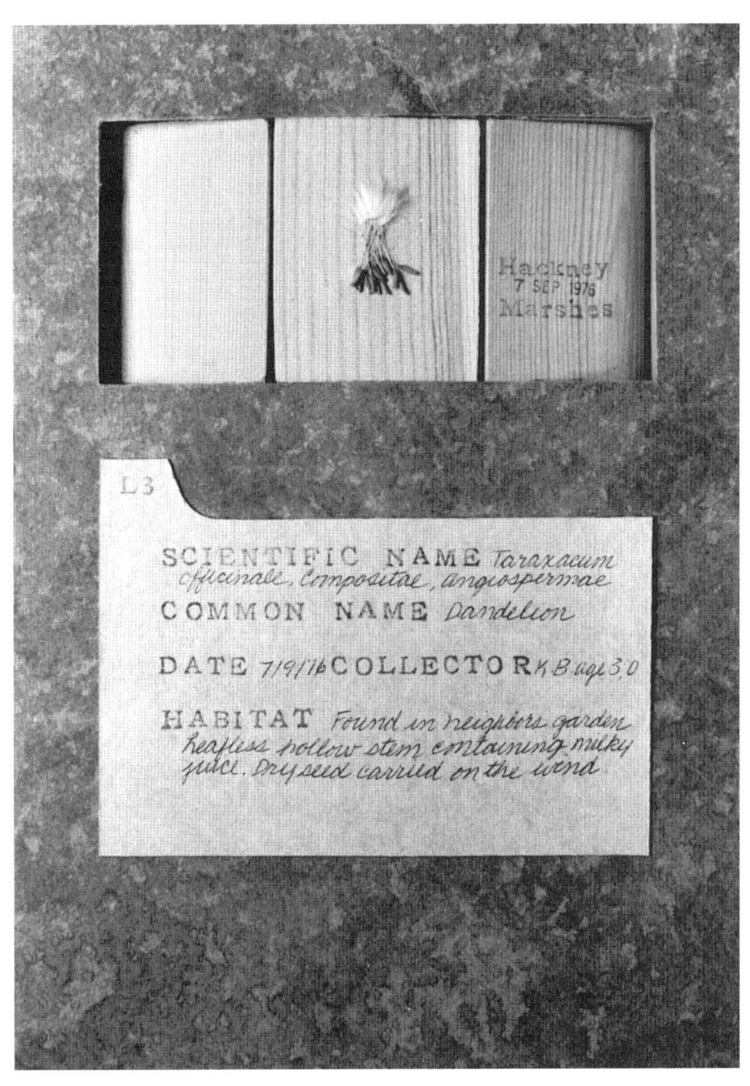
Hackney
7 SEP 1976
Marshes
L3
SCIENTIFIC NAME Taraxacum officinale, Compositae, Angiospermae
COMMON NAME Dandelion
DATE 7/9/76 COLLECTOR K.B. age 3.0
HABITAT Found in neighbors garden leafless hollow stem containing milky juice. Dry seed carried on the wind

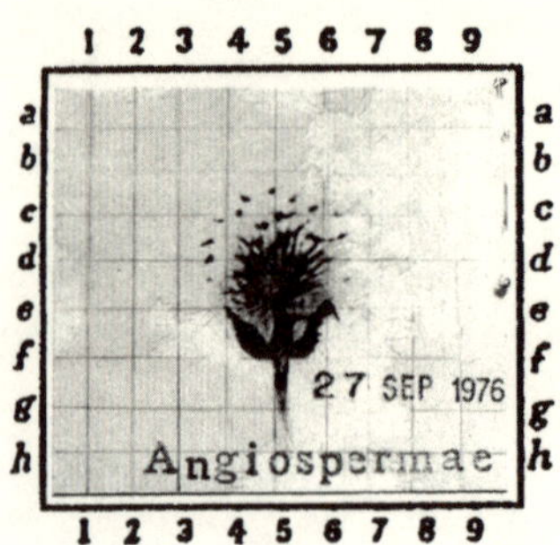

Fig. 3a

L3. RESEARCH III Homo sapiens (F)

Age 3;1, September 27, 1976.
(9:30 A.M. watching me take a bath)

K. What's that?
M. A breast.
K. Is that where babies drink their milk?
M. Yes.
K. Is there some now?
M. No, only when mummies have tiny babies. You used to drink your milk like that when you were little, but now you're a big boy and drink your milk from a cup.

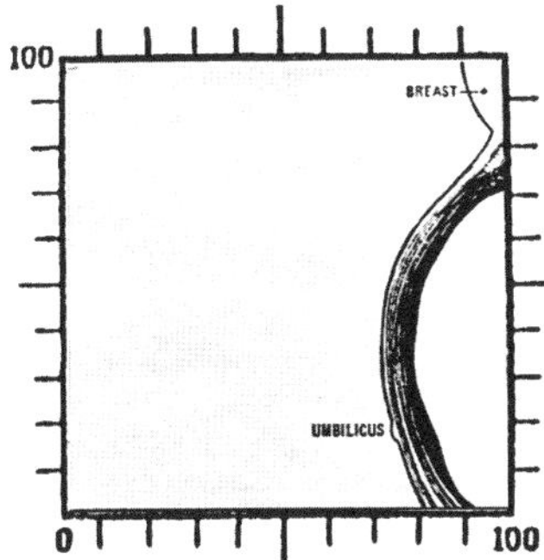

Fig. 3b

L3. INDEX C Homo sapiens (F)

CAESARIAN SECTION, CARPAL SYNDROME, CATHETER, CAPUT, CAUL, CAUTERIZATION, CEPHALHAEMATOMA, CERVICAL CANAL, CERVICAL CAP, CERVICAL 3MEAR, CERVICITIS, CERVIX-erosion of, incompetence of, carcinoma-in-situ of, CHORION, CHROMOSOMES, CLITORIS, CLIMACTERIC, COCCYX, COITUS, COLOSTRUM, CONCEPTION, CONDOM, CONSTIPATION, CONTRACEPTION, CONTRACEPTIVE CREAM, CONTRACEPTIVE PILL, CONTRACTION, CRAMP, CRAVINGS, CURETTAGE, CYSTITIS, CYTOPLASM, CYTO-TEST.

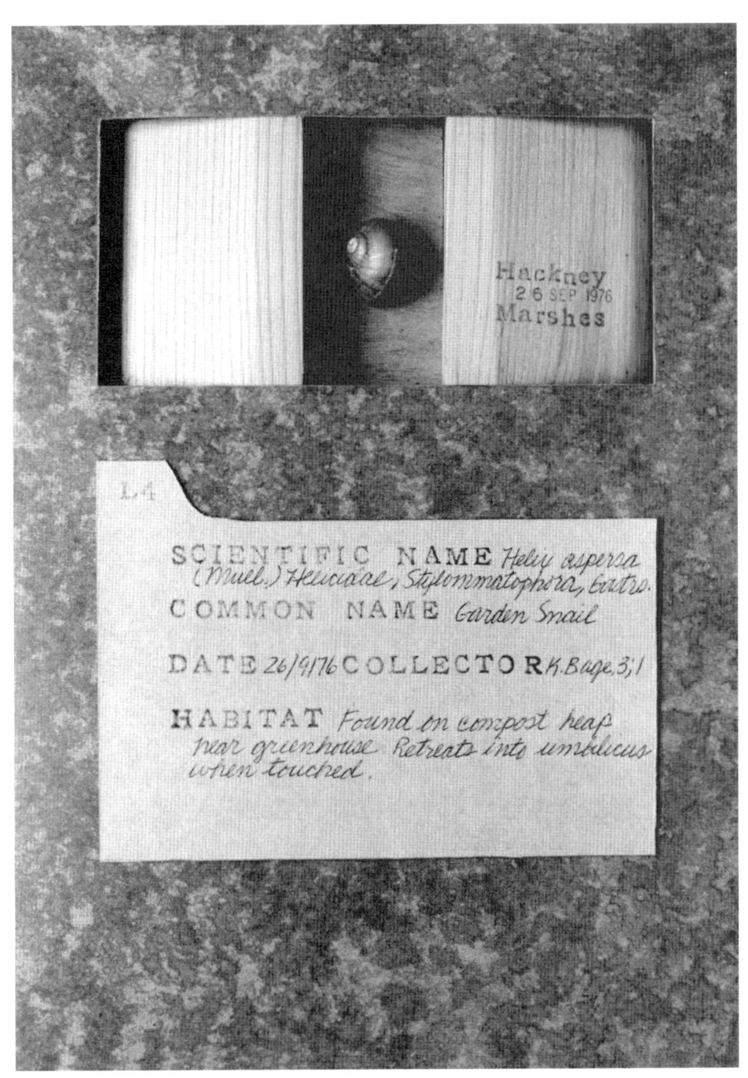
Hackney
26 SEP 1976
Marshes
L4
SCIENTIFIC NAME Helix aspersa
(Muel.) Helicidae, Stylommatophora, Gastro.
COMMON NAME Garden Snail
DATE 26/9/76 COLLECTOR K. Bage, 3;1
HABITAT Found on compost heap
near greenhouse Retreats into umbilicus
when touched.

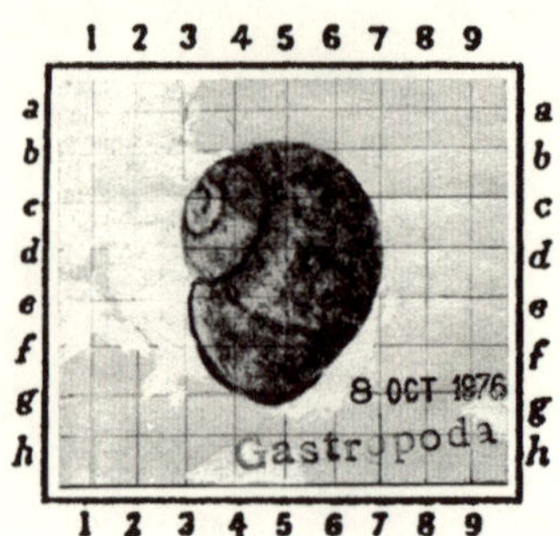

Fig. 4a

L4. RESEARCH IV Homo sapiens (F)

Age 3;1, October 8, 1976
(8:45 A.M. jumping up and down on our bed)

K. Mummy, do you have a hole in your tummy?
M. No.

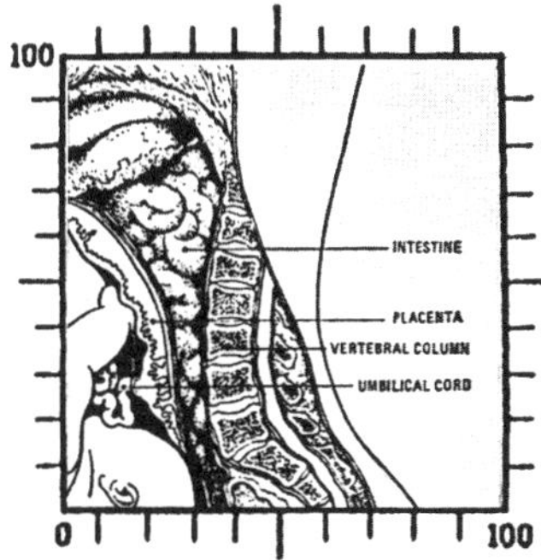

Fig. 4b

L4. INDEX D-E Homo sapiens (F)

DECOMPRESSION, DELIVERY DATE, DELIVERY POSITION, DEMAND FEEDING, DIAPHRAGM, DIET, DILATORS, DILATATION, DIURETIC, DAPTONE, DOUCHING, DRY LABOUR, FEAR OF DYING, DYSMATURITY, DYSMENORRHOEA, DYSPARUNIA, ECLAMPSIA, ECTOPIC PREGNANCY, EMBRYO, ENDOMETRIUM, ENEMA, ENGAGEMENT, ENGORGEMENT, EPIDURAL, EPISIOTOMY, ERGOMETRINE, EXERCISES.

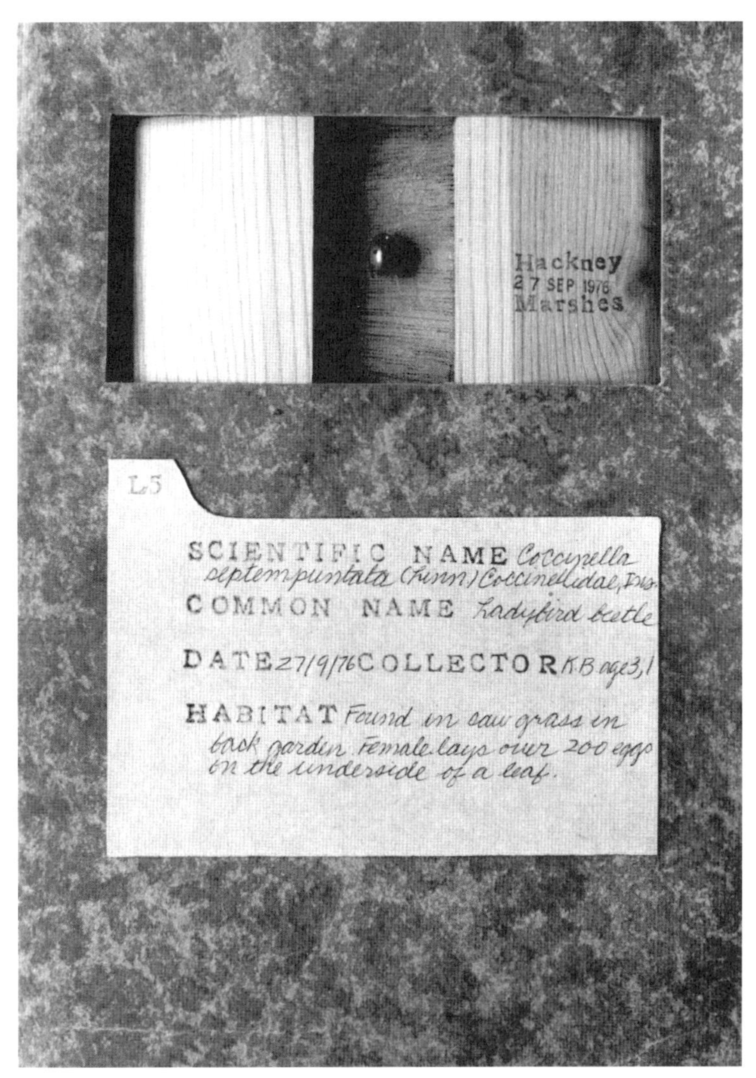
Hackney
27 SEP 1976
Marshes
L5
SCIENTIFIC NAME Coccinella septempuntata (Linn) Coccinellidae,
COMMON NAME Ladybird beetle
DATE 27/9/76 COLLECTOR K.B age 3,1
HABITAT Found in caw grass in back garden Female lays over 200 eggs on the underside of a leaf.

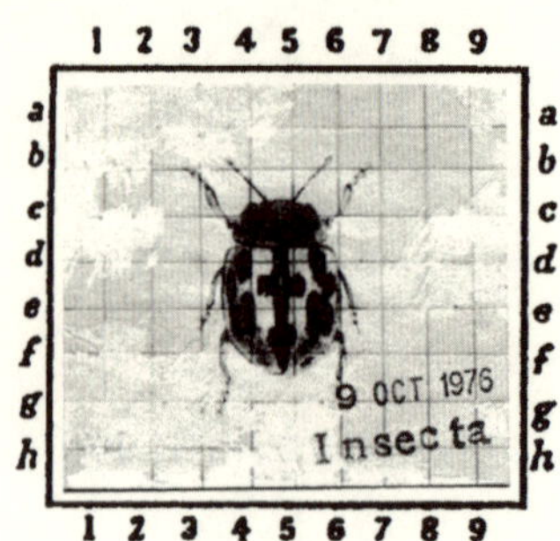

Fig. 5a

L5. RESEARCH V Homo sapiens

Age 3;1, October 9, 1976
(8:30 A.M. jumping on the bed again)

K. Mummy, do you have a baby in your tummy?
M. No, not now, but when you were a tiny baby, before you were born, you were in my tummy.

(8:00 P.M. eating supper)

K. When I was a tiny baby I was in Mummy's tummy. When I get big, I will give you (Sally) and Mummy a baby and when Daddy gets bigger he will have a baby.

R. Boys don't have babies.

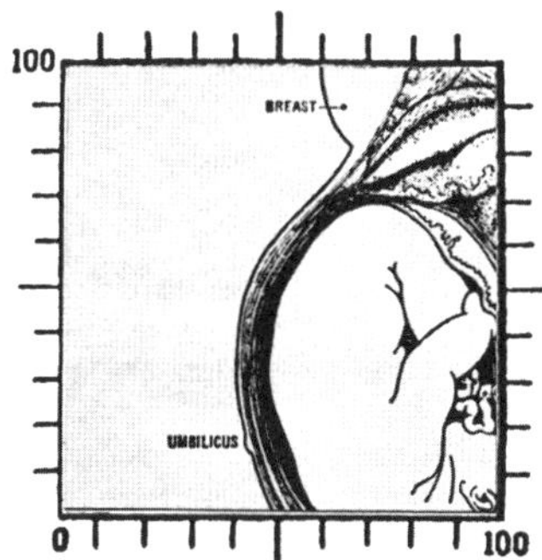

Fig. 5b

L5. INDEX F-G Homo sapiens (F)

FALLOPIAN TUBES, FALLS, FAINTNESS, FAMILY PLANNING, FERTILITY, FERTILIZATION, FIBROIDS, FIBROUS TISSUE, FOETUS, FOETAL DEATH, FOETAL DISTRESS, FOETAL STETHOSCOPE, FOLIC ACID, FONTANELLE, FORCEPS, FORGETFULNESS, FREQUENCY, FUNDUS, GENITAL TRACT, GERMAN MEASLES, GINGIVITIS, GLUCOSE TOLERANCE, GONORRHOEA, GRANULATION, GUTHRIE TEST.

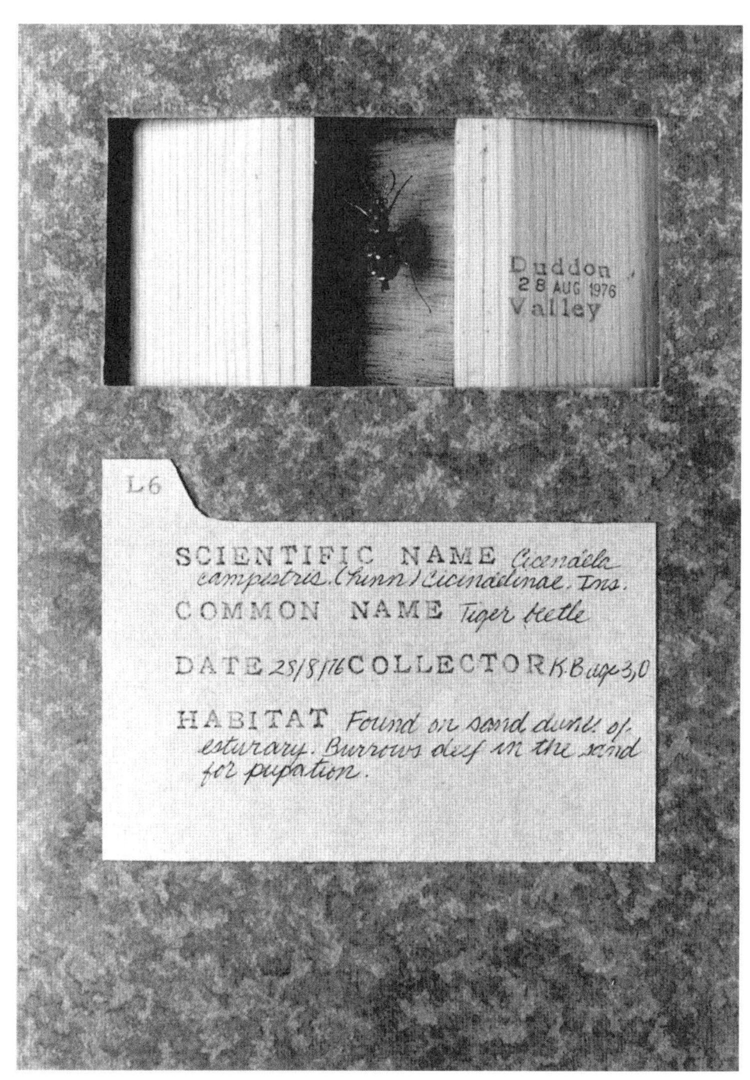
Duddon
28 AUG 1976
Valley
L6
SCIENTIFIC NAME Cicendela campestris. (Linn) Cicindelinae. Ins.
COMMON NAME Tiger beetle
DATE 25/8/76 COLLECTOR K.B age 3,0
HABITAT Found on sand dunes of estuary. Burrows deep in the sand for pupation.

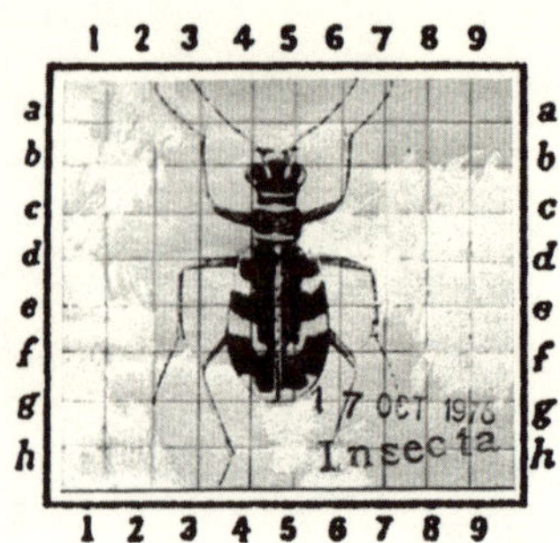

Fig. 6a

L6. RESEARCH VI Homo sapiens (F)

Age 3;1, October 17, 1976
(4:00 P.M. talking to Elona, who is pregnant)

K. Why don't I have a baby?
M. Only mummies ....ladies have babies.

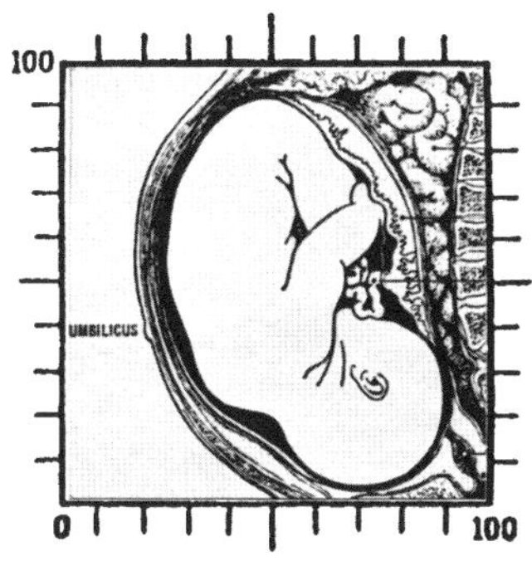

Fig. 6b

L6. INDEX H-I Homo sapiens (F)

HAEMORRHAGE, HAEMORROIDS, HEADACHES, HEART-BURN, HORMONES, HYDRAMNIOS, HYDATIDIFORM MOLE, HYMEN, HYPERTENSION, HYPOTENSION, HYS-TERECTOMY, HYSTEROTOMY, IMPLANTATION, INDUC-TION, INFECTION, INFERTILITY, INTERVENOUS INFUSION, INTERVENOUS DRIP, INTRA-UTERINE DEVICE, INTRA-UTERINE DEATH.

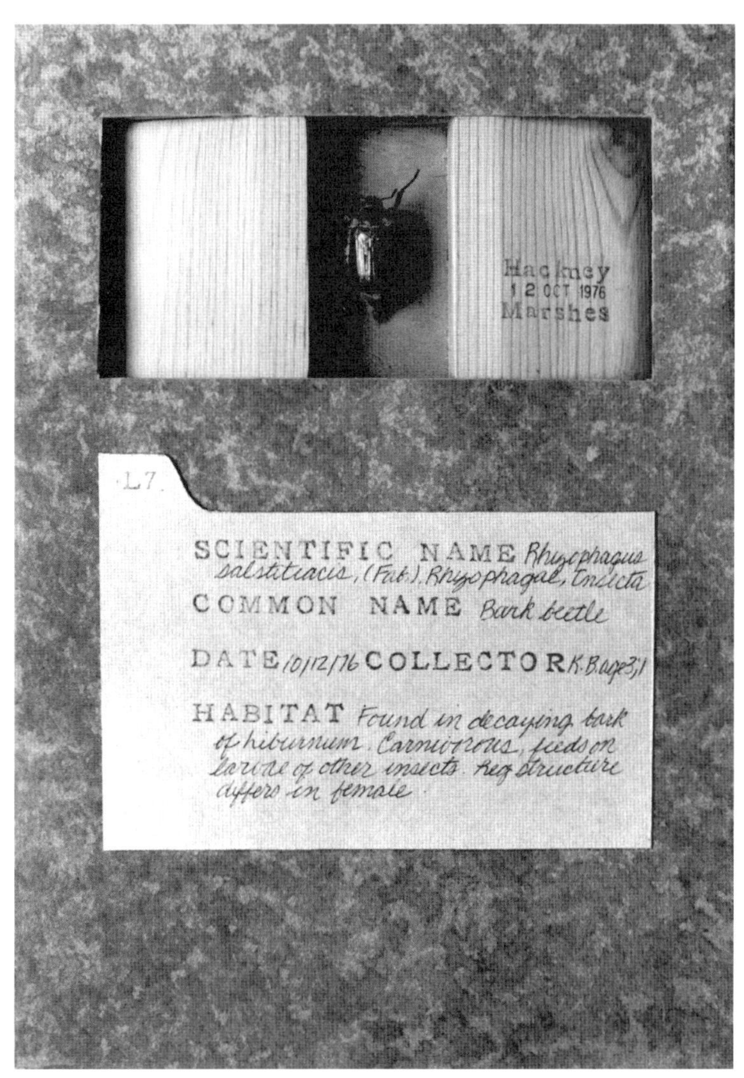
Hackney
12 OCT 1976
Marshes
L7.
SCIENTIFIC NAME Rhyzophagus salstitiacis, (Fab.). Rhyzophagae, Insecta
COMMON NAME Bark beetle
DATE 10/12/76 COLLECTOR K.B. age 3,1
HABITAT Found in decaying bark of hiburnum. Carnivorous, feeds on larvae of other insects. Leg structure differs in female.

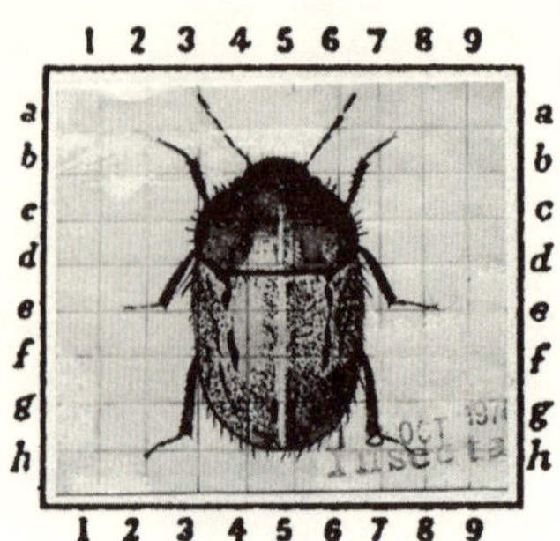

Fig. 7a

L7. RESEARCH VII Homo Sapiens (F)

Age 3;1, October 18, 1976
(7:30 P.M. getting ready for bed)

K. Will the badmen come and cut my willy off?
M. No, of course not.

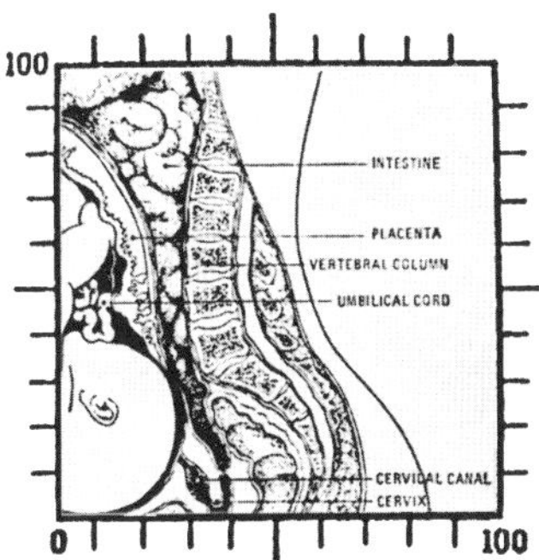

Fig. 7b

L7. INDEX L Homo sapiens (F)

LABIA MAJORA, LABIA MINORA, LABOUR-false labour, length of labour, normal labour (first stage, second stage, third stage), LABOUR PAINS, PROLONGED LABOUR, RAPID LABOUR, LACERATION, LACTATION, LEVATORS, LIFTING, LIGHTENING, LIE OF BABY, LINEA MIGRA, LITHOTOMY, LOCHIA, LOOP, LUBRICANT.

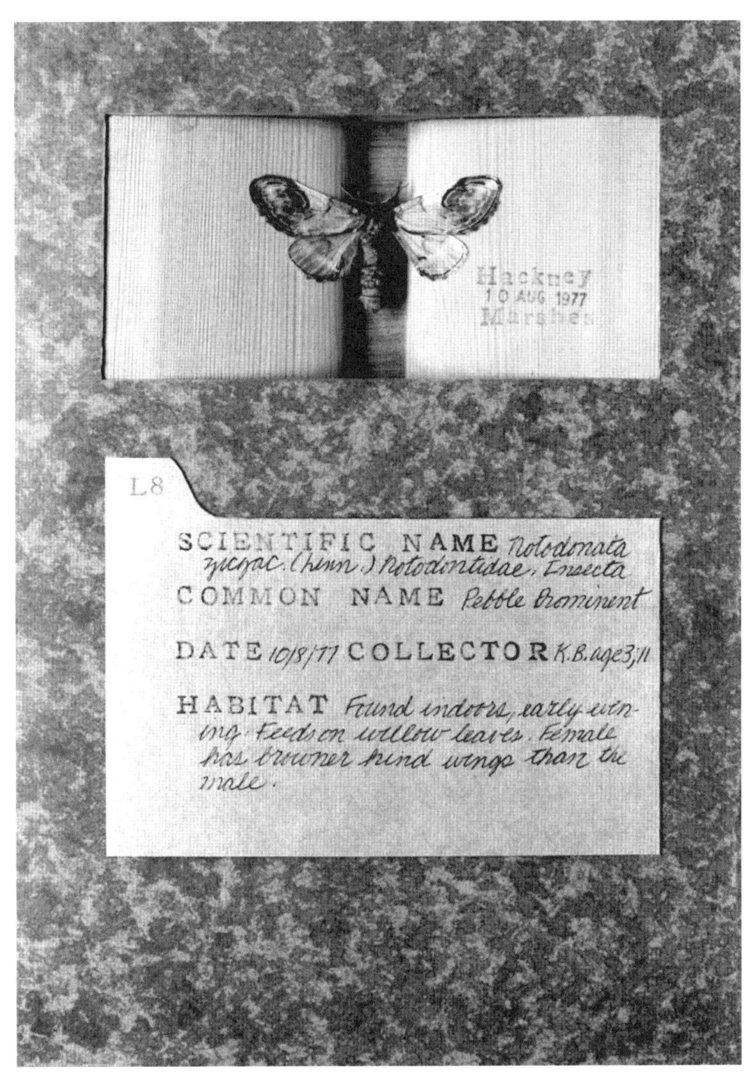
Hackney
10 AUG 1977
Marshes
L8
SCIENTIFIC NAME
COMMON NAME Pebble Prominent
DATE 10/8/77 COLLECTOR K.B. age 3;11
HABITAT Found indoors, early evening. Feeds on willow leaves. Female has browner hind wings than the male.

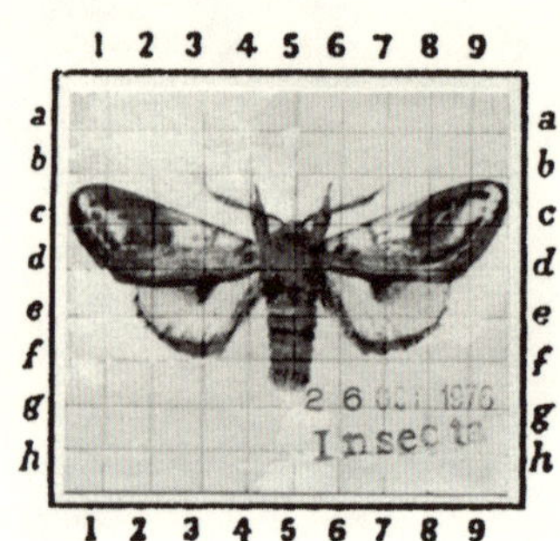

Fig. 8a

L8. RESEARCH VIII Homo sapiens (F)

Age 3;2, Oct. 26, 1976
(4:30 P.M. having tea)

K. I can't give you a baby, maybe Daddy can get you one in the shop.

M. You were my baby, now you're a big boy .... but I don't want another baby. Anyway, they don't come from shops.

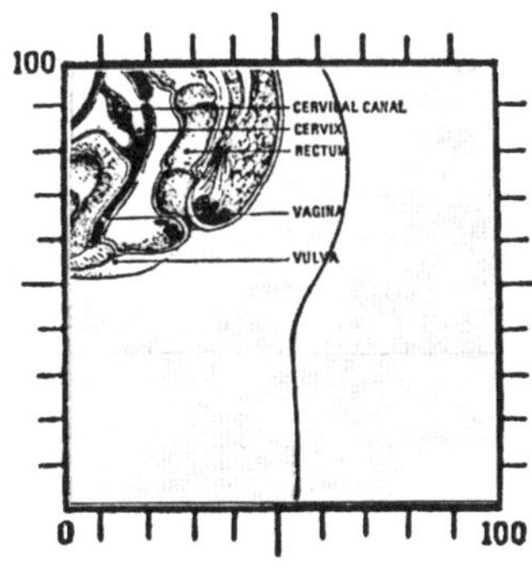

Fig. 8b

L8. INDEX M-N-O Homo sapiens (F)

MASTURBATION, MATERNITY, MECONIUM, MENARCHE, MENOPAUSE, MENORRHAGIA, MENSTRUAL CYCLE, MENSTRUATION, MISCARRIAGE, MONGOLISM, MOODS, MONILIA, MORNING SICKNESS, MOULDING, MOVEMENTS, MUCUS, MULTIGRAVIDA, MULTIPLE PREGNANCY, MYOMECTOMY, NATURAL CHILDBIRTH, NAUSEA, NECK-OF-THE WOMB, NERVOUSNESS, NIGHTMARES, NIPPLES-bleeding of, itching of, soreness of, shields for, NOSE BLEEDS, OEDEMA, OESTROGEN, OESTRIOL, ORGASM, OVARY, OVULATION, OVULAR PHASE, OVUM, OXYTOCIN.

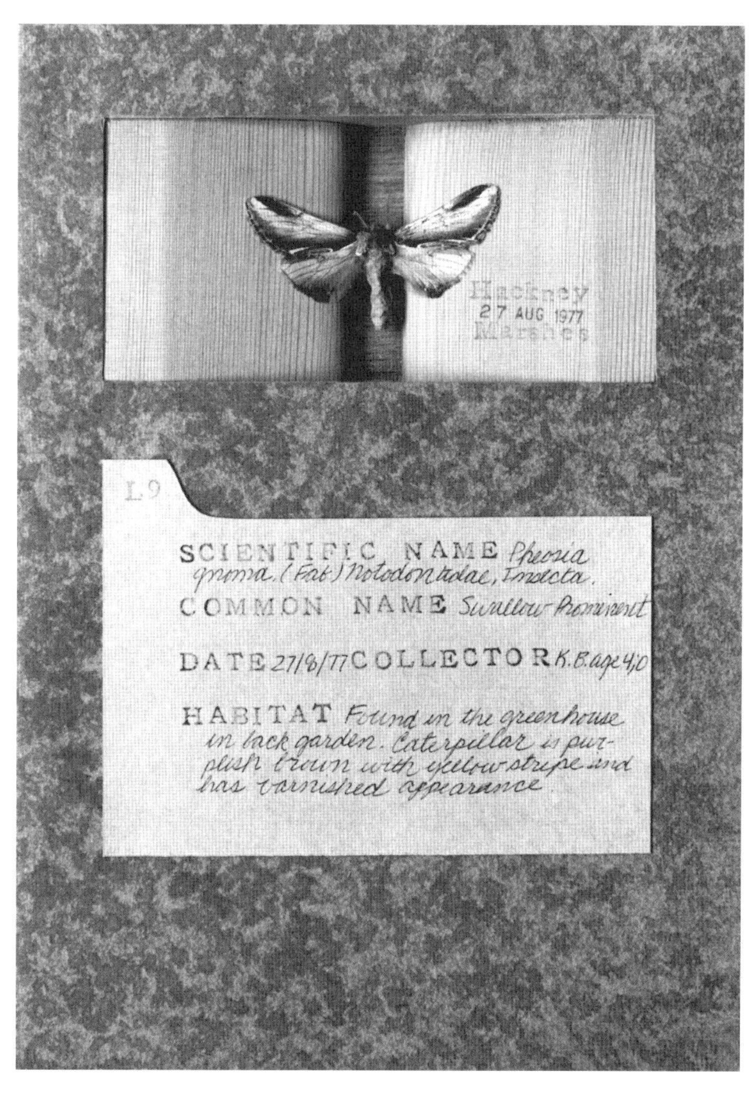
Hackney
27 AUG 1977
Marshes
L9
SCIENTIFIC NAME Pheosia
gnoma. (Fab) Notodontidae, Insecta.
COMMON NAME Swallow Prominent
DATE 27/8/77 COLLECTOR K.B. age 4,10
HABITAT Found in the greenhouse
in back garden. Caterpillar is pur-
plish brown with yellow stripe and
has varnished appearance.

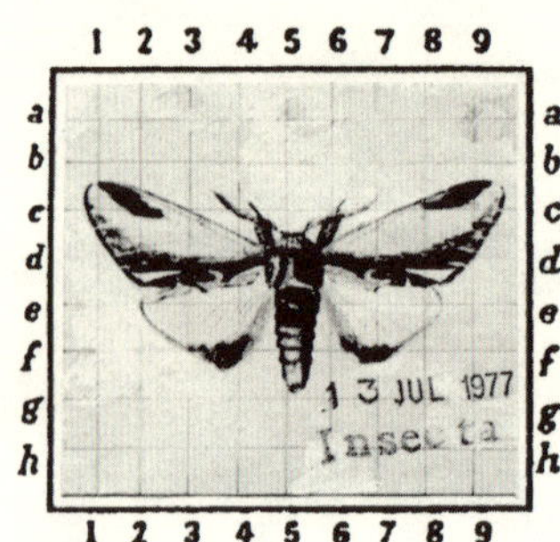

Fig. 9a

L9. RESEARCH IX Homo sapiens (F)

Age 3;10, July 13, 1977.
(8:00 P.M. coming into the bathroom)

K. Do babies come from bottoms?
M. No, ... from vaginas. Girls have three holes; one for poohs, one for wees, and one where babies come out - that's the vagina.

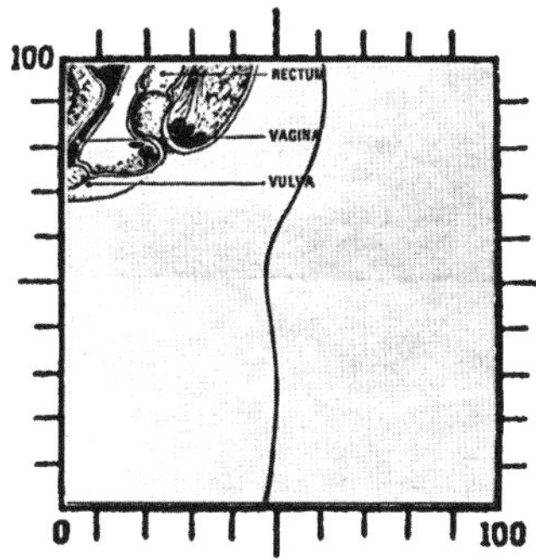

Fig. 9b

L9. INDEX P Homo sapiens (F)

PAIN-IN-THE-HANDS, PAIN-IN-THE-LEGS, PELVIC CAVITY, PELVIC EXAMINATION, PELVIC FLOOR, PELVIC INLET, PELVIC OUTLET, PELVIS, PERINEUM, PERIOD, PESSARY, PETHIDENE, PITUITARY GLAND, PLACENTA-removal of, retention of, separation of, PLACENTA PRAEVIA, PLASMA, POSITION OF BABY (L.O.A., L.O.L., L.O.P., R.O.P., R.O.L., R.O.A.) POST MATURITY, POST-NATAL, POST-PARTUM, POSTURE, PREGNANCY-diagnosis of, length of, symptoms of, PREMATURITY, PRE-MATURE DELIVERY, PRE-MENTRUAL TENSION, PRIMAGRAVIDA, PROLAPSE, PROGESTERONE, PROTEINURIA, PUBERTY, PUBIC BONE, PUBIC HAIR, PUERPERIUM, PUSHING, PYELITIS.

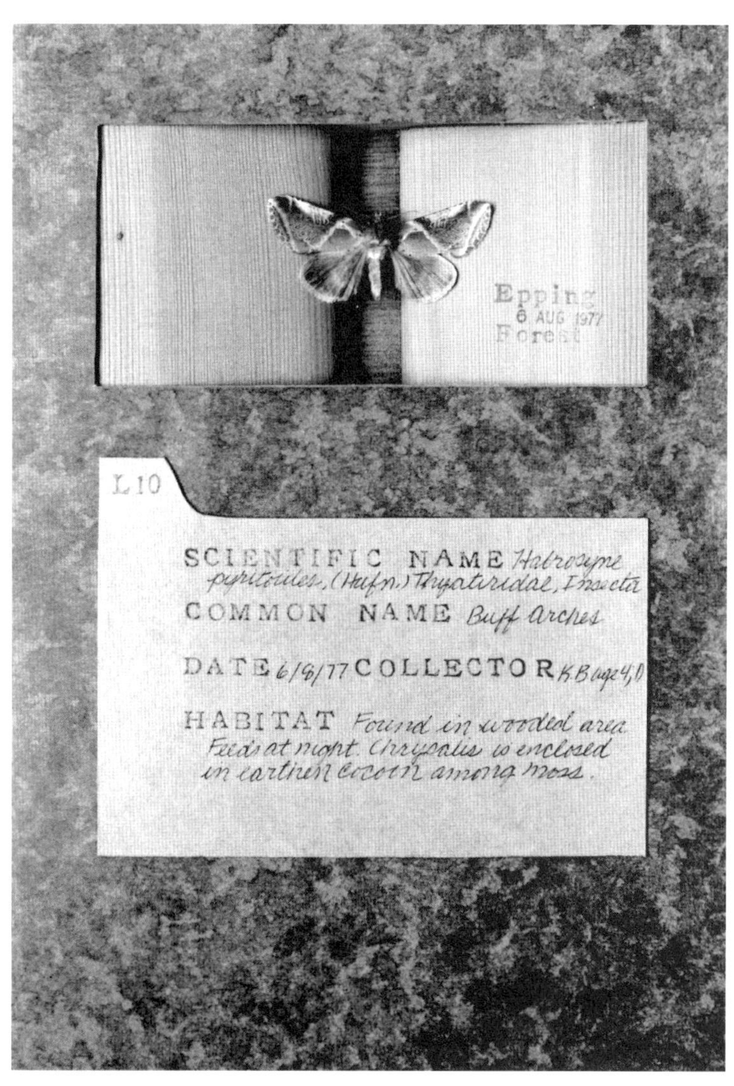
Epping
6 AUG 1977
Forest
L10
SCIENTIFIC NAME Habrosyne pyritoides, (Hufn.) Thyatiridae, Insecta
COMMON NAME Buff Arches
DATE 6/8/77 COLLECTOR K.B age 4,
HABITAT Found in wooded area. Feeds at night. Chrysalis is enclosed in earthen cocoon among moss.

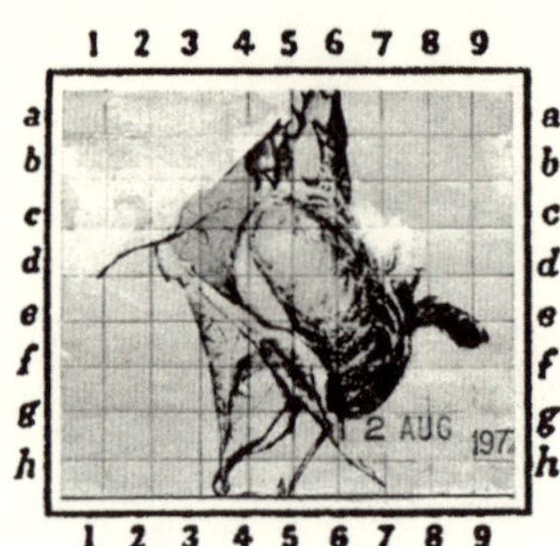

Fig. 10a

L10. RESEARCH X Homo sapiens (F)

Age 3;11, August 12, 1977
(2:00 A.M. coming into our bedroom)

K. You aren't kissing her on the lips are you?
R. Yes... (laughing) we're making a baby.
M. Oh Ray ... don't say that.
K. I don't want to sleep in my room. There's ghosts and snakes and spiders and crabs up there.

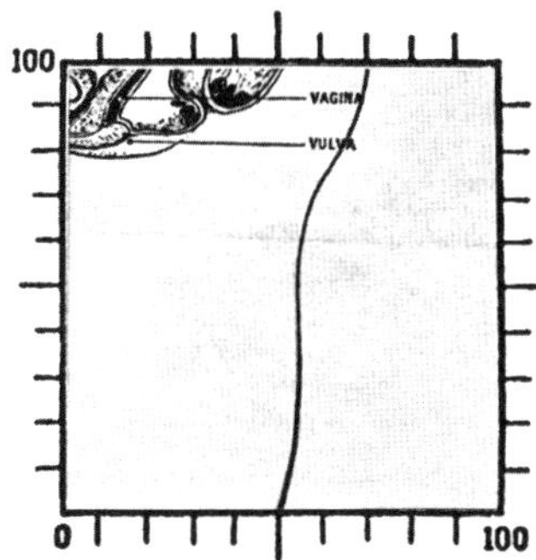

Fig. 10b

L10. INDEX R-S Homo Sapiens (F)

RECTUM, RED PALMS, RELAXATION, RHYTHM METHOD, RUBELLA, RUPTURED MEMBRANE, SACRUM, SALPINGECTOMY, SALPINGES, SALPINGITIS, SEXUAL INTERCOURSE-during pregnancy, after childbirth, after abortion, SHAKES, SHOCK, SHOW, SLEEPLESSNESS, SPECULUM, SPERM, SPERMICIDE, SPIDER NAEVI, SPINAL ANAESTHETIC, STERILIZATION, STERILITY, STILL-BIRTH, STITCHES, STRESS INCONTINENCE, STRETCH MARKS, SUPPOSITORIES, SUPINE SYNDRONE, SYMPHYSIS PUBIS, SYNTOMETRINE, SYPHILIS.

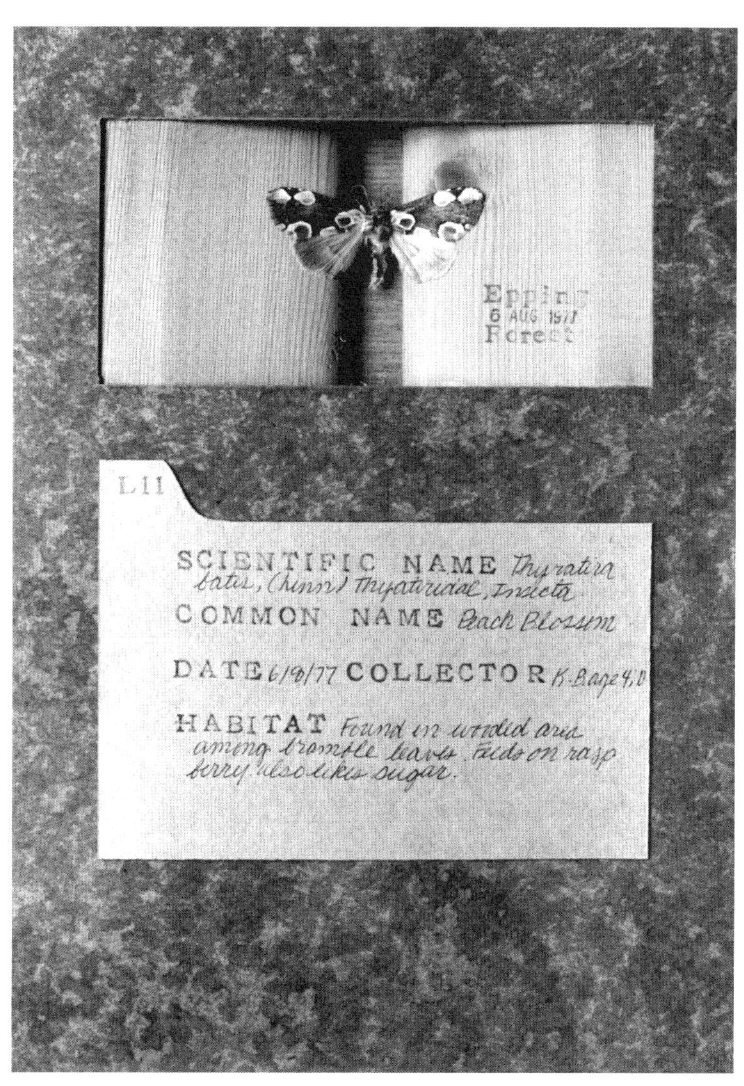
Epping
6 AUG 1977
Forest
L11
SCIENTIFIC NAME
COMMON NAME
DATE
COLLECTOR
HABITAT

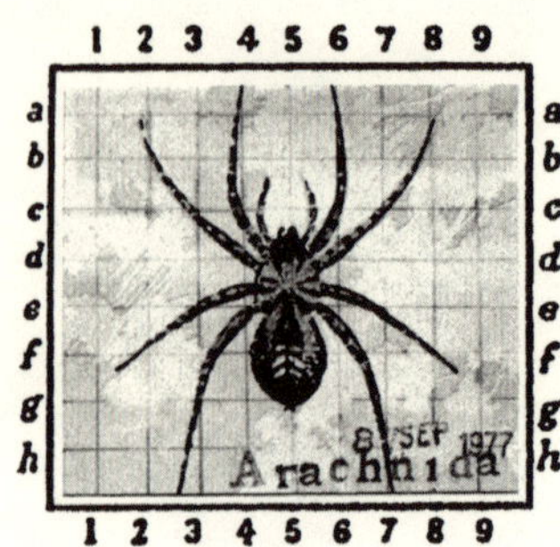

Fig. 11a

L11. RESEARCH XI Homo sapiens (F)

Age 4;1, September 8, 1977
(8:00 P.M. getting into his own bed)

K. Mens don't dance with mens, do they Mum?
They dance with womans.
M. Ummm... that's right.

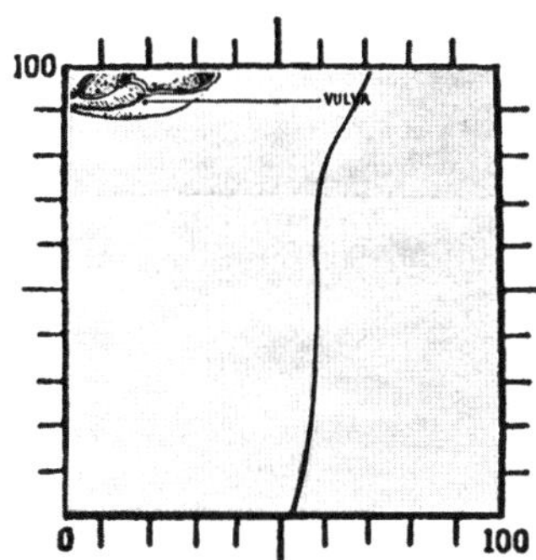

Fig. 11b

L11. INDEX T-U-V Homo sapiens (F)

TIREDNESS-during pregnancy, during labour, after delivery, in general, TOXAEMIA, TRICHOMONAS, TRILENE, TUBAL INSUFFLATION, TUBAL LIGATION, TUMOUR, TWINS, ULTRASOUND, UMBILICAL CORD, UMBILICUS, URETHRA, URINE TEST, UTERUS-action of, contraction of, cavity of, tubes of, retroversion of, VAGINA-vaginal bleeding, vaginal delivery, vaginal discharge, vaginal examination, VARICOSE VEINS, VAULT CAP, VENEREAL DISEASE, VENTEUSE, VERNIX, VERTEBRAL COLUMN, VERTEX, VITAMINS, VOMITING, VULVA.

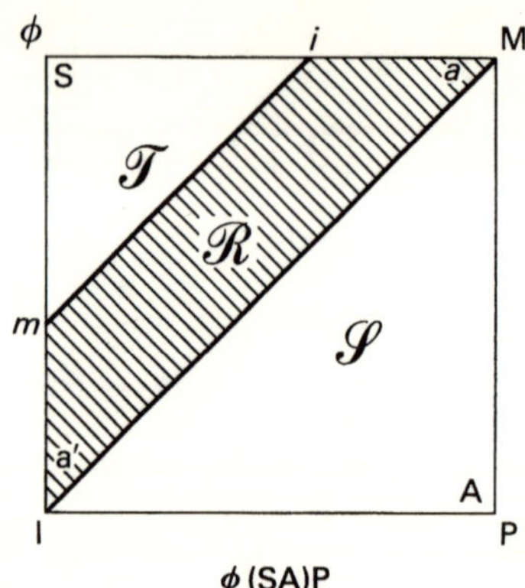

ϕ
i
M
S
a
𝒯
ℛ
m
𝒮
a′
A
I
P
ϕ (SA)P

(WHAT AM I?)

s

Experimentum Mentis V
On the Order of Things

The mother's relation to castration, to the Father and the Law, is called into question by the sexual researches of her child. These researches are crucial in structuring the castration complex. The consequences of this moment determine the child's sexual identity and his future choice of love object. For the mother this moment necessitates the representation of a double loss–the child as phallus and the body as feminine.

Castration privileges the phallus as signifier of desire. The desire of the mother is the phallus; the child wants to be the phallus. Because desire is always the desire of the Other, it includes the desire to know. To know the mother's body is to test the desire of the Other. When the child asks a question concerning the presence/absence of the penis, as in Research 1, L1, "Where is your willy Mummy?," it is not definitive simply because he hears or sees the mother's answer. He must acknowledge the fact that she does not have what it is that he is looking for. However, taking up this position requires a sacrifice for both the mother and the child. At first he denies the mother's lack. He searches with voyeuristic intensity for the evidence which will confirm the imaginary dominance of the phallic attribute. This search is motivated by his newly discovered pleasure in masturbation. Even the mother's bodily processes, such as micturition and defecation, are subject to the child's scrutiny. But she exhibits nothing. Moreover, she denies nothing. Her silence is imposed by the child's insistent misrecognition.

When the child repeatedly asks. "What's that?," as in Research III, L3, he already knows the answer is "A breast"; but what he does not know, and why he continues to ask, is what he himself is. For the child, at this moment, the mother still has the power to determine his relation to the signifier; to have or to be the phallus. In turn she asks herself the crucial yet unspoken question, "What am I?" It is unspoken because "I" is not the subject of a sentence but a place, the unconscious. In this place she is designated as feminine by a complex of archaic oral, anal, and vaginal drives, which recede from the site of speaking the more she tries to speak. It is the lacunae in the mother's answers to the child's questions that ultimately censor his research.

The child's spontaneous scopophilia provokes the mother's sense of "shame." This does not happen conspicuously at the level of these lived events, but at the level of the unconscious, as an effect of the re-presentation of the castrated image of her own mother.

Nevertheless, there is a reprieve at the founding moment of castration, that is the Father's promise. This promise is reiterated in the child's valorization of the mother's body, which he sees as having the phallus in the form of a baby, as in Research VI, L6, "Why can't I have a baby?" In pregnancy, the mother presents herself to herself in the mirror image of repletion and plenitude. However, the anatomy of fantasy is fragile and always entails the fear of falling back into disarray. It is the drive for self-mastery which underlies the illusion of unity. In this respect the mother is like her child. For him, the figure of the Phallic Mother is frightening, seductive and ultimately castrating. In part, this is because she is the one who first aroused the child's genital feelings by the constant and intimate care of his body. The mother's susceptibility to guilt for excessively gratifying or restricting her child (often in fantasy) is reinforced by pedagogy which urges her to take a "friendly but not indulgent" attitude towards his erotic activities. The child's displays of exhibitionism and "cruelty" are met with inhibition and compassion from the mother. Her dread of violence is motivated by a vicarious identification with the castration fears of her child (if he is a boy), her sexual partner and above all, her father. For the child, the threatening "badmen" of Research VII, L7, mark the intervention of the Law. Thus "I will give you a baby ..." of Research V, L5, becomes "I can't give you a baby ..." of Research VIII, L8, and subsequently introduces the theories about where babies come from, as in Research IX, L9, "Do babies come from bottoms?"

The mother's shame, inhibition, compassion and dread of violence are also intimately linked to her initial discovery of "the mystery of birth." It is precisely the effect of her mother's words with regard to childbirth and sexual intercourse which constitute the locus of her fear of pain, evisceration, rape and, in fact, of vaginal castration insofar as she represents, to herself, the motive of her fear—the loss of the body's "feminine interface." But the fear of femininity in the sense of "feminine drives" remains a source of anxiety because it appears to be unrepressed, anarchic, archaic and utterly unrepresentable. It is only represented, if ever, in the symbolic castration of the sexual act. This is also why the mother protects the child from witnessing the "violence" of "making love"; in so far as she desires to be the phallus for the Other (sexual partner), the mother's femininity is lost in the castrating moment of her enjoyment. For the child, accepting the mother's castration is often marked by symptomatic consequences, notably the snakes, spiders, ghosts of Research X, L10. But when he finally concedes that she does not have the phallus, the child takes up a masculine position in relation to the signifier, that is to have the phallus, as implied in the heterosexual imperative of Research XI, L11, "Men don't dance with mens ... they dance with womans." Thus theories about the birth of babies are turned into inquiries about sexual difference and these eventually give way, under the weight of repression, to questions about origins and the order of things.

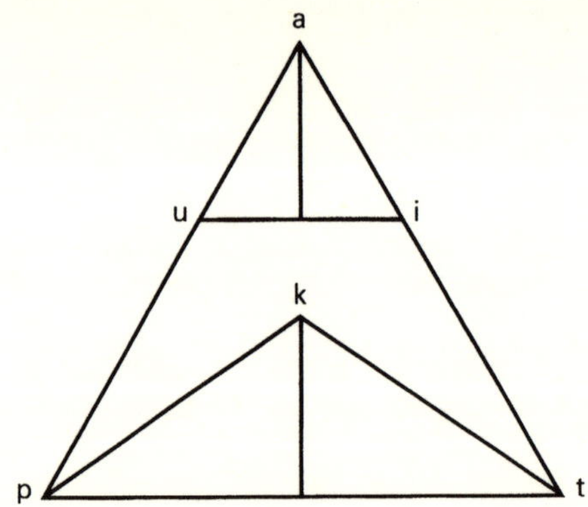
a
u
i
k
p
t

Documentation VI
Prewriting Alphabet, Exergue and Diary

The formative phase in which the child began to read and write was documented over a period of 18 months from January 1977 to April 1978. During this time (age 3.5–4.8), he started to identify certain letter shapes and map out a system of markings related to the traditional alphabet. Notations were made on his observations following "ABC sessions" (i.e., reading from favourite alphabet books as part of the bed-time story repertoire) and the documentation was concluded when he began to write his own name. At the same time he entered infants' school, an event which was equally significant for the mother because the learning process, once assumed to be a "private" discourse, was then clearly seen to be determined by an institutional context.

The documentation is inscribed on slates and set out in chronological order. Each inscription is divided into three registers (analogous to the Rosetta Stone) with the child's "hieroglyphic" letter-shapes (prewriting alphabet) in the upper portion; the mother's print-script commentary (exergue) in the middle section and her type-script narrative (diary) in the lower part.

Alphabet

The letter shapes deciphered in these inscriptions do not constitute a logical alphabet (there are 15 figures beginning with x and ending in B rather than 26 from A to Z); but they do demonstrate the child's propensity to develop a system of graphic representation.

Prewriting succeeds a mode of purposeful scribbling which already includes diagrammatic markings such as crosses and circles. At this moment, the significant difference is that the child's expressed intention in making these marks is *writing*. The x, called "a cross," ref. 3.501x, constitutes a kind of universal grapheme class. It is virtually the functional equivalent of all letters, as the commentary indicates, "he substitutes different letter names for the same mark"; as yet, the child does not recognize the distinctive features which are necessary to distinguish one letter or grapheme class from another. In ref. 6.6020, the distinctive feature of o, curvedness, displays an optimal contrast with the straight lines (ascenders) of x. o is generally associated with anything round, but at the same time it designates a more specific letter category than x in so far as when he writes o, he calls it "a round **and an o.**" The development of a graphemic system follows from this initial opposition of marks, but it is ultimately dependent upon filling in the gaps between x and o. The first split occurs on the side of curvedness between the closedness of o and the openness of e, ref. 3.6030. At this point an extensive number of variations or graphs are included in the grapheme class e, but together with x and o they comprise a triangle defining the distinctive features closedness-openness on the horizontal axis and straightness-curvedness on the vertical axis:

x

o e

In turn, straightness is differentiated by symmetry, x, versus asymmetry, r. The grapheme r, called "a hook," ref. 3.704r, also introduces curvedness into this category and by an extension of the "hook" produces n and m. Next the ascender l is marked by the addition of a feature-i which he calls "a dot and an i," ref. 3.805i, and c, significantly unnamed, ref. 3.806c, is marked by the addition of ascenders and descenders b, d, p, q, "a round and a straight," ref. 3.908p, thus combining the distinctive features of both axes of the triangle.

Then capital letter configurations arise from combinations, additions or subtractions of ascenders; first placing an emphasis on the distinctive feature straightness as in E, F, "a straight one and another straight one," ref. 3.909E, and later introducing curvedness as in R, ref. 4.113R. This is followed by the letters K and B, ref. 4.414K-4.515B, which are constructed with the specific intention of writing his own name. By this time, the child's discrimination of distinctive features is adequate enough to categorize most letters of the alphabet and designate them by a spoken name. In addition, he recognizes that letters such as E and e constitute alternatives for a single grapheme class and that, although they have no distinctive features in common, they are equated when identifying a letter category in reading. The concept of reading also implies directionality; as evidenced in ref. 4.515K, the child's name is insistently printed from left to right, and significantly, previous inversions and reversals of letters such as ɘ q ɔ are corrected in this process. As a result, his letters effectively represent the minimal contrasts necessary to distinguish a word in writing and at this moment his "writing" articulates the letter as a material locus, a visual configuration, a concept and a category name.

Exergue

The commentary and quotations set out below the child's inscription identify the letter as material support of a concrete discourse. Within this space, emphasis is placed on the intersubjective relations between mother and child in the act of reading and writing. Thus the gaps, omissions and inversions of the prewriting alphabet are crucial for the mother in deciphering the child's text. His incipient agraphia–the provocative ə, ref. 3.603e, the unspoken ɔ, ref. 3.806c, the overstated E, ref. 4.012 H, insofar as it is symptomatic of a resistance to the repression of Oedipal sexuality, implicates the mother and gives a place to her fantasies as well as those of the child. In this sense the intertextuality of alphabet and exergue efface the distinction between an object-letter and a subject who deciphers it. The hieroglyphic residue of the child's letter-shapes–the ideographic x, ref. 3.501x, the pictographic i, ref. 3.805i, the phonographic s, ref. 3.1111s–undermine a notion of the alphabet as absolute representation, i.e., as a system of arbitrary signs purged of all figurative regressions.

On the one hand, the repression, condensation and displacement of graphemic signifiers in the child's text suggest a writing anterior to speech, an insistence of the letter in the discourse of the unconscious which is resistant to signification as such. And on the other hand, the graphic rhetoric of children's books referred to in the mother's annotations to the child's script, such as A is for apple, B is for balloon, C is for cake, etc., implies a certain coagulation of the signified, underlining the logocentric bias of the system of language to which the letter ultimately subscribes; a system that privileges naming and the proper name and that pronounces the beginning of writing with the child's inscription of his father's name.

Diary

The diary narrative inserts the intersubjective discourse of the letter into a complex of institutional practices and systems of representation which produce the social subordination of the mother. First, there is the representation of a specific socio-economic category. The diary events surrounding the child's entry into infants' school "take place" in an urban, industrial, multi-racial, working-class area of the inner city often designated as disadvantaged or "deprived," ref. 3.806c. In sociological rhetoric, "disadvantage" is constituted by a signifying chain of percentages concerning one-parent families, working mothers, low income, poor housing, inadequate transport, overcrowded schools, accidents, disease, pollution, illiteracy and crime. The place the mother occupies as an effect of the signifying chain is inevitably that of failure or at best a victim of circumstance; but the position she takes up in the process of representing this place to herself is by no means fixed as one of resignation; in ref. 3.704r it is resistance, in ref. 3.908p, denial, in ref. 3.1111s, disassociation. Ultimately, it is not the mother's hopes, aspirations and ambitions for her child that are lacking, but the possibility of their realization which is circumscribed by the economic constraints, social practices and political effects of separation from the means of production, possession and "advantage."

Second, there is the construction of the agency of the mother/housewife. In this position the mother is assigned certain responsibilities, moral attributes and legal statuses by the education authority. For instance in ref. 4.414K, the form of address employed by the headmistress, i.e., "Mrs.", at once confirms the parent's legal status as wife and her moral attribute as mother, implying the child's "legitimacy." It is to this agent/addressee that the school sends all memoranda concerning the dates of term, of holidays, the requirements for school outings, bazaars and benefits, the cost of school dinners, the rules and regulations concerning absenteeism, tardiness, fires, floods, the lending of library books, and the lending of a helping hand, such as supervising the playgroup, ref. 3.501x.

In addition, the local health authority, in collaboration with the school, administers a medical service which consists primarily of monitoring the child's health (illness, immunization, physical growth, mental progress and general social adjustment), and which designates the mother as guarantor of his well-being. This process of surveillance is epitomized by the yearly check-up, ref. 3.909E, and the mother's attendance is "strongly advised." Unavoidably, the child's symptom is read as a sign of her capacity/incapacity to fulfill the agency of the mother/housewife at the level of the attributes deemed essential to that agency such as common sense, practicality and discipline mediated by an intimate, "natural" bond with the child. However, the mother never sufficiently corresponds to the agency this institutional discourse defines and that is demonstrated by the father's participation in the realization (also always partial) of those capacities, for instance when the mother is working, ref. 4.113R. Nor does the father ever conform to the agency of the father/husband fulfilling the function of breadwinner or possessing a "natural" aptitude for authority, etc. On the one hand, there is often conflict between the husband and the wife over responsibility for the child, ref. 4.414K, but on the other hand, there is unmitigated deference shown by both parents towards the assumed authority of the headmistress/teacher in matters concerning childcare, ref. 3.807m. Thus, the mother's secondary social status is not necessarily a result of the subordination of women by men, but rather it is an effect of the position occupied as the agent of childcare within the legal, moral, medical and pedagogic discourses of the educational institution. But there is a difference for the mother with respect to that position because these discourses also assign a place to the child which radically displaces her representation of him as a part of herself. Consequently, the school becomes the site of a struggle for "possession" of the child; it is a struggle the mother always loses and it is this sense of "loss" which produces a specific form of subordination for the woman in her capacity as the mother/housewife.

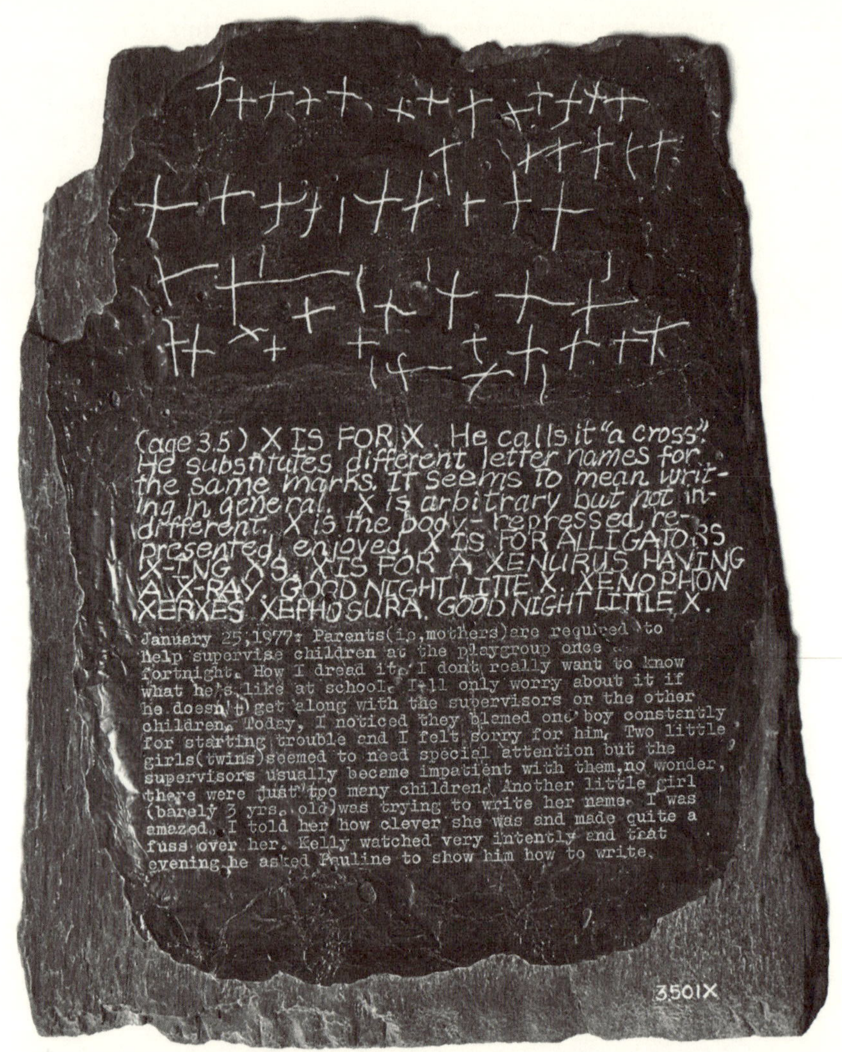
(age 3.5) X IS FOR X. He calls it "a cross".
He substitutes different letter names for
the same marks. It seems to mean writing in general. X is arbitrary but not in-
different. X is the body - repressed, represented, enjoyed. X IS FOR ALLIGATORS
X-ING X'S. X IS FOR A XENURUS HAVING
A X-RAY. GOOD NIGHT LITTE X. XENOPHON
XERXES XEPHOSURA. GOOD NIGHT LITTLE X.
January 25, 1977: Parents (i.e., mothers) are required to
help supervise children at the playgroup once a
fortnight. How I dread it. I don't really want to know
what he's like at school. I'll only worry about it if
he doesn't get along with the supervisors or the other
children. Today, I noticed they blamed one boy constantly
for starting trouble and I felt sorry for him. Two little
girls (twins) seemed to need special attention but the
supervisors usually became impatient with them, no wonder,
there were just too many children. Another little girl
(barely 3 yrs. old) was trying to write her name. I was
amazed. I told her how clever she was and made quite a
fuss over her. Kelly watched very intently and that
evening he asked Pauline to show him how to write.
3.501X

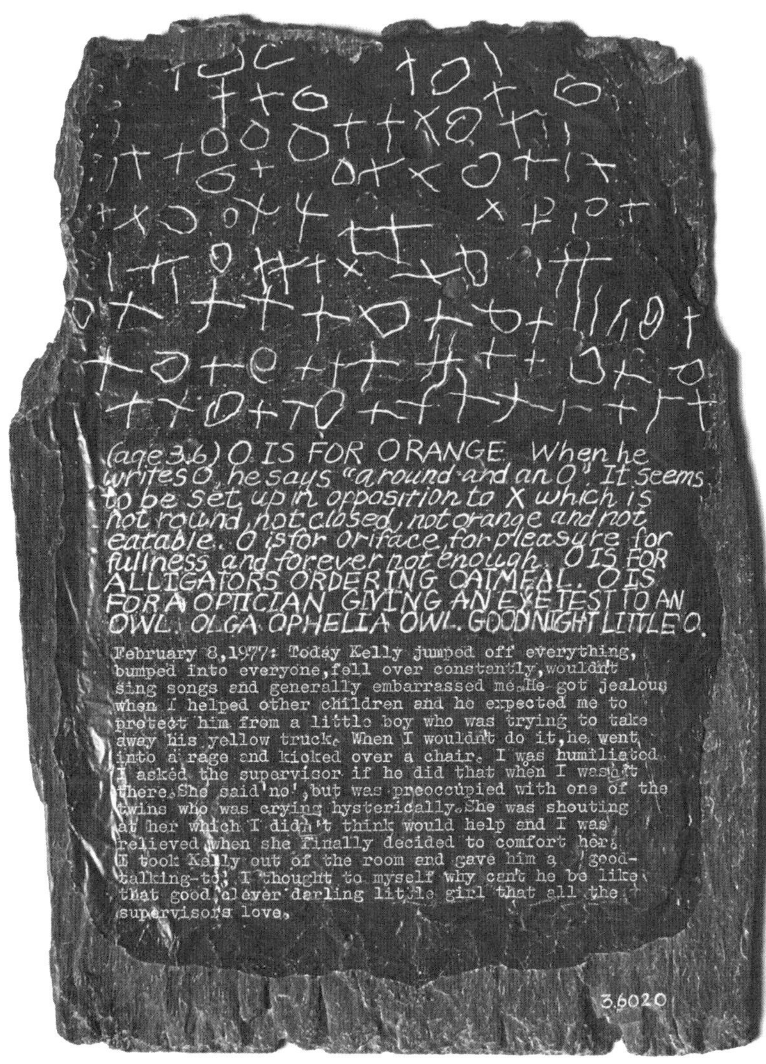
(age 3.6) O IS FOR ORANGE. When he
writes O, he says "a round and an O". It seems
to be set up in opposition to X which is
not round, not closed, not orange and not
eatable. O is for oriface, for pleasure, for
fullness and forever not enough. O IS FOR
ALLIGATORS ORDERING OATMEAL. O IS
FOR A OPTICIAN GIVING AN EYE TEST TO AN
OWL. OLGA OPHELIA OWL. GOODNIGHT LITTLE O.
February 8,1977: Today Kelly jumped off everything,
bumped into everyone,fell over constantly,wouldn't
sing songs and generally embarrassed me. He got jealous
when I helped other children and he expected me to
protect him from a little boy who was trying to take
away his yellow truck. When I wouldn't do it,he went
into a rage and kicked over a chair. I was humiliated.
I asked the supervisor if he did that when I wasn't
there. She said 'no',but was preoccupied with one of the
twins who was crying hysterically. She was shouting
at her which I didn't think would help and I was
relieved when she finally decided to comfort her.
I took Kelly out of the room and gave him a 'good-
talking-to'. I thought to myself why can't he be like
that good,clever darling little girl that all the
supervisors love.
3.6020

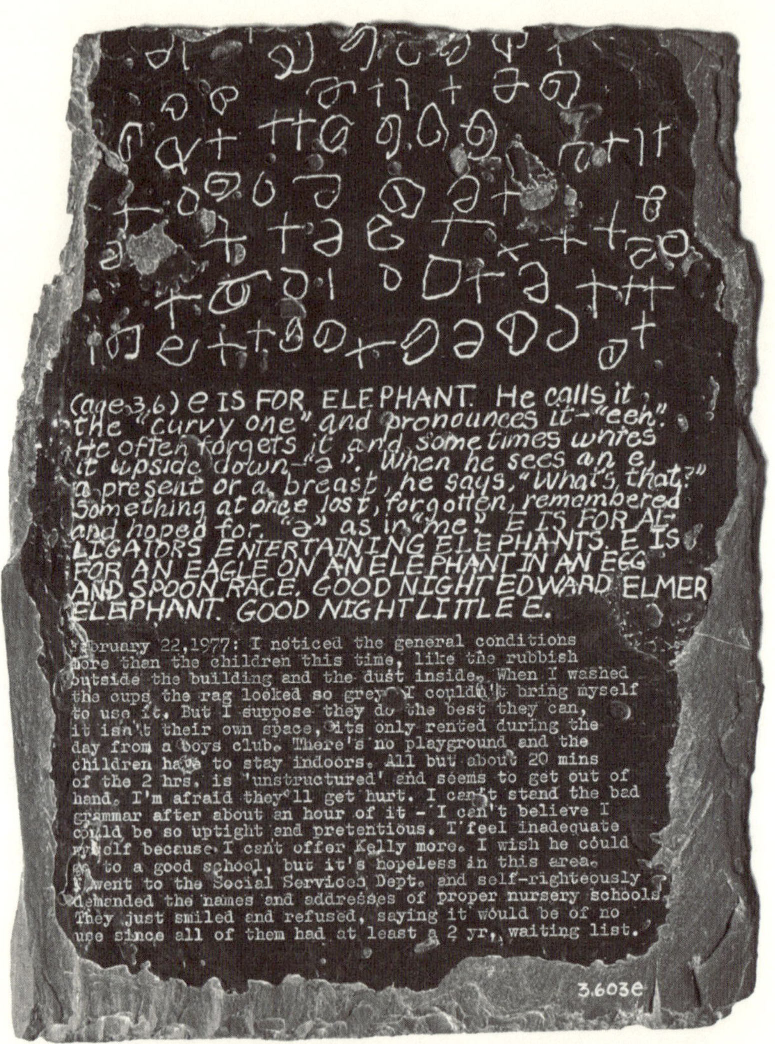
(age 3,6) e IS FOR ELEPHANT. He calls it
the "curvy one" and pronounces it—"eeh".
He often forgets it and sometimes writes
it upside down—"ə". When he sees an e,
a present or a breast, he says, "What's that?"
Something at once lost, forgotten, remembered
and hoped for. "ə" as in "me." E IS FOR AL-
LIGATORS ENTERTAINING ELEPHANTS. E IS
FOR AN EAGLE ON AN ELEPHANT IN AN EGG
AND SPOON RACE. GOOD NIGHT EDWARD ELMER
ELEPHANT. GOOD NIGHT LITTLE E.
February 22,1977: I noticed the general conditions
more than the children this time, like the rubbish
outside the building and the dust inside. When I washed
the cups the rag looked so grey I couldn't bring myself
to use it. But I suppose they do the best they can,
it isn't their own space, its only rented during the
day from a boys club. There's no playground and the
children have to stay indoors. All but about 20 mins
of the 2 hrs. is 'unstructured' and seems to get out of
hand. I'm afraid they'll get hurt. I can't stand the bad
grammar after about an hour of it - I can't believe I
could be so uptight and pretentious. I feel inadequate
myself because I can't offer Kelly more. I wish he could
go to a good school, but it's hopeless in this area.
I went to the Social Services Dept. and self-righteously
demanded the names and addresses of proper nursery schools.
They just smiled and refused, saying it would be of no
use since all of them had at least a 2 yr. waiting list.
3.603e

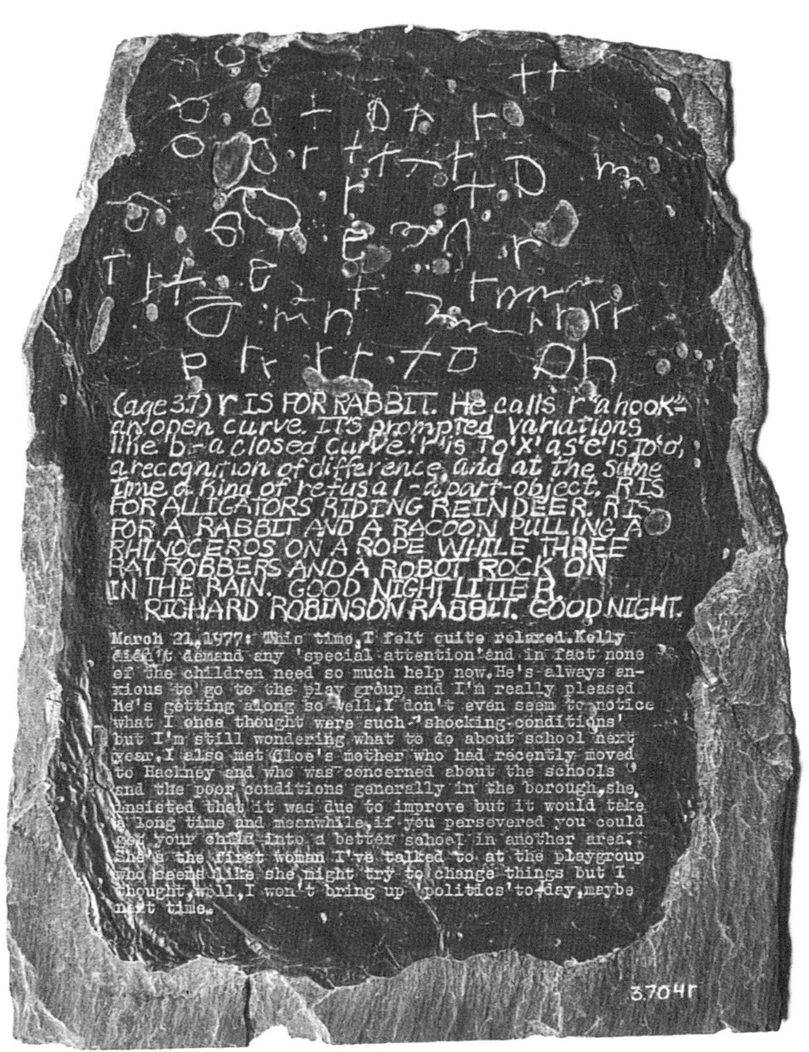
(age 3.7) r IS FOR RABBIT. He calls 'r' a hook—
an open curve. IT'S prompted variations
like 'b'—a closed curve. 'r' is to 'x' as 'e' is to 'o',
a recognition of difference and at the same
time a kind of refusal—a part-object. R IS
FOR ALLIGATORS RIDING REINDEER. R IS
FOR A RABBIT AND A RACOON PULLING A
RHINOCEROS ON A ROPE WHILE THREE
RAT ROBBERS AND A ROBOT ROCK ON
IN THE RAIN. GOOD NIGHT LITTLE R.
RICHARD ROBINSON RABBIT. GOOD NIGHT.
March 21, 1977: This time, I felt quite relaxed. Kelly
didn't demand any 'special attention' and in fact none
of the children need so much help now. He's always anxious to go to the play group and I'm really pleased
he's getting along so well. I don't even seem to notice
what I once thought were such 'shocking conditions'
but I'm still wondering what to do about school next
year. I also met Cloe's mother who had recently moved
to Hackney and who was concerned about the schools
and the poor conditions generally in the borough, she
insisted that it was due to improve but it would take
a long time and meanwhile, if you persevered you could
get your child into a better school in another area.
She's the first woman I've talked to at the playgroup
who seems like she might try to change things but I
thought, well, I won't bring up 'politics' to-day, maybe
next time.
3.704r

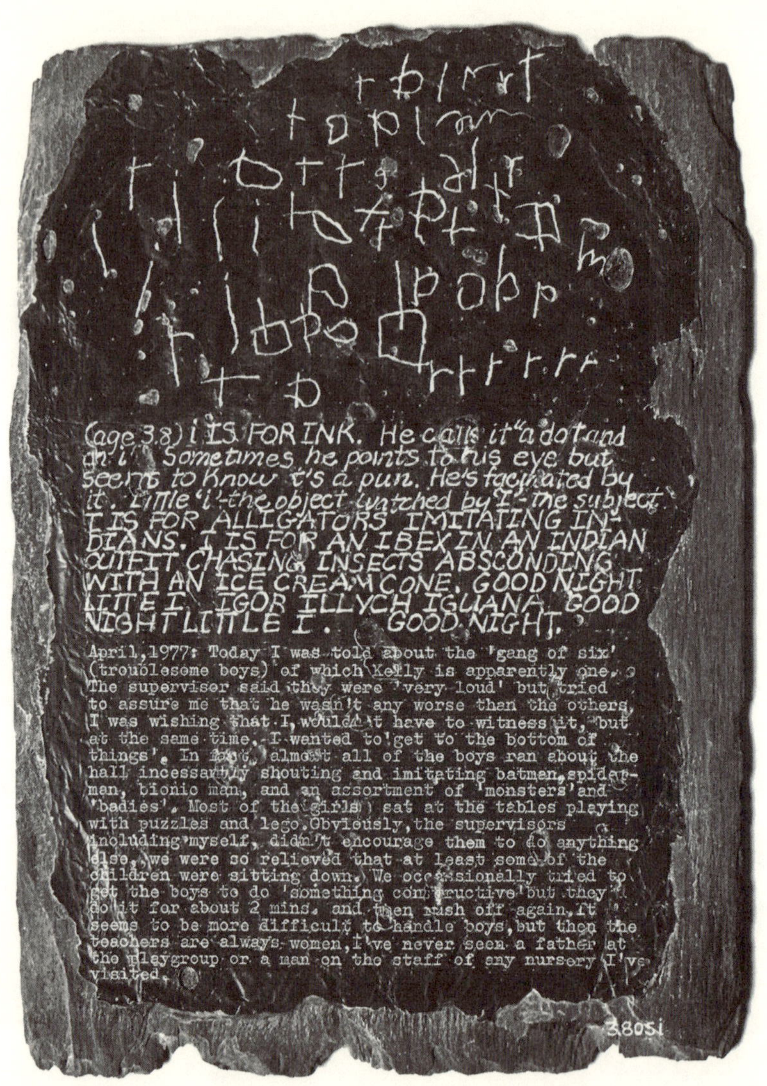
(age 3.8) i IS FOR INK. He calls it "a dot and an i" Sometimes he points to his eye but seems to know it's a pun. He's facinated by it. Little 'i'-the object watched by 'I'-the subject.
I IS FOR ALLIGATORS IMITATING IN-DIANS. I IS FOR AN IBEX IN AN INDIAN OUTFIT CHASING INSECTS ABSCONDING WITH AN ICE CREAM CONE. GOOD NIGHT LITTE I. IGOR ILLYCH IGUANA. GOOD NIGHT LITTLE I. GOOD NIGHT.
April, 1977: Today I was told about the 'gang of six' (troublesome boys) of which Kelly is apparently one. The supervisor said they were 'very loud' but tried to assure me that he wasn't any worse than the others. I was wishing that I wouldn't have to witness it, but at the same time, I wanted to 'get to the bottom of things'. In fact, almost all of the boys ran about the hall incessantly shouting and imitating batman, spider-man, bionic man, and an assortment of 'monsters' and 'badies'. Most of the girls sat at the tables playing with puzzles and lego. Obviously, the supervisors including myself, didn't encourage them to do anything else, we were so relieved that at least some of the children were sitting down. We occassionally tried to get the boys to do 'something constructive' but they do it for about 2 mins. and then rush off again. It seems to be more difficult to handle boys, but then the teachers are always women, I've never seen a father at the playgroup or a man on the staff of any nursery I've visited.
3.805i

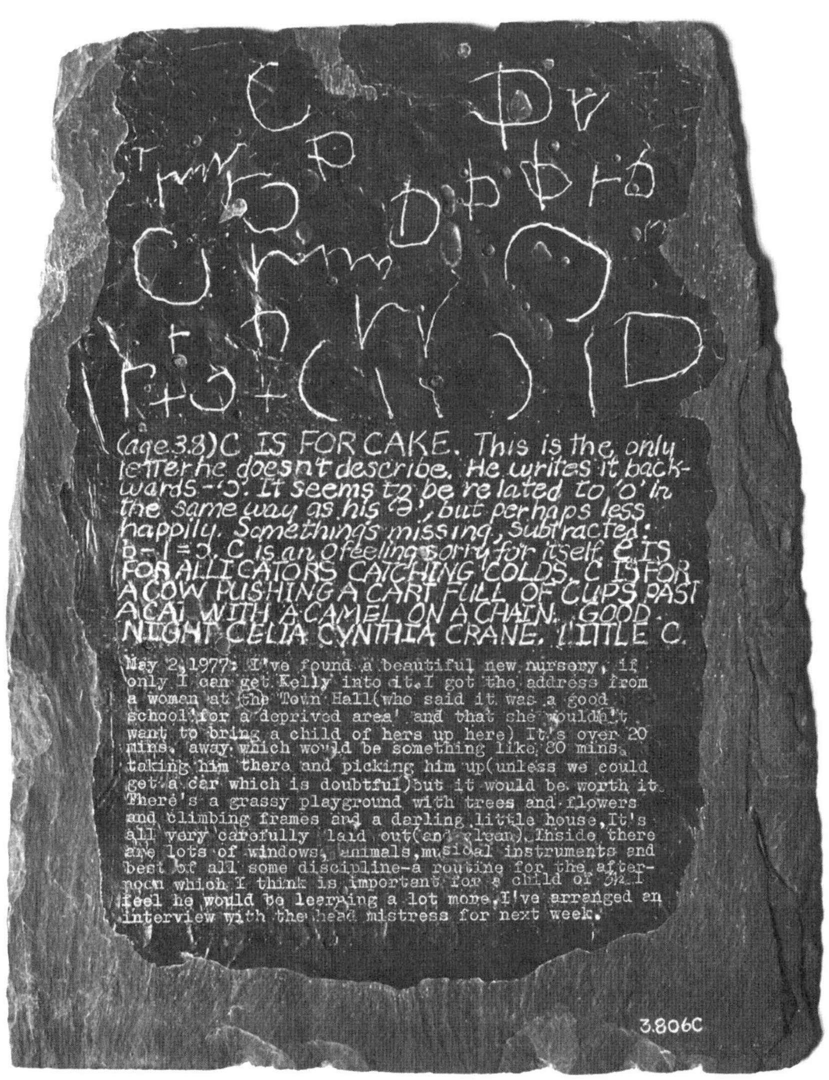
(age 3.8) C IS FOR CAKE. This is the only
letter he doesn't describe. He writes it backwards–'Ɔ'. It seems to be related to 'o' in
the same way as his 'ə', but perhaps less
happily. Something's missing, subtracted:
b–l = Ɔ. C is an O feeling sorry for itself. C IS
FOR ALLIGATORS CATCHING COLDS. C IS FOR
A COW PUSHING A CART FULL OF CUPS PAST
A CAT WITH A CAMEL ON A CHAIN. GOOD
NIGHT CELIA CYNTHIA CRANE. LITTLE C.
May 2,1977: I've found a beautiful new nursery, if
only I can get Kelly into it. I got the address from
a woman at the Town Hall(who said it was a good
school for a deprived area' and that she wouldn't
want to bring a child of hers up here) It's over 20
mins. away which would be something like 80 mins.
taking him there and picking him up(unless we could
get a car which is doubtful)but it would be worth it.
There's a grassy playground with trees and flowers
and climbing frames and a darling little house. It's
all very carefully laid out(and clean). Inside there
are lots of windows, animals, musical instruments and
best of all some discipline-a routine for the afternoon which I think is important for a child of 3½. I
feel he would be learning a lot more. I've arranged an
interview with the head mistress for next week.
3.806C

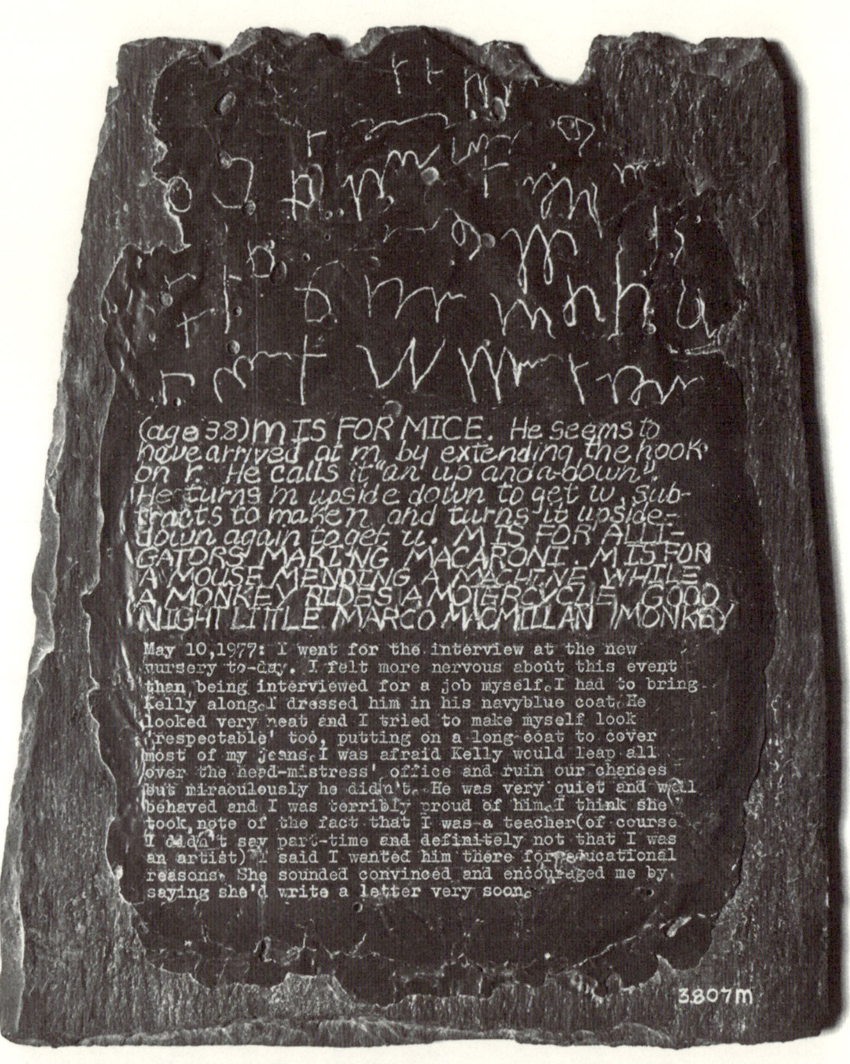
(age 3.8) m IS FOR MICE. He seems to
have arrived at m by extending the hook
on r. He calls it "an up and-a-down".
He turns m upside down to get w, sub-
tracts to make n and turns it upsidedown again to get u. M IS FOR ALLI-
GATORS MAKING MACARONI. M IS FOR
A MOUSE MENDING A MACHINE WHILE
A MONKEY RIDES A MOTERCYCLE. GOOD
NIGHT LITTLE MARCO MACMILLAN MONKEY
May 10,1977: I went for the interview at the new
nursery to-day. I felt more nervous about this event
than being interviewed for a job myself. I had to bring
Kelly along. I dressed him in his navyblue coat. He
looked very neat and I tried to make myself look
'respectable' too, putting on a long coat to cover
most of my jeans. I was afraid Kelly would leap all
over the head-mistress' office and ruin our chances
but miraculously he didn't. He was very quiet and well
behaved and I was terribly proud of him. I think she
took note of the fact that I was a teacher(of course
I didn't say part-time and definitely not that I was
an artist) I said I wanted him there for educational
reasons. She sounded convinced and encouraged me by
saying she'd write a letter very soon.
3807m

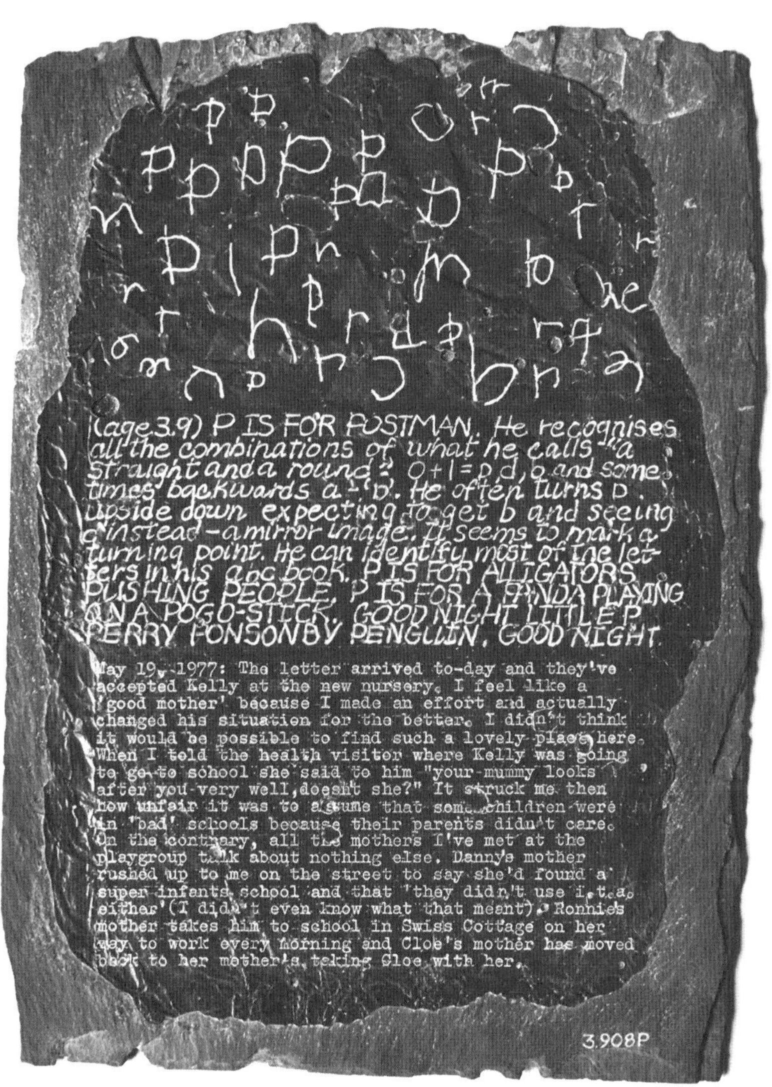
(age 3.9) P IS FOR POSTMAN. He recognises
all the combinations of what he calls "a
straight and a round": O+I = p d, b and sometimes backwards a-'D'. He often turns D
upside down expecting to get b and seeing
d instead – a mirror image. It seems to mark a
turning point. He can identify most of the letters in his abc book. P IS FOR ALLIGATORS
PUSHING PEOPLE. P IS FOR A PANDA PLAYING
ON A POGO-STICK. GOODNIGHT LITTLE P.
PERRY PONSONBY PENGUIN. GOOD NIGHT.
May 19, 1977: The letter arrived to-day and they've
accepted Kelly at the new nursery. I feel like a
'good mother' because I made an effort and actually
changed his situation for the better. I didn't think
it would be possible to find such a lovely place here.
When I told the health visitor where Kelly was going
to go to school she said to him "your mummy looks
after you very well, doesn't she?" It struck me then
how unfair it was to assume that some children were
in 'bad' schools because their parents didn't care.
On the contrary, all the mothers I've met at the
playgroup talk about nothing else. Danny's mother
rushed up to me on the street to say she'd found a
super infants school and that 'they didn't use i.t.a.
either' (I didn't even know what that meant). Ronnie's
mother takes him to school in Swiss Cottage on her
way to work every morning and Cloe's mother has moved
back to her mother's, taking Cloe with her.
3.908P

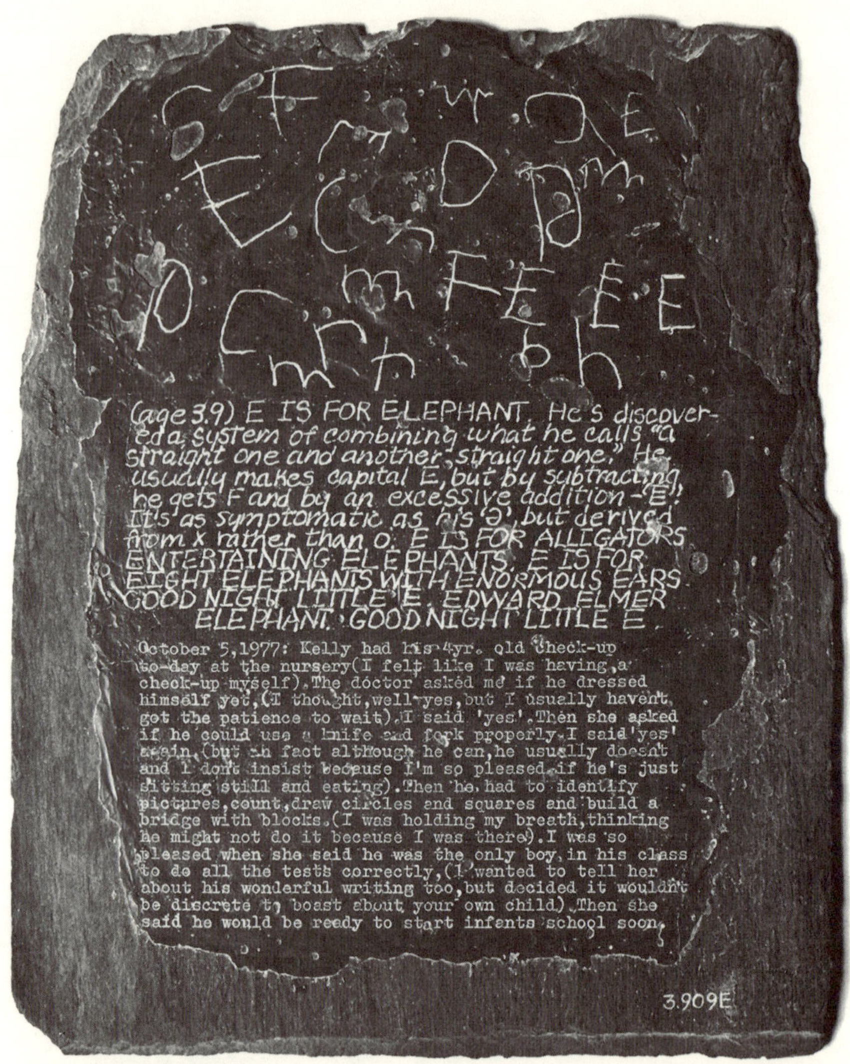
(age 3.9) E IS FOR ELEPHANT. He's discovered a system of combining what he calls "a straight one and another straight one." He usually makes capital E, but by subtracting, he gets F and by an excessive addition - 'E'! It's as symptomatic as his 'ə', but derived from x rather than o. E IS FOR ALLIGATORS ENTERTAINING ELEPHANTS. E IS FOR EIGHT ELEPHANTS WITH ENORMOUS EARS GOOD NIGHT LITTLE E. EDWARD ELMER ELEPHANT. GOOD NIGHT LITTLE E.
October 5,1977: Kelly had his 4yr. old check-up to-day at the nursery(I felt like I was having a check-up myself).The doctor asked me if he dressed himself yet,(I thought,well-yes,but I usually haven't got the patience to wait).I said 'yes'.Then she asked if he could use a knife and fork properly.I said'yes' again.(but in fact although he can,he usually doesn't and I don't insist because I'm so pleased if he's just sitting still and eating).Then he had to identify pictures,count,draw circles and squares and build a bridge with blocks.(I was holding my breath,thinking he might not do it because I was there).I was so pleased when she said he was the only boy in his class to do all the tests correctly,(I wanted to tell her about his wonderful writing too,but decided it wouldn't be discrete to boast about your own child).Then she said he would be ready to start infants school soon.
3.909E

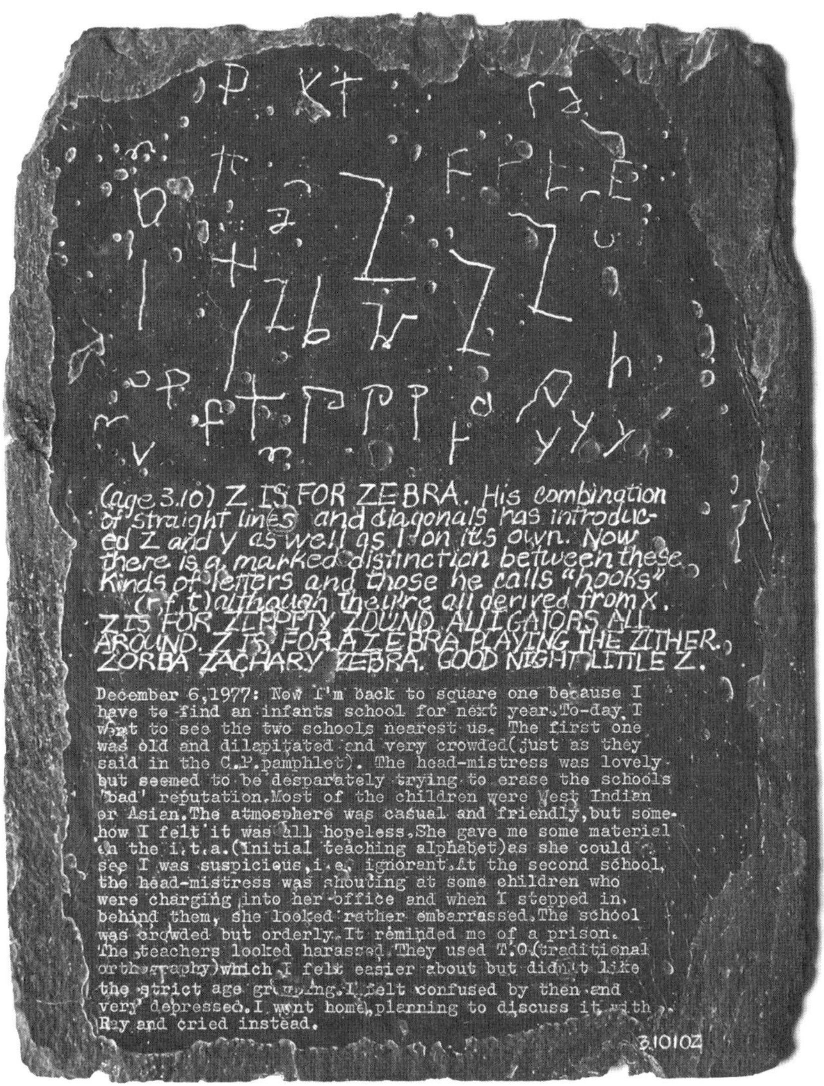
(age 3.10) Z IS FOR ZEBRA. His combination of straight lines and diagonals has introduced Z and y as well as l on its own. Now there is a marked distinction between these kinds of letters and those he calls "hooks" (r, f, t) although they're all derived from x.
Z IS FOR ZEPPITY ZOUND ALLIGATORS ALL AROUND. Z IS FOR A ZEBRA PLAYING THE ZITHER. ZORBA ZACHARY ZEBRA. GOOD NIGHT LITTLE Z.
December 6,1977: Now I'm back to square one because I have to find an infants school for next year.To-day I went to see the two schools nearest us. The first one was old and dilapitated and very crowded(just as they said in the C.P.pamphlet). The head-mistress was lovely but seemed to be desparately trying to erase the schools 'bad' reputation.Most of the children were West Indian or Asian.The atmosphere was casual and friendly,but somehow I felt it was all hopeless.She gave me some material on the i.t.a.(Initial teaching alphabet)as she could see I was suspicious,i.e. ignorant.At the second school, the head-mistress was shouting at some children who were charging into her office and when I stepped in behind them, she looked rather embarrassed.The school was crowded but orderly.It reminded me of a prison. The teachers looked harassed.They used T.O.(traditional orthography)which I felt easier about but didn't like the strict age grouping.I felt confused by then and very depressed.I went home,planning to discuss it with Ray and cried instead.
3.10.10Z

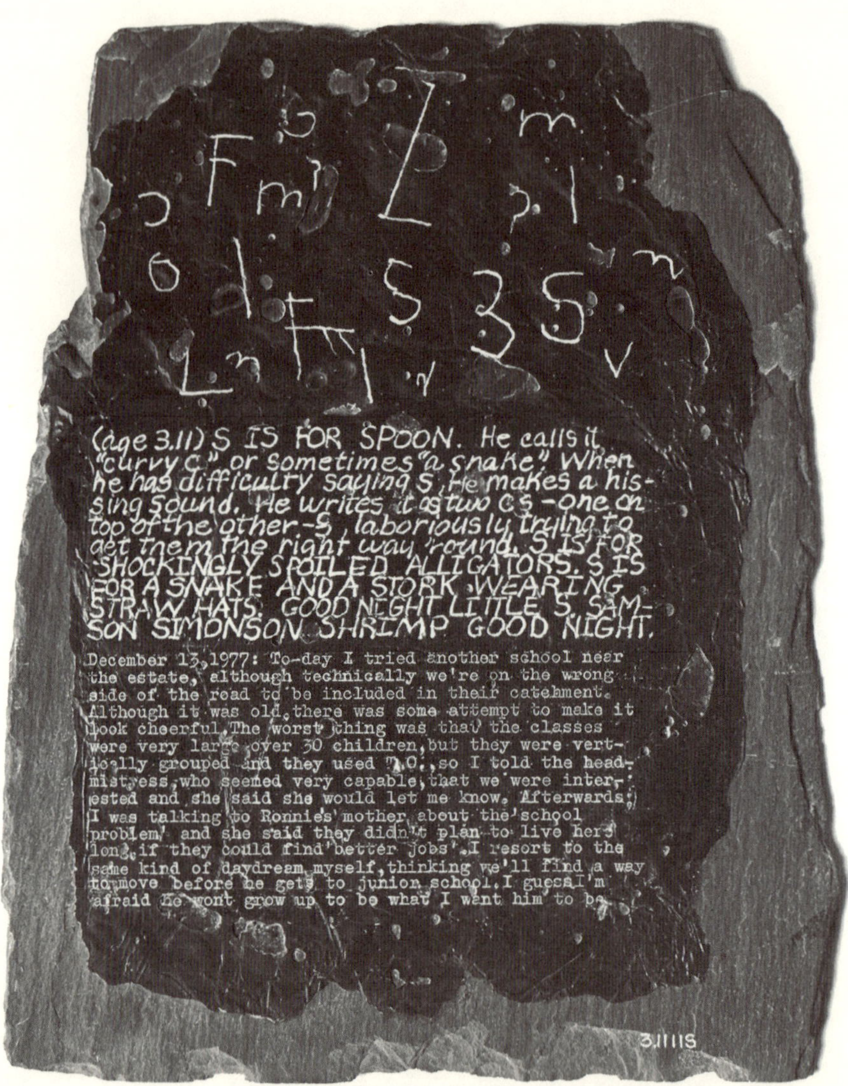
(age 3.11) S IS FOR SPOON. He calls it "curvy C" or sometimes "a snake". When he has difficulty saying S, He makes a hissing sound. He writes it as two C's - one on top of the other - S, laboriously trying to get them the right way 'round. S IS FOR SHOCKINGLY SPOILED ALLIGATORS. S IS FOR A SNAKE AND A STORK WEARING STRAW HATS. GOOD NIGHT LITTLE S. SAMSON SIMONSON SHRIMP. GOOD NIGHT.
December 13, 1977: To-day I tried another school near the estate, although technically we're on the wrong side of the road to be included in their catchment. Although it was old, there was some attempt to make it look cheerful. The worst thing was that the classes were very large, over 30 children, but they were vertically grouped and they used T.O., so I told the headmistress, who seemed very capable, that we were interested and she said she would let me know. Afterwards I was talking to Ronnie's mother about the school problem, and she said they didn't plan to live here long, if they could find better jobs. I resort to the same kind of daydream myself, thinking we'll find a way to move before he gets to junion school. I guess I'm afraid he wont grow up to be what I want him to be.
3.11.1S

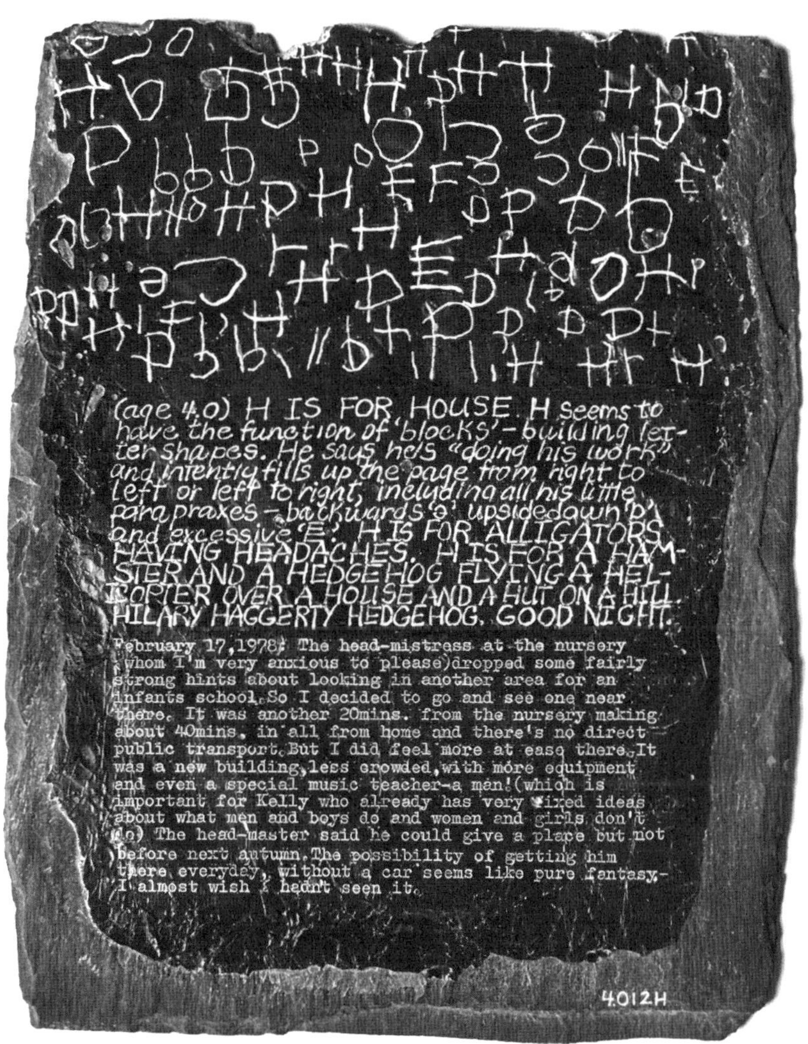
(age 4.0) H IS FOR HOUSE. H seems to have the function of 'blocks' – building letter shapes. He says he's "doing his work" and intently fills up the page from right to left or left to right, including all his little parapraxes – backwards 'e' upsidedown 'p' and excessive 'E'. H IS FOR ALLIGATORS HAVING HEADACHES. H IS FOR A HAMSTER AND A HEDGEHOG FLYING A HELICOPTER OVER A HOUSE AND A HUT ON A HILL. HILARY HAGGERTY HEDGEHOG. GOOD NIGHT.
February 17, 1978: The head-mistress at the nursery (whom I'm very anxious to please) dropped some fairly strong hints about looking in another area for an infants school. So I decided to go and see one near there. It was another 20mins. from the nursery making about 40mins. in all from home and there's no direct public transport. But I did feel more at ease there. It was a new building, less crowded, with more equipment and even a special music teacher – a man! (which is important for Kelly who already has very fixed ideas about what men and boys do and women and girls don't do) The head-master said he could give a place but not before next autumn. The possibility of getting him there everyday, without a car seems like pure fantasy – I almost wish I hadn't seen it.
4.012H

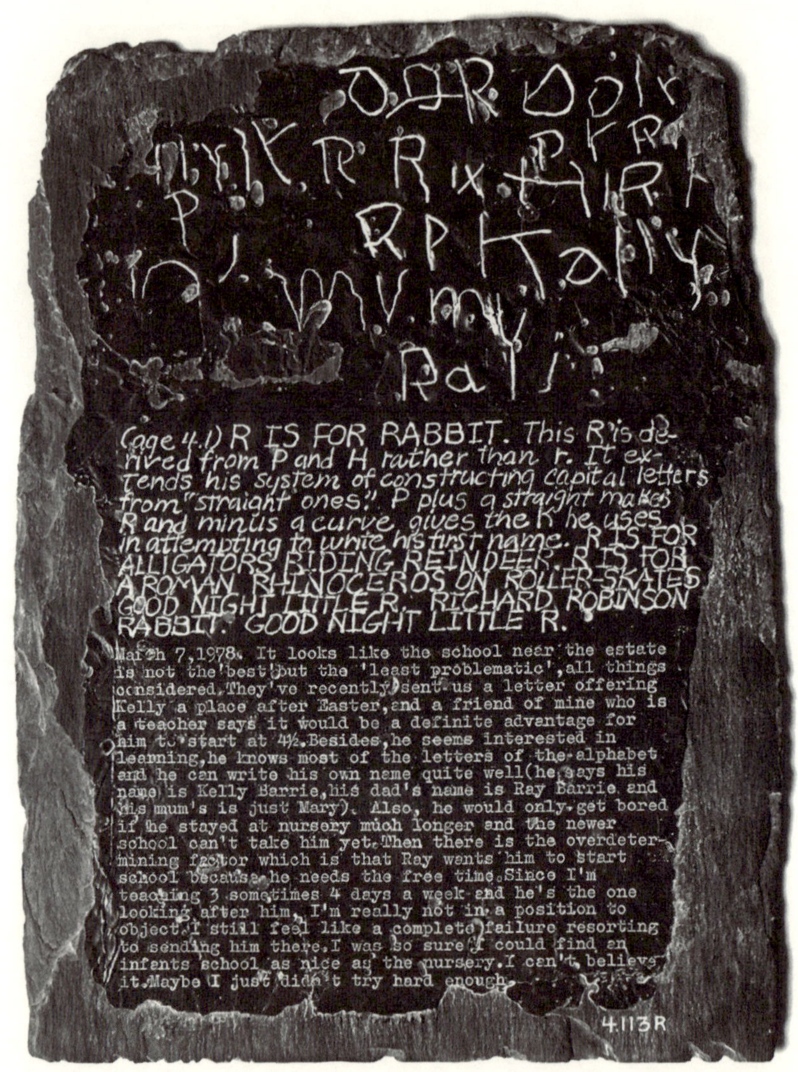
(age 4.1) R IS FOR RABBIT. This R is derived from P and H rather than r. It extends his system of constructing capital letters from "straight ones." P plus a straight makes R and minus a curve gives the K he uses in attempting to write his first name. R IS FOR ALLIGATORS BIDING REINDEER. R IS FOR A ROMAN RHINOCEROS ON ROLLER-SKATES GOOD NIGHT LITTLE R. RICHARD ROBINSON RABBIT. GOOD NIGHT LITTLE R.
March 7,1978. It looks like the school near the estate is not the best but the 'least problematic',all things considered. They've recently sent us a letter offering Kelly a place after Easter,and a friend of mine who is a teacher says it would be a definite advantage for him to start at 4½.Besides,he seems interested in learning,he knows most of the letters of the alphabet and he can write his own name quite well(he says his name is Kelly Barrie,his dad's name is Ray Barrie and his mum's is just Mary). Also, he would only get bored if he stayed at nursery much longer and the newer school can't take him yet.Then there is the overdetermining factor which is that Ray wants him to start school because he needs the free time.Since I'm teaching 3 sometimes 4 days a week and he's the one looking after him, I'm really not in a position to object.I still feel like a complete failure resorting to sending him there.I was so sure I could find an infants school as nice as the nursery.I can't believ it.Maybe I just didn't try hard enough.
4.113R

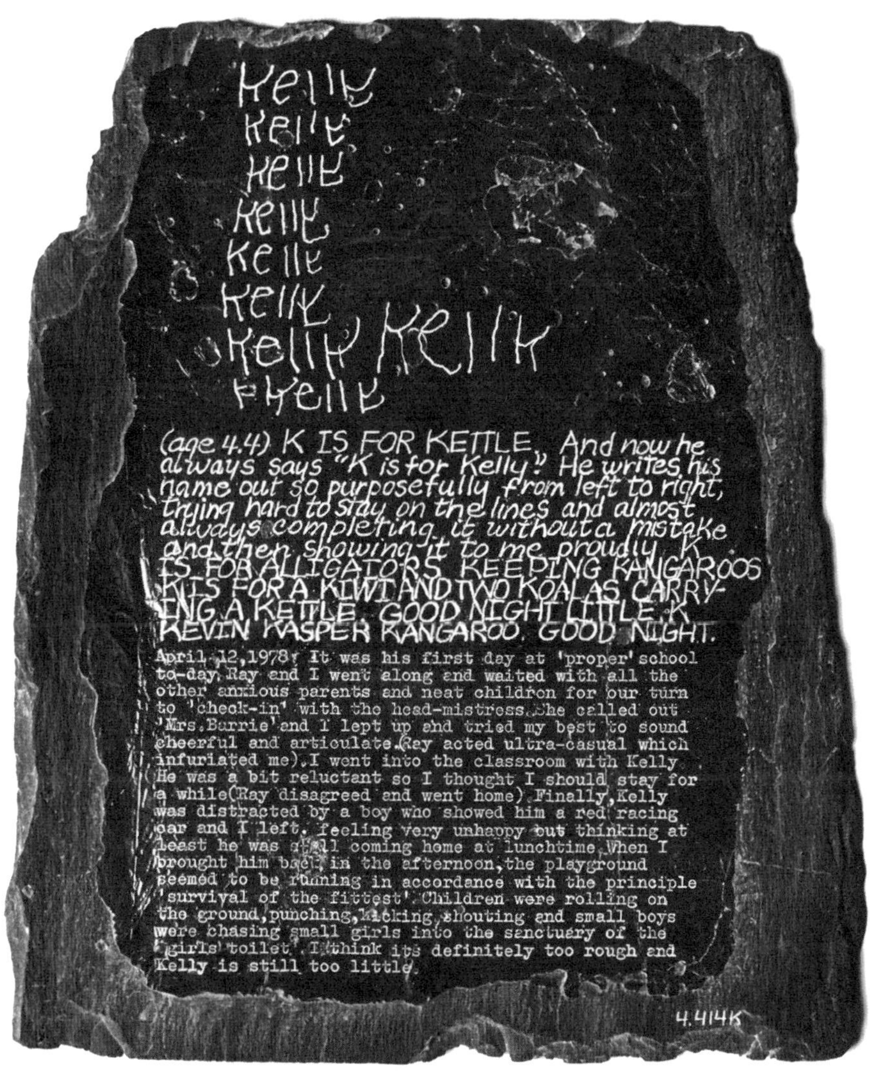
Kelly
Kelly
Kelly
Kelly
Kelly
Kelly
Kelly Kelly
Kelly
(age 4.4) K IS FOR KETTLE. And now he always says "K is for Kelly." He writes his name out so purposefully from left to right, trying hard to stay on the lines and almost always completing it without a mistake and then showing it to me proudly. K IS FOR ALLIGATORS KEEPING KANGAROOS K IS FOR A KIWI AND TWO KOALAS CARRYING A KETTLE. GOOD NIGHT LITTLE K KEVIN KASPER KANGAROO. GOOD NIGHT.
April 12,1978: It was his first day at 'proper' school to-day. Ray and I went along and waited with all the other anxious parents and neat children for our turn to 'check-in' with the head-mistress. She called out 'Mrs. Barrie' and I lept up and tried my best to sound cheerful and articulate.(Ray acted ultra-casual which infuriated me). I went into the classroom with Kelly. He was a bit reluctant so I thought I should stay for a while(Ray disagreed and went home). Finally, Kelly was distracted by a boy who showed him a red racing car and I left, feeling very unhappy but thinking at least he was still coming home at lunchtime. When I brought him back in the afternoon, the playground seemed to be running in accordance with the principle 'survival of the fittest'. Children were rolling on the ground, punching, kicking, shouting and small boys were chasing small girls into the sanctuary of the 'girls' toilet'. I think its definitely too rough and Kelly is still too little.
4.414K

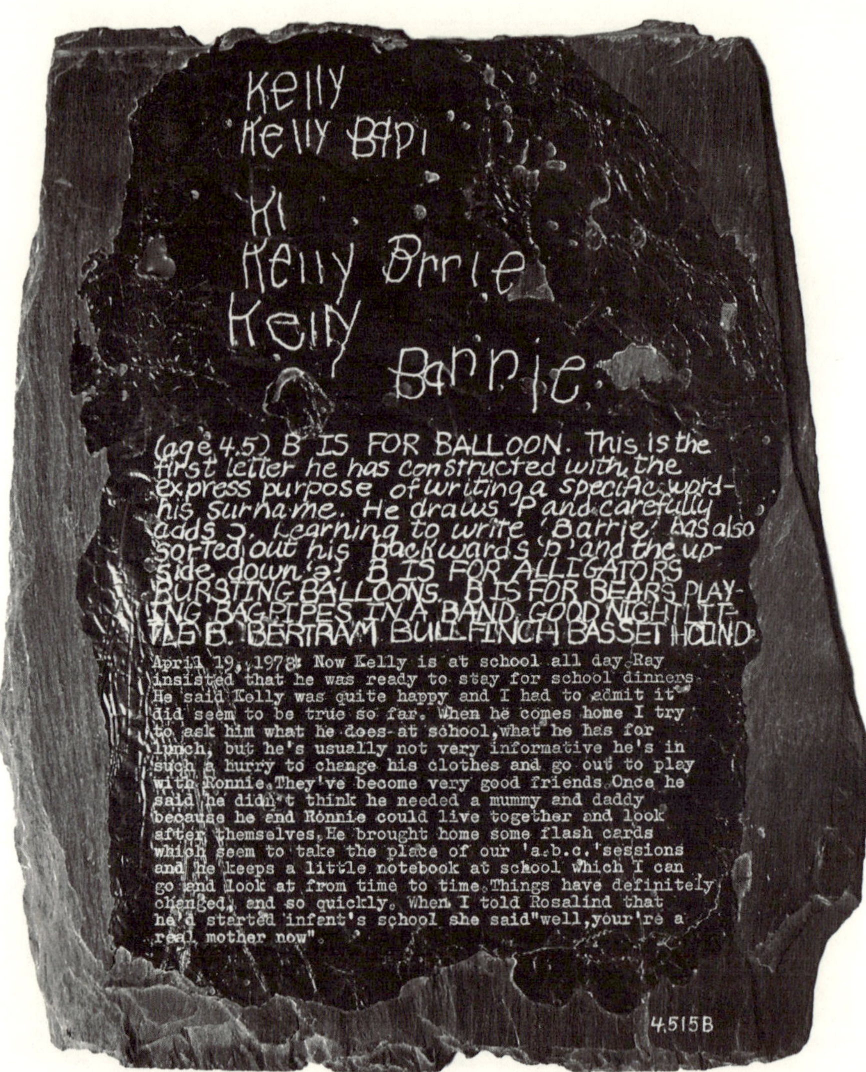
Kelly
Kelly Bapi
Ki
Kelly Brrie
Kelly
Barrie
(age 4.5) B IS FOR BALLOON. This is the first letter he has constructed with the express purpose of writing a specific word- his surname. He draws P and carefully adds ɔ. Learning to write 'Barrie' has also sorted out his backwards 'p' and the upside down 'ə'. B IS FOR ALLIGATORS BURSTING BALLOONS. B IS FOR BEARS PLAYING BAGPIPES IN A BAND. GOOD NIGHT LITTLE B. BERTRAM BULLFINCH BASSET HOUND
April 19, 1978: Now Kelly is at school all day. Ray insisted that he was ready to stay for school dinners. He said Kelly was quite happy and I had to admit it did seem to be true so far. When he comes home I try to ask him what he does at school, what he has for lunch, but he's usually not very informative he's in such a hurry to change his clothes and go out to play with Ronnie. They've become very good friends. Once he said he didn't think he needed a mummy and daddy because he and Ronnie could live together and look after themselves. He brought home some flash cards which seem to take the place of our 'a.b.c.' sessions and he keeps a little notebook at school which I can go and look at from time to time. Things have definitely changed, and so quickly. When I told Rosalind that he'd started infant's school she said "well, your're a real mother now".
4.515B

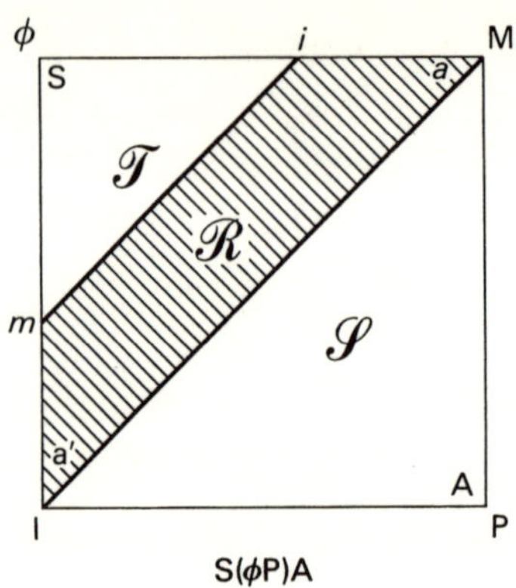

S(ϕP)A

(WHAT WILL I DO?)

Experimentum Mentis VI
On the Insistence of the Letter

Prewriting emerges as postscript to the Oedipus complex and as a preface to the moment of latency. Insofar as the child's sexual researches are repressed by the Law and the Father, they are sublimated in the body of the letter; but it is the mother who first censors the look, who wipes the slate clean with her silence and prepares the site of inscription. For the mother, the child's text is a fetish object; it desires her. The polymorphous perversity of the letter explores the body beyond the limit of the look. The breast (e), the hook (r), the lack (c), the eye (i), the snake (s); forbidden anatomies, incestuous morphologies; the child's alphabet is an anagram of the maternal body. For the child the grapheme-as-body-in-the-position-of-the-signifier plays with difference, not the difference of the founding moment of castration, the ultimatum of being or having, but rather a replay of differences and separations already sanctioned in the structuring and dissolution of the Oedipus complex. A cross (x), a round (o), an up and a down (n, m), a straight and a round (p, b, d, q); pairs of graphemic oppositions designate the symbolic function of presence and absence in a double movement of memory and forgetting. Feces, mark, imprint, utterance–a residue of corporality subtends the letter and overflows the text. The gift unfolds the child's desire to-be-what-she-wants-him-to-be; but the letter constructs the cannot-be of his autonomy and instigates the unexpected pleasure of deferment.

With the inscription of his proper name, the child is instituted as the author of his text. Each purposeful stroke disfigures the anagram, dismembers the body. The mother is dispossessed of the phallic attributes of the pre-Oedipal instance, but only as if retracing a vague figure of repletion on a distant screen. Fading, forgetting–she cannot remember although "it seems like only yesterday." This wound to her narcissism is now a caricature: a tearful bliss, a simulated ecstasy, a veritable stigmata in the Name-of-the-Father. With the child's insistent repetition of the Name, he appropriates the status of the Father, the dead Father, the absent Father, the precondition of the "word." The incestuous meaning of the letter is ciphered by the paternal metaphor. But at the same time, this introduces the possibility of "truth," the truth of the mother–that is, the fiction of the "real mother," not the Madonna, but the Pieta, dispelling imputations of guilt with patience, self-sacrifice, long-suffering and resignation. Resignation punctuated with protests: "he is too little... he is too young... they are too rough... it is too far." In fantasy, the mother endures an endless series of threats to the child's well-being; sickness, accident, death. Her castration fears take the form of losing her loved objects, primarily her children; but underlying this is the fear of losing love, that is, the fear of being unable to reconstitute her narcissistic aim, of being unable to see herself as infinitely good and unconditionally loved. Ultimately, it is the fear of her mother's death and of her own death as the imaginary stake in the representation of that loss. This negation is constituted by a recognition of unbearable dependence; but it is also an affirmation of life since the child's independence is implicated in the renunciation he imposes on her desire.

The effects of repressing Oedipal pleasure for both the mother and the child are evaded through sublimation, that is, through their mutual inscription in an order of extrafamilial discourse and social practice. But the very movement towards a nonparental ideal that prompts the child's creative initiatives or indiscretions and constructs the representation of his social place, returns the mother to the site of the family, to the parental ideal of her own mother and to the representation of maternal femininity. Such a circuitous passage is problematic; being the phallus, she cannot have it; not having it, she cannot represent herself as subject of desire. She finds it difficult to assume responsibility for her pleasure without guilt; to provoke her sexual partner, to slight her child. Fearing failure, she is distracted from the projects which interest her most. There is a reprieve; another child, the fullness of the dyad, the sweetness of that imaginary encapsulation which reduces the "outside world" to absurdity. But there is also the inevitable moment of separation reiterating a lack always already inscribed and impossible to efface. She asks herself "What will I do? ... when he starts school... when he grows up... when he leaves home... when he leaves me..." This moment signifies more than separation; it articulates a rupture, a rent, a gap and a confrontation–a confrontation not only because of the way in which her desire, as desire of the child, to-be-what-she-wants-him-to-be, is produced within a field of social and economic constraints; but also because of the way in which the dialectic of desire, the movement of subject and object with its insistence on bisexuality, continually transgresses the system of representation in which it is founded. The construction of femininity as essentially natural and maternal is never finally fixed but forever unsettled in the process of articulating her difference, her loss. And it is precisely at such moments that it is possible to desire to speak and to dare to change.

Notes

Schema R, Experimentum Mentis I-VI

	KEY
S	the subject
I	the Imaginary (at upper left)
R	the Real (shaded area)
S	the Symbolic (at lower right)
a	the figure of the Imaginary other of the "stade du miroir"
a´	the identification of the (child's) ego through the identification with the ideal of the ego (the paternal "imago")
ø	the phallus (Imaginary object)
I	the ideal of the ego
P	the position of the Name-of-the-Father in the locus of the Other
M	the signifier of the primordial object ("das Ding" – cf. Freud on negation) – the mother, who is the "real" "Other"
(i)	the two Imaginary end-points of all later narcissistic relationships
(m)	the ego (m) and the specular image (i)
iM	the axis of desires (object choice)
mI	the axis of identifications (narcissism)
SA	the metaphorical relationship between the subject and the Other or between the phallus (ø) and the Name-of-the-Father (P)

Wilden, A., *The Language of the Self*, Johns Hopkins University Press, 1968, p. 294.

Schema R, Documentation IV

In 1966 Lacan explained that schema R is to be read in three dimensions. J.A. Miller adds the following comment in *Les Cahiers de l'analyse* no. 1-2: The surface R is to be taken as the flattening out of the figure obtained by joining i to I and m to M, that is, by the twisting which characterizes the Moebius strip. The presentation of the schema in two dimensions is thus related to the cut which enables the strip to be laid out flat. It will be realized that the line IM cannot refer to the relationship of the subject to the object of desire: the subject is only the cutting of the strip, and what falls out of it is called "the object a."

Wilden, A., *The Language of the Self*, Johns Hopkins Press, 1968, p. 296.

Figure I, Documentation I

Metabolism in the First Year of Life.

Abt, I. A., *Pediatrics*, W.B. Sanders Co., 1923, p. 664.

Figure 2, Documentation II

A summary of the characteristics of holophrastic speech and the ages (with two children) at which they first emerge. It should be understood that the transition from holophrastic speech is gradual, not abrupt.

McNeill, D., *The Acquisition of Language*, Harper and Row, Publishers, 1970, p. 24.

Figure 3, Documentation III

Take a square ABCD (in perspective). Produce AD and BC to intersect at V.

The point V is the central vanishing point (on the horizon or eye level). Produce the diagonal AC to meet the eye level: this gives the distance point DP. Mark off a number of equal divisions along AG passing through B. Join these points to DP and V. The intersections on VG will give the horizontal co-ordinates and the intersections along AB will give the orthogonal co-ordinates.

Dubery, F., Willats, J., *Drawing Systems*, Studio Vista, 1972, p. 56.

Figure 4, Documentation IV

As regards all visible objects, three things must be considered. These are the position of the eye which sees (b), that of the object seen (a), and the position of the light which illuminates the object (c).

Richter, I.A., *Selections from the Notebooks of Leonardo da Vinci*, Oxford University Press, 1952, p. 130.

Figure 5, Documentation V

The Cartesian co-ordinates applied to the known pelvic outline of Archaeopteryx (ancient bird) with the co-ordinates of the pelvis of Apatornis superimposed on it and three intermediate systems interpolated to give the hypothetical types leading up to Apatornis.

Thompson, D.W., *Growth and Form*, Cambridge University Press, 1969, p.307.

Figure 6, Documentation VI

PHONEMIC PATTERNING: Ordinarily child language begins and the aphasic dissolution of language preceding its complete loss and ends with what psychopathologists have termed the "labial stage." In this phase, speakers are able to produce only one type of utterance, which is usually transcribed as /pa/. From the articulatory point of view, the two constituents of this utterance represent polar configurations of the buccal tract ... This polarity between the minimum and the maximum of energy appears primarily as a contrast between two successive units—the optimal consonant and the optimal vowel. Thus the elementary phonemic frame, the Syllable, is established (Consonant + Vowel).

After the appearance of the contrast CV, founded upon one attribute of sound, loudness, the utilization of the other basic attribute, pitch, is psychologically inferable. Thus, the first tonality opposition is instituted: grave/acute, in other words, the concentration of energy in the lower vs. upper frequencies of the spectrum. In /p/ the lower end predominates, while in /t/ the upper is stronger... At this stage, the pole of high and concentrated energy /a/ contrasts with the lower energy stops /p/ and /t/. Both the stops are opposed to each other by a predominance of one or the other end of the frequency spectrum, as the gravity and acuteness poles. These two dimensions underlie a TRIANGULAR pattern of phonemes... The tonality opposition, originally consonantal, may in turn be extended to the vocalic pattern: it is naturally the diffuse vowel (founded in opposition to the compact vowel /a/) that splits into grave and acute, complementing the vocalic apex of the overall triangle by a /u/—/i/ base-line. In this way, the originally single primary triangle is partitioned into two autonomous two-dimensional patterns—the consonantal and the vocalic triangle.

Jakobson, R. and Halle, M., *Fundamentals of Language*, Mouton, The Hague, 1975, pp. 50-3.

References

The books listed are coded according to their use as sources and references at various points throughout the *Post-Partum Document*. Thus DOC. refers to Documentation, EXP. to Experimentum Mentis and INTRO. to Introduction.

Abt, I.A., *Pediatrics*, W.B. Sanders Co., 1923; DOC. I.

Adams, P. and Minson, J., "The Feminine Body and Feminist Politics," *m/f*, no. 3, 1979; DOC.VI.

Barthes, R., *The Pleasure of the Text*, Jonathan Cape, 1976; EXP. VI.

Bloom, L., *One Word at a Time*, Mouton, 1975; DOC. II.

Breen, D., *The Birth of the First Child*, Tavistock Publications, 1975; EXP. I.

Coward, R., Cowie, E., and Lipshitz, S., *Psychoanalysis and Patriarchial Structures*, Patriarchy Conference paper, 1976; EXP. I, II, III.

Coward, R., and Ellis, J., *Language and Materialism*, Routledge & Kegan Paul, 1977; EXP. VI.

Delmar, R., *Engels Origins of the Family, Private Property and the State*, in Mitchell, J., Oakly, A. (eds), *Rights and Wrongs of Women*, Penguin, 1976; INTRO.

Derrida, J., *Of Grammatology*, Johns Hopkins University Press, 1975; DOC. II, VI.

Dolto, F., *Dominique, the Analysis of an Adolescent*, Souvenir Press, 1971; EXP. I, II, III.

Dolto, F., *Le Complexe d'Oedipe, psychoanalyse et pediatrie*, Editions du Seuil, 1971; EXP. IV, V, VI.

Foucault, M., *The Order of Things, An Archaeology of the Human Sciences*, Tavistock Publications, 1970; DOC. V.

Foucault, M., *The Archaeology of Knowledge*, Tavistock Publications, 1972; DOC. V, VI.

Freud, S., *The Interpretation of Dreams*, 1900, Standard Edition, Hogarth Press, 1964, vol. VII; EXP. VI.

Freud, S., *Fragment of an Analysis of a Case of Hysteria*, 1905, Standard Edition, vol. VII; EXP. VI.

Freud, S., *Three Essays on Sexuality*, 1905, Standard Edition, vol. VII; EXP. V.

Freud, S., *Analysis of a Phobia in a Five-Year-Old Boy*, 1909, Standard Edition, vol. X; EXP. V.

Freud, S., *Leonardo da Vinci and a Memory of his Childhood*, 1910, Standard Edition, vol. XI; EXP. V.

Freud, S., *On Narcissism: An Introduction*, 1914, Standard Edition, vol. XIV; EXP. I, II, III, IV, V, VI.

Freud, S., *The Ego and the Id*, 1923, Standard Edition, vol. XIX; EXP. I, II, III.

Freud, S., *Negation*, 1925, Standard Edition, vol. XIX; EXP. VI.

Freud, S., *Some Physical Consequences of the Anatomical Distinction Between the Sexes*, 1925, Standard Edition, vol. XIX; EXP. V.

Freud, S., *Inhibitions, Symptoms and Anxiety*, 1926, Standard Edition, vol. XX; EXP. V, VI.

Freud, S., *Fetishism*, 1927, Standard Edition, vol. XXI; EXP. V.

Freud, S., *Female Sexuality*, 1931, Standard Edition, vol. XXI; EXP. IV.

Freud, S., *Femininity*, Lec. XXXIII, *The New Introductory Lectures*, 1933, Standard Edition, vol. XXII; EXP. IV.

Freud, A., *Normality and Pathology in Childhood*, 1966, Hogarth Press, 1973; EXP. IV, V.
Gordon, C., "Birth of the Subject," *Radical Philosophy*, no. 17, 1977; DOC. V.
Kellog, R., *Analysing Children's Art*, Mayfield Publishing Co., 1970; DOC. III.
Klein, M., *The Role of the School in the Libidinal Development of the Child*, 1923, in *The Writings of Melanie Klein*, vol. I, The Hogarth Press, 1975; EXP. VI.
Klein, M., *Early Stages of the Oedipus Complex*, 1928, in *The Writings of Melanie Klein*, vol. I, The Hogarth Press, 1975; EXP. VI.
Kristeva, J., "Maternité selon Giovanni Bellini," *Peinture*, nos 10/11, 1975; EXP. VI.
Kristeva, J., "The Subject in Signifying Practice," *Semiotexte*, vol. 1, no. 3, 1975; EXP. VI.
Kristeva, J., "Signifying Practice and Mode of Production," Eng. trans. Nowell-Smith, G., *Edinburgh Magazine*, no. 1, 1976; EXP. III.
Kristeva, J., "Femme/Mère/Pensée," *Art Press*, no. 5, 1977; EXP. IV.
Lacan, J., *The Mirror Phase as Formative of the Function of the I*, 1949, in *Ecrits*, trans. Sheridan, A., Tavistock Publications, 1977; EXP. I, II, III.
Lacan, J., *The Function and Field of Speech in Psychoanalysis*, 1953, in *Ecrits*, trans. Sheridan, A., Tavistock Publications, 1977; DOC. VI.
Lacan, J., "Some Reflections on the Ego," *International Journal of Psychoanalysis*, no. 34, 1953; EXP. I, II, III.
Lacan, J., *On a Question Preliminary to Any Possible Treatment of Psychosis*, 1955-56, in *Ecrits*, trans. Sheridan, A., Tavistock Publications, 1977; EXP. VI.
Lacan, J., *The Insistence of the Letter in the Unconscious*, 1957, in *Ecrits*, trans. Sheridan, A., Tavistock Publications, 1977; EXP. II, VI.
Lacan, J., *The Signification of the Phallus*, 1958, in *Ecrits*, trans. Sheridan, A., Tavistock Publications, 1977; EXP. I, II, III, IV, V, VI.
Lacan, J., *The Subversion of the Subject and the Dialectic of Desire in the Freudian Unconscious*, 1960, in *Ecrits*, trans. Sheridan, A., Tavistock Publications, 1977; EXP. IV, V.
Lipshitz, S., *Freud's Fetishism and a Step Beyond*, Radical Philosophy Conference paper, 1976; EXP. V.
McNeil, D., *The Acquisition of Language*, Harper & Row, 1970; DOC. II.
Mannoni, M., *The Child, his "Illness" and the Others*, Tavistock Publications, 1970; EXP. I, II, III.
Mitchell, J., *Woman's Estate*, Penguin Books, 1971; INTRO.
Mitchell, J., *Psychoanalysis and Feminism*, Allen Lane, 1974; EXP. I, II, III.
Montrelay, M., "Inquiry into Femininity," 1970, Eng. trans. Adams, P., *m/f*, no. 1, February 1978; EXP. IV, V.
Piaget, J., *The Child's Conception of the World*, 1929, Paladin, 1973; DOC. V.
Piaget, J., and Inhelder, B., *The Psychology of the Child*, 1966, Routledge & Kegan Paul, 1969; DOC. II, III.
Plaza, M., "Phallomorphic Power and the Psychology of Women," trans. David, M., and Hodges, J., *Ideology and Consciousness*, no. 4, 1978; EXP. VI.
Rose, J., *The Imaginary – the Insufficient Signifier*, BFI Seminar paper, 1975; EXP. I, II, III.
Saussure, F., *Course in General Linguistics*, Fontana/Collins, 1974; DOC. VI.
Smith, F., *Understanding Reading*, Holt, Rinehart & Winston, 1971; DOC. VI.
Wilden, A., *The Language of the Self*, Johns Hopkins University Press, 1968; EXP. I, II, III; DOC. IV.
Winnicott, D.W., *The Child, the Family and the Outside World*, Penguin Books, 1964; DOC. IV.

Selected Bibliography

Apter, E., *Feminizing the Fetish, Psychoanalysis and Narrative Obsession in Turn-of-the-Century France*, ch. 5, Cornell University Press, Ithaca, 1991.

Barry, J., Flitterman, S., "The Politics of Art Making," *Screen*, vol. 21, no. 2, 1980, London.

Berger, M., *Minimal Politics: Performativity and Minimalism in Recent American Art*, Distributed Art Publishers, New York, 1997.

Blazwick, I., "Work in Progress," *NowHere Louisiana*, vol. II, Texts, 1996, Louisiana Museum of Art.

Carson, J., "(Re)Viewing Mary Kelly's Post-Partum Document," *Documents*, Fall, 1998, New York.

Cowie. E., "Introduction to the Post-Partum Document," *m/f*, nos. 5 and 6, 1981, London.

Fraser, A., "On the Post-Partum Document," *Afterimage*, March 1986, New York.

Freiberg, F., "The Post-Partum Document: Maternal Archaeology," *Lip*, no. 7, 1982 Melbourne, Victoria.

Gourlay, S., "The Discourse of the Mother, Radical Theoretical Practice & Feminist Production," *Fuse*, Summer, 1984, Toronto.

Grace, H., "From the Margins: A Feminist Essay on Women Artists," *Lip*, no. 2, 1981, Melbourne, Victoria.

Isaak, J., "Our Mother Tongue," *Vanguard*, vol. ii, no. 3, 1982, Vancouver, British Columbia.

Isaak, J., "Mary Kelly," *The Revolutionary Power of Women's Laughter*, Protetch McNeil, New York, 1983.

Iverson, M., "The Bride Stripped Bare by Her Own Desire," *Discourse*, no. 4, 1981, Berkeley, California.

Iverson, M., Crimp, D., Bhabha, H., *Mary Kelly*, Phaidon Press Limited, London, 1997.

Jones, A., *Body Art/Performing the Subject*, ch. 1, University of Minnesota Press, Minneapolis, 1998.

Kelly, J., "Mary Kelly," *Studio International*, no. 1, 1977, London.

Kelly, J., "Mary Kelly," *Studio International*, no. 3, 1978, London.

Kelly, M., *Imaging Desire*, collected writings, MIT Press, Cambridge, 1996.

Kelly, M., et. al., "A Conversation on Recent Feminist Art Practices," *October*, no. 71, Winter, 1995, Cambridge.

Kent, S., "Mary Kelly," *Hayward Annual '78*, The Arts Council of Great Britain, 1978, London.

Linker, K., "Representation and Sexuality," *Art After Modernism: Rethinking Representation*, ed. Brian Wallis, The New Museum of Contemporary Art, New York, 1984.

Lippard, L., "Issue and Tabu," *Issue*, Institute of Contemporary Art, 1980, London.

Maloon, T., "Mary Kelly, Interview," *Artscribe*, no. 13, 1978, London.

Mastai, J., *Social Process/Collaborative Action: Mary Kelly 1970-1975*, Charles H. Scott Gallery, Emily Carr Institute of Art and Design, Vancouver, British Columbia, 1997.

Mulvey, L., "Post-Partum Document," *Spare Rib*, no. 53, 1976, London.

Mulvey, L., "Mary Kelly and Laura Mulvey in Conversation," *Afterimage*, March, 1986, New York.

Nash, M., "Mary Kelly," *Un Certain Art Anglais*, Arc II, Musee d'Art Moderne de la Ville de Paris, 1979, Paris.

Osborne, C., "Post-Partum Document," *Feminist Review*, Winter, 1984, London.
Owens, C., "Posing," *Difference: On Sexuality and Representation*, The New Museum of Contemporary Art, New York, 1985.
Owens, C., "The Discourse of Others: Feminists and Postmodernism," *The Anti-Aesthetic*, ed. Hal Foster, Bay Press, Port Townsend, 1983.
Paoletti, J. *The Critical Eye/I*, Yale Center for British Art, New Haven, 1984.
Parker, R., Pollock, G., *Old Mistresses: Women, Art and Ideology*, ch. 5, Routledge, London, 1982.
Parker, R., Pollock, G., *Framing Feminism*, Pandora Press, London, 1987.
Pollock, G., *Vision and Difference*, ch. 7, Routledge, London, 1988.
Smith, P. "Mother as the Site of her Proceedings," *Parachute*, no. 26, 1982, Montreal, Ontario.
Taylor, P., "Vision in Disbelief," *Artforum*, October, 1982, New York.
Weinstock, J., "A Lass, a Laugh (and a Lad)," *Art in America*, June, 1983, New York.
Yee, L., *Division of Labor: "Women's Work" in Contemporary Art*, Bronx Museum of the Arts, New York, 1995.

Appendix

Post-Partum Document review

Laura Mulvey
Spare Rib, no. 40, 1976

Traditionally, the ability to produce children and the emotional relationship that ensues have been held up as the reason for women's lack of creativity. Now, with the women's movement, it is beginning to be possible to bring motherhood, with all the deeply traumatic emotions and unrecognized elements involved, into the kind of examination it desperately needs. Mary Kelly's exhibition *Post-Partum Document* is a crucial contribution to this. As an artist, she forces into public view the unacceptable combination of roles mother/artist – a slap in the face for old guard concepts of the artist as freewheeling genius; as a feminist, she focuses on the contradictory emotions that necessarily come with motherhood, which have been almost taboo as a subject for art in male-dominated culture.

It is quite clear from the attention Mary Kelly's exhibition has received in the establishment press that it was a direct provocation to conventional concepts of "art." It is the form of the exhibition, its emphasis on work rather than art-object-for-critical-evaluation, that causes so much outrage. A painting of a mother changing her baby's nappy would be easily overlooked as kitsch, but not so with dirty nappy liners annotated and placed within a discourse that needs work to be unravelled, and refuses to place the figure of the mother on view.

The exhibition comes within a radical art practice which refuses to see art works as purely objects in themselves but rather takes an exhibition as space to give documentation the force of argument. It deprives the object of any market value and its meaning only truly emerges if the work put in by the artist is complemented by work put in by the spectator in reading the documentation and understanding the theories. But the complexity of the language in *Post-Partum Document* and the many different ideas presented simultaneously did place a great burden on the spectator.

Mary Kelly described her previous exhibition *Women and Work*, produced collectively with Kay Hunt and Margaret Harrison, as "a document on the division of labor in a specific industry, showing the changes in the labor process and the constitution of the labor force during the implementation of the Equal Pay Act. At the same time, we were discovering how the division of labor in industry was underpinned by the division of labor in the home and that the central issue for women was in fact reproduction." Real objects, records (written, taped, filmed, videoed) were collected together as evidence focusing attention on a particular economic situation. Individually, they may have been disparate without meaning, but linked and organized by the artists, the whole could take on a new level of significance.

In the *Post-Partum Document*, Mary Kelly uses her relationship with her infant son as her raw material. The exhibition has two distinct parts: objects and records acting as factual evidence of the past, framed and hung on the gallery walls, and written, separate documentation using Freudian psychoanalysis to give a commentary and structure to the actual exhibits.

The first room contained the (now famous) nappy liners and baby's vests dating from the period in which the child's needs and the mother's work meet to produce a complementary relationship (the dyad). At this point, the mother's frustrated helplessness can be soothed by pleasure, partly through the eroticism of physical interdependence and partly through narcissistic satisfaction at their completeness as a couple. The second room contained an infinitely more complex record of the child's gradual acquisition of language and the mother's notes as she tries to cope with the sense of loss that overcomes her as the child takes his first steps to social independence. The completeness of the two is broken as the father as authority and the nursery school introduce the child to another world of "law and culture."

In its appearance and presentation, Mary Kelly's exhibition reduces the passion involved in this process to the minimum; her aim is to distance the emotion by putting the dilemma into a wider context: the way women's unconscious is shaped by the patriarchy. The exhibits themselves are touchingly reminiscent of women's traditional means of self-expression (her diary showing so much self-doubt, painfully collected and guarded memorabilia). She organizes this material in an attempt to turn the most unspoken and culturally repressed of everyday experiences (mother-child relationship) into an art work inspired by feminism and psychoanalysis.

Mary Kelly's use of psychoanalysis is a direct result of recent work by feminists (Juliet Mitchell's book *Psychoanalysis and Feminism* and the conference on patriarchy held last May in London), and growing interest within the women's movement. This interest stems from the realisation that biological difference becomes overlaid by a cultural concept of sexual difference suited to the needs of a particular social order, which psychoanalytic theory can help us to understand. Thus "femininity" can be understood not as a natural essence but as a complicated edifice which the patriarchy demands in order to give "masculinity" meaning and strength. The little girl enters society "negatively"; her lack of penis gives the phallus significance and allows the male to fear castration.

Mary Kelly evokes the impact that producing a child has on women whose unconscious desires are formed within the confines of the castration complex: "During the antepartum period (gestation inside the mother's body) and continuing during the breast-feeding phase of early postpartum, the mother's negative place in the patriarchal order—more precisely the Symbolic—can be 'misrecognized' because in a sense the child *is* the phallus for her." ("Experimentum I." Weaning from the Breast.) As the child grows through the various stages of increasing independence from his mother, she experiences a sense of loss that Mary Kelly describes as reliving her own previous Oedipal drama, undergoing castration for the second time and relearning the fact of her negative place in the symbolic order. Within these terms, the mother has two possible roads open; recognition and acceptance of her secondary place or rebellion against it. Her rebellion takes the form of fetishisation of the child (as substitute phallus), clinging to the couple relationship and refusing to allow the child to emerge as an independent entity. Part of the fascination of the *Post-Partum Document* lies here: the exhibition in all of its obsessive detail fetishizes the child, but in this case the mother has reconciled her "natural capacity" with her work as an artist. The art object as fetish replaces the child as potential fetish.

The exhibition throws a spotlight on the need to explore further the labyrinthine unconscious structures that lie behind the natural-looking facade "motherhood," but Mary Kelly is limited by a theory biased—though not invalidated—by patriarchal assumptions. The influence of the French psychoanalyst Jacques Lacan is heavily apparent in the *Post-Partum Document.* But one important aspect of the exhibition prevails: it gives a voice to the pain and pleasure women have lived as mothers, understood by each other, despised as domestic by dominant culture. Mary Kelly's work comes in the footsteps of some of the very few women in the past who managed to be "artists" and constantly returned to the mother-child relationship in their work, women such as Mary Cassatt, Berthe Morisot and Julia Margaret Cameron.

Our Mother Tongue: The *Post-Partum Document*

Jo-Anna Isaak
Vanguard, April 1982

What strikes me is that women often keep out of the way or on the sidelines of the most interesting and unusual advancements of our culture, and when it is a question of feminine production, they demonstrate if not sentimentalism, at least romanticism. In any event, they do not view themselves as a part of the development of the avant-garde and the new epistemes. What we must do is to help women to understand that these modern breaks with tradition and the development of new forms of discourse are harmonious with the women's cause. By participation in this activity of subversion (which exists on a linguistic, family and social level) and in the growth of new epistemes they will be able to see this as well.

Julia Kristeva

As a child living amongst Kwakiutl people, I once saw a shaman chant and dance about the bed of a dying woman. Later, as an adult living amongst white men, I read an account of this event by Lévi-Strauss:

> That the mythology of the shaman does not correspond to an objective reality does not matter. The sick woman believes in the myth and belongs to a society which believes in it. The tutelary spirits and malevolent spirits, the supernatural monsters and magical animals are all part of a coherent system on which the native conception of the universe is founded. The sick woman accepts the mythical beings, or more accurately she has never questioned their existence. What she does not accept are the incoherent and arbitrary pains, which are an alien element in her system but which the shaman, calling upon a myth, will reintegrate within a whole where everything is meaningful.[1]

What the shaman does according to Lévi-Strauss is:

> provide the sick woman with a *language*, by means of which inexpressible psychic states can be immediately expressed. And it is the transition to this verbal expression—at the same time making it possible to undergo in an ordered and intelligible form a real experience that would otherwise be chaotic and inexpressible—which induces the release of the physiological process, that is, the reorganization, in a favourable direction, of the process to which the sick woman is subjected.[2]

As a woman living amongst the signifying practices of men, I am familiar with the politics of the process by which the woman's pain went unspoken and was made intelligible *as what it was not.*

I have outgrown my fear of the shaman *who was there*, now I fear the objectified language of the text which hides a speaker who pretends *not* to be there. For behind this seemingly transparent text is a man who participates in the structures of domination in this form of society (call it the paternal, the phallic, the symbolic). He speaks from that position, taking for granted the history of imperialism which has provided for the very possibility of his speaking of "native conceptions" as something other than his own. He takes for granted everything that makes his production of this text possible. He also takes for granted a relation to the sick woman and her pain. It is only through the reader's collusion in the systems of domination on which this text is predicated that this manner of speaking can survive, be credible, make sense. It is only in this manner of speaking that it is possible to *treat pain as a problem in understanding.*[3]

I have used this example in order to identify a language usage, a method of speaking, with a method of domination which is integral to capitalism and its ruling apparatus—more specifically its forms of patriarchal domination. I do so in order to introduce a work which disrupts this language usage and the power structure which it presupposes. Mary Kelly's *Post-Partum Document* is both an answer to and an examination of woman's silence within and alienation from the symbolic order as it is constituted within a capitalist society.

The work, begun in 1973 with the birth of her child, is an extended documentation of the mother-child relationship. It covers the first six years of the child's development and is divided into six sections including, in all, approximately 135 pieces. Each section examines a stage in the constitution of a woman's identity in and through significant moments in her child's development: for instance, weaning from the breast, weaning from the holophrase (learning to speak), weaning from the dyad (periodic separation from the mother), the first questions about sexuality and the collection of cathected objects, which represent loss, not only of the child but of the maternal body, and finally the child's entry into the law of the father—learning to write, starting school. The child's entry into the patriarchal order is experienced by the mother both as a loss and as re-enactment of her own initial negative entry into language and culture. "The whole project, not only the visible art work, but the process itself is about the relation of writing to the mother's body."[4]

The *Post-Partum Document* presents the viewer with very personal visual material which functions as the mother's memorabilia (fantasy stains, casts of the child's hand, scrawls, verbal utterances set out in typeface, gifts to the mother such as insects and shells), together with a narrative commentary and a series of diagrams which refer the viewer to a further text which reworks this data and explores its psychological and social significance. The memorabilia in this elaborate theoretical context consists of hermetic Lacanian diagrams which suggest a reading based on psychoanalysis, a second series of diagrams which provide a kind of exploration of the empirical procedures in the work (graphs, taxonomic information accompanying the botanical and zoological specimens) and anatomical diagrams. These memorabilia contest and parody the male prerogative over theory. Concomitantly, the mode of presentation (framed transparent boxes containing these "emblems of desire" of "la mère qui jouit"[5]) traverses the whole iconography of the museum display and the fetishism attached to commodities by the art market. The installation is a palimpsest simultaneously addressing an interconnecting set of theoretical, scientific and aesthetic discourses.

> *"When I use a word," Humpty Dumpty said in rather a scornful tone, "it means exactly what I choose it to mean - neither more or less."*
> *"The question is," said Alice, "whether you* can *make words mean so many different things."*
> *"The question is," said Humpty Dumpty, "which is to be master—that's all."*
>
> *Lewis Carroll*

The political force whose presence is partner in the *Post-Partum Document* is the women's movement, more specifically that part of it which addresses the issues of subjectivity and ideological oppression. The work functions as part of an ongoing debate over the relevance of psychoanalysis to the theory and practice of both Marxism and feminism. Mary Kelly addresses woman's estrangement from language in terms of Lacanian psychoanalytic theory in which the production of the subject is primarily a question of positionality in language. But it is not a question of her playing Anna to their Sigmund Freud, for she contextualizes the patriarchal bias of Lacanian and Freudian theory within a Marxian critique of the biological as an ideology which rationalizes the political. The intent and the effect of this theoretical merging is to bring the viewer and the materiality of the work together in such a way that the reading of the text becomes a subversive act. The process of understanding how meanings are produced and organized in language leads to the undermining of the bourgeois order—shattering its belief in a transparent text.

Lacan's theories, which form the principal structuring element of the *Post-Partum Document*, are a re-working of Freudian concepts within a linguistic paradigm. Language and the unconscious are treated not as separate entities, but language is seen to function as a passageway, and the only one, to the unconscious, to that which has been repressed and which has the potential to disrupt the established symbolic order, what Lacan has called the "No" or the "Name of the Father." The "Name of the Father" designates that which determines submission to the law and to any "conventional language." In French *nom* (name) and *non* (no) are homophonic words. Lacan has used this resemblance to underline the role of the father in the child's coming to language and the child's separation from the desired mother. In the Lacanian paradigm, this entry into language marks the passage into the symbolic order governed by the laws of language; it is the "Oedipal moment" which, if the child is female, is the moment of her "negative" entry into language, the awareness "of not having the privileged signifier of the culture" (Mary Kelly).

This initial "negative" entry into language and culture is reiterated in the mother-child relationship where for a brief period of time the mother, at least in the realm of the imaginary, exists outside of the power of the phallus. It is a period of "reprieve" in which the mother and the child in the fullness of the dyad experience "the sweetness of that imaginary encapsulation which reduces the 'outside world' to absurdity. But there is also the inevitable moment of separation, reiterating a 'lack' always already inscribed and impossible to efface" (Mary Kelly, Notes to the *Post-Partum Document*).

But this reading is only one of several inscriptions found in the text, for the work also evidences what Mark Nash calls "a healthy materialist distance from this ideology of the 'natural.'"[6] The Lacanian theory is displaced in the work through the reiteration of the primacy of the material and historical over the "natural." Thus "femininity" is revealed not as a natural essence but as a complicated edifice which the patriarchy constructs in order to represent "masculinity" as power.[7]

> *I learned to battle with the canvas, to come to know it as a being resisting my wish (dream), and to bend it forcibly to this wish. At first it stands there like a pure chaste virgin ... and then comes the wilful brush which first here, then there, gradually conquers it with all the energy peculiar to it, like a European colonist ...*
>
> *Wassily Kandinsky*

The complex nexus of art, sexuality and politics so succinctly articulated by the quote from Kandinsky reprinted on this page is a commonplace metaphor within the discourse of modern art, yet it exists very comfortably within the myth of the artist working outside the conventions and laws of society *"pour épater le bourgeois."* It does so because the struggle of accession of radical son to rooted father takes place on the site of woman's body. "Pictures are made the way princes get children," Picasso remarked, "with the shepherdess." Or, in less pastoral terms: "The paradox of phallocentrism in all its manifestations is that it depends on the image of the castrated woman to give order and meaning to its world."[8] Woman's body has been not just confiscated from her – it has been turned into the stranger on display. This masculine specularization of the "Other" is a necessary component in the libidinal economy of men as it has developed in our culture, which is distinct from the libidinal economy of women as it has been repressed in our culture:

> Women's desire most likely does not speak the same language as man's desire, and it probably has been covered over by the logic which has dominated the West since the Greeks.
> In this logic, the prevalence of the gaze, discrimination of form, and individualization of form is particularly foreign to female eroticism. Woman finds pleasure more in touch than in sight and *her entrance into a dominant scopic economy signifies, once again, her relegation to passivity:* she will be the beautiful object.[9]

Confronted with an established cultural apparatus in which the male appropriation of the scopic drive defines the women irrefutably as object-image of the look, women have traditionally remained on the margins of the dominant art practice. Currently, in women's art practice there is a proliferation of forms of signification in which the artist participates in the iconography of victimization and presents either her own body or the bodies of other women as signifiers, as objects of the gaze. In some cases, this is done in an attempt to deconstruct the system of exchange from within. For instance, in Adrian Piper's *Guerrilla Theatre* the "goods" are rendered valueless within the exchange system of the libidinal economy of men because they are made ugly. In other cases, there is an attempt to extract a vicarious pleasure by assuming both the "feminine" position as the object of the look and the "masculine" position as subject of the scopic drive. Cindy Sherman, for example, makes photographic pieces using herself in various costumes to represent imaginary female characters engaged in obscure melodramas, the subtext of which is always sexual accessibility. In an installation at Artists Space she appeared in the gallery every day—dressed up as a movie starlet—where she watched the viewer watching her act out the role of object of his gaze. In both cases, there is a constant referencing to male desires which correspond only slightly, or not at all, to woman's desire.

The *Post-Partum Document* displaces the fetishistic implications of conventional codes of representation by a deliberate absence of images of the female body. Yet fetishism, so much assumed to be the realm of masculine disavowal, is reinscribed in the work through the mother's fetishization of the child. This is in turn displaced when the cathected objects are installed as the standard reified objects in an art practice. "The 'art objects' are used as fetish objects, explicitly to displace the potential fetishization of the child, and implicitly to explore the typically fetishistic function of representation" (Mary Kelly). From there the reading of the entire installation moves to an exploration of the iconography of the museum, which as she says, "I've always thought of as a vast metaphor for the exploration of the mother's body."[10] The radical potential of the *Post-Partum Document* lies precisely in this convergence of readings and articulation of voices, "in so far as the 'feminine' is *said*, it is profoundly subversive" (Mary Kelly). "A woman's body, with its thousand and one thresholds of ardour—once, by smashing yokes and censors, she lets it articulate the profusion of meanings that run through it in every direction—will make the old single-grooved mother tongue reverberate with more than one language."[11]

NOTES

1 Claude Lévi-Strauss, *Structural Anthology* (Harmondsworth, Middx., 1972), p. 197.

2 *Ibid.*, p. 198.

3 I am indebted to and would like to direct the reader to the work of Dorothy E. Smith, Professor of Sociology, at Ontario Institute for Studies in Education, Toronto. In particular, I refer to her essay "Using the Oppressor's Language," *Resources for Feminist Research*, no. 5, July, 1979. Her method of reading through the seemingly transparent text to the structures of domination on which it is based is closely akin to that of the French Feminist's use of the neologism "phallologocentric," which serves both as an invective and as a method of analysis. Jacques Derrida uses the term "logocentrism" to disqualify and to deconstruct the mystification implicit in Western philosophical discourse—the paradigm of normative thinking. Luce Irigaray and Hélène Cixous append the prefix "phallo" in order to take the term a step further and use it to deconstruct the mystification implicit in the linguistic manifestations of phallocentrism.

4 Mary Kelly, conversation with Paul Smith, *Parachute*, no. 26, 1982.

5 Julia Kristeva, *Des Chinoises* (Paris: des femmes, 1974), pp. 30-1 (*About Chinese Women*, trans. Anita Barrows (New York, 1977)). The figure of the "mother who knows sexual pleasure" is the most severely repressed "feminine" figure in Western culture.

6 Mark Nash, review of Mary Kelly's *Post-Partum Document*, *Artscribe*, no. 10, January, 1978.

7 "If, on the other hand, one considered the family, women, and the sexual difference in the way they determine a social ethic, one could say after seeing their problems in China that the basic question there is the building of a society whose active power is represented by no one. No one can appropriate it for himself if no one is excluded from it, not even women—those last slaves, necessary supports to the power of masters—whose separation from power assures that it is representable and is to be represented (by fathers, by legislatures)." Julia Kristeva, "Women of China," *Signs*, Autumn, 1975, p. 81.

8 Laura Mulvey, "Visual Pleasure and Narrative Cinema," *Screen*, vol. 16, no. 3, Autumn, 1975, p. 6.

9 Luce Irigaray, "This Sex Which is Not One," *New French Feminism: An Anthology*, eds Elaine Marks and Isabelle de Courtirron, Amherst, Mass. 1980, p. 101.

10 Witness the title of the *Times* review of the Picasso exhibition: "Picasso, Modernism's Father, Comes Home to MoMA." For an analysis of MoMA as the labyrinthine female body see Carol Duncan and Alan Wallach, "The Museum of Modern Art as Late Capitalist Ritual: An Iconographic Analysis," *Marxist Perspectives*, Winter, 1978, pp. 28-51. "Like the church or temple of the past, the museum plays a unique ideological role. By means of its objects and all that surrounds them, the museum transforms ideology in the abstract into living belief."

11 Hélène Cixous, "The Laugh of the Medusa," *New French Feminisms*, p. 256.

The Bride Stripped Bare by Her Own Desire: Reading Mary Kelly's *Post-Partum Document*

Margaret Iversen
Discourse, no. 4, 1981

This is a sustained effort of research and production. It is a work of art which is both personal and political: an almost cryptic record of the mutual relationship between a mother and child, as well as a critically distanced analysis of women's insertion into Patriarchy. It reminds me in many ways of Marcel Duchamp's monumental self-portrait, *The Bride Stripped Bare by Her Bachelors, Even.* There frustrated desire is delayed in glass, caught as on a photographic plate, fetishized, and accompanied by copious notes which do not so much explain the visual signs as constitute another register of signification. Duchamp's work announces a radically new form of art which is further explored by Kelly. This kind of art articulates a way of thinking about the self now decisively decentered by the writings of Marx, Saussure, Freud and, most prominently in PPD, the neo-Freudian, Jacques Lacan. In Kelly's own words:

> Although it is a self documentation of the mother-child relationship (myself and my son), the *Post-Partum Document* does not describe the unified, transcendental subject of autobiography, but rather the de-centered, socially constituted subject of a mutual discourse.[1]

The original impetus for the work, quite apart from the artist's pregnancy, was given by a cluster of contemporary debates. Most important of these was the tendency within the women's movement to reflect on the subjective moment of their oppression, informally in consciousness-raising groups, and rigorously in books such as Juliet Mitchell's, *Psychoanalysis and Feminism* (1974).[2]

PPD as a feminist intervention has been much discussed. It is, in fact, intended to provide a focus and occasion for debating the contribution of psychoanalysis to our understanding of the way women internalize their oppression. The Document plots, in six stages, the mother's pleasure in narcissistic identification with her child, her subsequent re-experience of castration with the "loss" of her child, and her consequent re-recognition of her inferior status within phallocentric culture. The work attempts to explain the way in which motherhood seals feminine psychology. Each installation of the Document has prompted lively discussion and some outraged reactions—the "Dirty Nappies" or diapers, as the first document was dubbed, became something of a *cause célèbre* in London.

Yet this exclusive emphasis on the specifically feminist issues has tended to eclipse any consideration of Kelly's remarkable artistic practice. PPD is also artistically polemical. It confronts directly the professional woman artist's inhibited attitude to her child-rearing role, challenging that ideological construct which opposes creation to procreation as mutually exclusive functions.

It is, at the same time, a critical response to a type of feminist art which focuses on the female body, most often the artist's own. Kelly thinks that body art, while producing welcome new definitions of women, also takes gestural expressionism to its ultimate conclusion along with all its essentialist implications: "It leads to a practice which is very diverse, but which could be characterized as being concerned with excavating a kind of essential femininity, either cultural or biological."[3] Its sexual imagery, often intended as a parody, also makes it extremely vulnerable to sexist appropriation and exploitation.[4] In sharp contrast to this strand of feminist art practice, Kelly refrains from directly representing the female body, with the exception of sections of a diagram taken from a medical self-help text book. This restraint follows from the theoretical assumptions "that femininity is not a pre-given entity, but a representation of difference constructed within specific discourse."[5] There is no pre-social femininity, no essential core which can be reached beneath the layers of discourse, clothes, artistic conventions.

Kelly also conceived the work as a critique of the reductive and deductive logic of conceptual art, which she views as an extension of Greenbergian formalism. Joseph Kosuth deduced and embraced the logical consequence of Greenberg's position. In his seminal article, "Art After Philosophy," Kosuth defends the notion of art as "an analytic proposition." Art defines itself; it makes tautologous statements which do not, like synthetic propositions, depend for their validity on experience.

> A work of art is a kind of proposition presented within the context of art as a comment on art.[6]

Kelly's art is a comment on the art of the recent past only in the respect that it counterpoints this self-reflexive model. PPD addresses itself to a wide range of extra-artistic concerns and, at the same time, questions this category of the extra-artistic. The boundaries separating art, literature and science, knowledge and pleasure, are systematically transgressed. I am reminded of the parenthetical question put by Roland Barthes in his *The Pleasure of the Text*: "(and yet: what if knowledge were delicious?)."[7]

While some modernism remains locked in a reductive formalism, Kelly's kind of modernism reinterprets the radical break effected by the original avant-garde. The Cubists did not efface representational values; they did make palpable the problematic status of representation. The visual sign was wrested from its comfortable, naturalized reference to the world and split, becoming a two-sided sign comprising a material signifier provisionally linked to a signified. This gesture gave movements such as Dada and Surrealism a space in which to explore the manifold possibilities of signification. The modernist impulse originally meant not a contraction, but rather an expansion of possible signifying practices. This expansion opened onto political, psychological, epistemological and semiological questions which were subsequently nearly forgotten.

Kelly's exploration of sign systems is, once again, pointed. Her work makes use of two types of sign outside the dominant tradition of Western art history since the Renaissance: writing and what in Charles Sanders Peirce's typology of signs is called the index. Peirce grouped all signs under three categories which in practice overlap.[8] The *icon* represents its object by means of some similarity or resemblance. This category is, in its turn, subdivided into images which represent simple qualities of objects (portraits, for example) and diagrams which represent relational qualities. The *index* signifies by means of some causal or existential link with its object (a footprint, sundial, weathervane), while the symbol signifies by virtue of a conventional rule. These types infrequently occur unmixed. Thus, for example, photography combines aspects of the icon and index; hieroglyphic script combines the *symbol* and icon.

PPD displays a near absence of images, while symbols and indexical signs are set in montage-like juxtaposition. This opposition runs through the work like a leitmotiv accumulating connotations. Kelly herself speaks of two levels in the work—"my lived experience as a mother and my analysis as feminist of that experience."[9]

Yet within the context of PPD, the extreme dissimilarity of these modes of signification acquire a special point and poignancy. The traumatic effect of the mother's experience is recapitulated in Kelly's art by the use of very private, vestigial signs (traces, stains, molds, fragments) on the one hand, and an utterly abstract scientific discourse on the other. The intimacy of the index, its relation to the sense of touch, is like an impression on memory which resists verbalization. These mute, sensuous traces recall for the mother her Imaginary identification for the child. The satisfaction and pleasure of mothering flow from this mis-recognition of the baby as part of herself, supplementing her lack. "The child is a means whereby the woman perhaps disguises her lack, her negative place."[10] Briefly, mistakenly, the mother makes up for her lost phallus, the privileged signifier of our culture.

This reversion to the Imaginary is, according to Lacan, a form of neurosis. But as Fredric Jameson points out in his helpful article, "Imaginary and Symbolic in Lacan," for Lacan, "the apprenticeship of language is (also) an alienation of the psyche ... there can be a hypertrophy of the Symbolic at the Imaginary's expense."[11] The diagrams, algorithms and footnotes to PPD are a sort of hypertrophy of the symbolic. I believe Kelly is simultaneously serious about Lacan's theory and perhaps gently parodying it—a self-conscious witness to women's alienated position in relation to the Symbolic order. The juxtaposition of private traces and theoretical discourse represents the dialectic of desire and alienation which is the condition of the subject and of the maternal subject most acutely.

This reading is appropriate, but partial. The psychoanalytic theory must also be seen as a way of coping with the inevitable loss of the child. Lacan argues that language or the Law is also a salutary release from immediacy: the abstract Name-of-the Father supersedes the physical father; a paternal function replaces a brute presence. Kelly's analysis is, equally, a release from the immediacy of lived experience.

These antagonistic registers of signification are literally superimposed in a very affective piece which, for me, serves as a key to the more complex documents (see "Introduction," pp. 3-6). The series consists of tiny baby's undershirts, carefully folded by the mother. These emotionally cathected objects are crossed by the folded, intersecting lines of a Lacan diagram concerning intersubjectivity. Each unit of the series adds one line to the completion of the diagram, until finally the T-shirt is literally crossed out, denied. This imaginary works on various levels. Firstly, it indicates that the mother is acknowledging her baby as a separate individual, relinquishing her fetishistic attachment to the child and attempting to understand the structure of their intersubjective relationship. Secondly, the metaphor of folded material and intersecting lines hints at Lacan's contention that the unconscious, its condensations and displacements, is structured like a language.[12] Thirdly, it indicates that representation takes place at the site of a lack. The pleasure of the body is denied for a discourse of the Other: the accession to language coincides with the Oedipal fear of castration. In this series, the distancing of the fetish object, the baby, here displaced as the T-shirt, is an image of the mother's re-experience of castration and re-affirmation of the symbolic order. Representation, like desire itself, is dependent on the notion of a lack. Or to put it in terms of the Genesis myth, knowledge implies Paradise lost and the effort to regain it.

This last mentioned consideration is crucial to our understanding of the Document. The objects in the work are fetish objects, compensating for the mother's sense of lack. Kelly makes this point herself in a published interview:

> That's why all the objects in the work are fetish objects, very explicitly, to displace the fetishizing of the child and also to make an implicit statement about the fetishistic nature of representation.[13]

In each section of the Document, a fetish object is "delayed in glass" to mark a stage of separation and loss. I want now to describe these objects and the stages they represent.

Parts I, II and III document the three stages of separation after birth as described by Lacan—weaning from the breast, weaning from the holophrase and weaning from the dyad. All three chart a progressive empirical development. Weaning from the breast is measured in terms of the progressive introduction of solid food. Fecal stains on the diaper liners, which measure the infant's ability to digest its food, are analysed and accompanied by feeding charts. One senses that it is not so much the process of weaning, as the painstaking regulation of the baby's diet, which drives a wedge between the natural symbiosis of mother and child.

Part II documents a loss of a different kind. At first, single word utterances of the child and the mother's interpretations or glosses form an intersubjective discourse. As the child learns to form patterned speech, dependence on the mother declines and her narcissistic identification is threatened. The last recorded utterance of this series is the full sentence, "See the baby" (looking in the mirror). The child's imaginary identification with the mother is thus also ruptured at this stage by his finding a coherent, ideal self in the mirror, by mastering speech, and by his desire to be in the father's place. It should be noted that each of these steps in the construction of an independent ego involves an identification with another: the mirror image, the language of another, the father. This is what is meant by Lacan's decentering of the notion of I. Kelly presents the recorded utterances and glosses on blocks of type which are printed below. The reverse face type and rectified imprint allude to the deciphering of cryptograms, as well as to the psychological effect of mirroring.

"Documentation III" marks the moment of actual separation when the child begins nursery school. The process of extrafamilial socialization is traced in diaries of recorded conversations between mother and child superimposed on daily examples of scribblings produced at school. The splitting of the dyad is indicated in the diaries by the child's use of the pronoun "I," by allusions to the father's presence and, visually, by the increasing concentricity of the drawings – an index of ego-formation. A revised perspective schema forms a grid on each drawing which marks off the immediate transcribed conversations from the mother's later reflections on them (the conversation viewed as object, from a distance, in perspective). The child's indexical traces (stains, word-imprints, scribblings) imply physical proximity; perspective construction implies a gap between viewer and viewed.

"Documentation IV" is disarmingly romantic. It deals with the pleasure of maternal femininity and the incest taboo. The anxiety of separation is alleviated by "transitional objects," comforting fetishes, or as Kelly says "emblems of desire," "representations of a pleasure now sublimated, lost."[14] In this case, a blanket serves for the child, imprints of her son's small hand, for the mother. The document juxtaposes these two registers in a developmental series. Stamped on the surface of the sensual handmolds is Lacan's Schema R, which represents the subject's position within the fields of the Imaginary, Symbolic and Real. Successive units of the series complete the diagram and weaken the handprint in a way very similar to the T-shirt series. The loss represented here is more than the mother's pleasure in the child's body; it is also a sublimation of a pleasure in her own body as feminine, motherly, like her mother's. The lower register consists of fragments of a blanket, carefully arranged and inscribed like soft shards in an archaeological museum. The inscriptions transcribe the mother's confessional diary, commenting on her ambivalent reference to "my baby/my big boy," the child's growing sexual curiosity, and his verbal formulation of a fully formed ego's capacity for object love, "I love you, Mummy."

Increasing curiosity about the mother's body and, by extension, the world is the theme of "Documentation V." Specimens of insects and flowers gathered by the three-year old boy are mounted on entomological pinning blocks and classified in a manner which simulates a style of exhibition typical of the nineteenth century, the moment when interest in origins and evolution was most intense. Other components of the document suggest the displaced meanings of these specimens; the child's questions about sex appear under xeroxed specimens, and entries in a medical text-book index are printed under sections from a diagram of full-term pregnancy. The child's comings and goings, fetching and questioning, his extravagant biological fantasies, traverse the mother's body in an endless discourse of desire.

The sixth and final section covers the period in which the child begins to read and write. Here again the logic of unconscious desire governs the process. Kelly has incised examples of her son's prewriting on tablets of slate. The slates, which are divided into three registers of different kinds of writing, visually mimic the Rosetta Stone.[15] The mother's commentary in script follows the "hieroglyphic" letter shapes, and a typed narrative fills the lower section. The documented process of constructing the alphabet is fascinating. It demonstrates the truth of Saussure's contention that language is made up, not of positive terms, but of differences: X, which initially indicates all writing, becomes in the second unit X versus O, straightness versus roundness. The rest of the letters "fill the gap" between this primary contrast. The closedness of O contrasts with the openness of e; p, d, b, q are rotations of a straight and a round. Against Saussure, we are shown that the logic of the differences are specifically graphic, and that the archaeology of script uncovers residues of non-arbitrary, pictographic modes of signification.

The footnotes to this document inform us that writing coincides with the moment when the child's sexual researches are repressed—"a postscript to the Oedipus complex." Yet sexuality becomes sublimated in the body of the letter. The lack, C, the eye, I, the Excessive, E, the snake, S. The polymorphous perversity of these letters, their bizarre pictographic anatomies, inversions, rotations, are speaking the language of the unconscious —until, in the last unit of the series, the purposeful inscription of the child's proper name, the Name-of-the-Father, finally arrests the play of signifiers and makes them conform to a cultural order.

Throughout this essay I have focused on the artistic practice of PPD—on its opposition to gestural expressionism, on the polyphony of its modes of signification, and on its extra-artistic concerns. *Post-Partum Document* and many other contemporary works of art founded on a similar ideological conception play on and criticize our habitual aesthetic response. This accounts for the difficulties we may encounter viewing installations of the work. Each of the units in a series has a self-contained visual interest, but its near-repetition makes us scan the series for differences. We refer to footnotes and diagrams, and gradually pick out a narrative thread. As we move between visual interest, theory and narrative, we make different discourses, different modes of signification, inform each other. Rather than confirming some *a priori* unity of consciousness, this artistic practice "pictures" the construction of the subject within an ensemble of social relations and discourses. Yet PPD is far from conceptual or academic. It requires study but, here at least, knowledge *is* delicious.

NOTES

1 Mary Kelly, "Notes on Reading the Post-Partum Document," *Control*, no. 10, Nov. 1977.

2 Juliet Mitchell, *Psychoanalysis and Feminism* (Allen Lane: 1974, Pelican Books: 1975).

3 "Mary Kelly," interviewed by Terence Maloon, *Artscribe*, no. 13, 1978.

4 Lucy Lippard's account of women's body art in *From the Center* is both sympathetic and critical.

5 Mary Kelly, "On Femininity," *Control*, no. 11, Nov. 1979.

6 Joseph Kosuth, "Art after Philosophy," reprinted in *Minimalism*, ed. G. Battock, p. 163.

7 Roland Barthes, *The Pleasure of the Text*, trans. R. Miller (New York: Hill and Wang, 1975), p. 23.

8 A relatively readable account of the typology of signs is found in Charles Sanders Peirce, *Letters to Lady Welby*. Otherwise, secondary sources include Roman Jacobson, "Quest for the Essence of Language" in his *Selected Writings*, and Peter Wollen, *Signs and Meaning in the Cinema*.

9 "Mary Kelly," interviewed by T. Maloon, *Artscribe*, no. 13, 1978.

10 *Ibid.*, p. 17.

11 Fredric Jameson, "Imaginary and Symbolic in Lacan: Marxism, Psychoanalytic Criticism and the Problem of the Subject," *Yale French Studies*, Psychoanalysis and Literature Issue, p. 351.

12 "... what the psychoanalytic experience discovers in the unconscious is the whole structure of language." Jacques Lacan, "The Agency of the Letter in the Unconscious or Reason since Freud," *Écrits*, trans. Alan Sheridan (Tavistock: 1977), p. 147.

13 "Mary Kelly," interviewed by T. Maloon, *Artscribe*, no. 13, p. 17.

14 Mary Kelly, "On Femininity," *Control*, no. 11, Nov. 1979.

15 The appearance of incised tablets is produced by a very clever process which involves tracing and typing onto tin foil, using the foil as a template to form a resin mold on the slate, and then filling the molded letter shapes with a white paste.

Mother as Site of Her Proceedings: Mary Kelly's *Post-Partum Document*[1]

Paul Smith
Parachute, no. 26, 1982

For the moment our writing must be performed at the edge of a certain impossibility, on the line which is marked between body and history (and where neither body nor history are not the loci of difficulties). And we have recently been accustoming ourselves to the sound of women re-claiming their propinquity to the body, as if in answer to men's camping on the side of history, from where the iron-ring of patriarchy is guarded. What, perhaps, we have not often enough seen reconnoitred is the very place where the line is drawn, the no-man's-land as it were, the space which is constituted by writing itself—writing understood as the praxis which transgresses fixed positions and their moral interpretations. This is a space which is approached at certain moments by such as Luce Irigaray or Jean Louis Schefer. And my enthusiasm for Mary Kelly's *Post-Partum Document* is in part due to the fact that, within an art-practice (always a language), it works towards such a writing-space; towards, in fact, the place where *Post-Partum Document* ends as it claims that "it is possible to desire to speak and to dare to change."[2]

Post-Partum Document proceeds, through a documentation of the mother-child relationship, to a remarking of the continual movement of disruption and inconsistency in the social and psychical positioning of both mother and child. What is at stake, probably first and foremost, is the mother's experience of loss as the child accedes to the Symbolic realm; so already the work is not so much the record of the child's "development," but more the exploration of the mother's experience of maternity itself as it is felt and represented. The work constitutes a mapping-out of the mother's desires as they too are subjected to the Symbolic at the same time as the child's; it takes its force from a certain negation of the social contract by the dialectic of desire: the child becoming other constantly re-presents the mother's lack. Since it always emphasizes the contradictions inherent to the social world's representation of the mother, this sense of loss constitutes always a transgression of that system which would posit the mother as unitary subject, the provider of love and comfort and thus the guarantor of social/symbolic cohesion.

So the work demonstrates, finally and carefully, that the supposed homogeneity of the Symbolic is continually prone to disruption: even as that ironring imposes itself by absorbing the child into its institutions (language itself, the family, the education system), it inflicts a loss upon the mother who watches the child depart. That maternal loss, a reimposition of the castration anxiety in a way, is so often denied through the mother's fetishization of the child, her initial narcissistic satisfaction cushioning its loss by assuming the traditional role of mother/housewife, a role always natural and essential within patriarchy. The acceptance of the role would always involve to some degree or other what Irigaray would see as the *interdiction* of the woman, a sort of decreed silence.[3] If the mother can act and speak it can only be *for* the child. So, within that already established context, Mary Kelly is guilty simply by dint of having produced this work: she should, should she not, have rather spent her time exercising the characteristic qualities of the maternal role, demonstrating the mother's natural capacity as original support for social conversation? By mere force of speaking in this mode which is not for the child, Mary Kelly transgresses (and, of course, this work is never a chronicle of child-development, still less the story of the child's acquisition of language): she speaks by and for herself, by and for maternal fantasies.

The recognition that the mother-as-given is not the mother-as-experienced cuts across the representations, exactly, of motherhood in culture. Hence Mary Kelly's exploration of the very site of herself as mother, her direct questioning of her representations, assumed or transgressed. And here (perhaps, to some other eyes, a paradox) I see the initial *political* force of this work: in its recognition that it is on the psychic that ideology works, through representation, and that the political is primarily inscribed there, on site as it were. (Here, Lacan suggesting that nothing like the ego pre-exists the Symbolic; Freud that male/female roles—and so motherhood—are conventional impositions upon the one libido.)

An important decision in Mary Kelly's practice is thus not to employ her own (photographic/filmic) image in the work. Such an image is always recuperable into the passes of ideology, and, it seems to me, is forever a witness to a fixity, provoking the confidence that here is a position, and positions are always interpretable.[4] But perhaps here the "rigorous non-use of the image"[5] is not simply a strategy against the problems of representing women, against any homogeneous notion of femininity, against *Schaulust* itself:[6] perhaps there is also another knowledge, arising from the perception that in art the body is intrinsically a problem for representation, is always a prey to rational geometry. The mother's body would be, of course, especially much of a problem: it is simply beyond figuration because of the loss that it bespeaks. The mother's body is properly inscribed (for men and women) as absence of devolved image, as lack of geometry—it predates the father. It exists at the level, for representation, of primal repression where figurability is not thought and pictorial experience does not exist. But what does exist there is still the letter, the mark of desire, the cut of separation inscribed.

That's one way of getting to Mary Kelly's preeminent concern for the language in her work. Another is to note the return of the repressed, as it were, in the diary-narrative that runs throughout the work. Yet as it returns—a writing which might take the risk of acting as if image of the subject "I"—it is immediately thrown into the arena guarded by other discourse. These, always positing a truth, always presenting a knowledge, always nonetheless differentiate themselves from one another and, as representations, as together subtending a plenitude, they continually belie their own urge for that plenitude—they contradict. In Mary Kelly's work this is crucial, that there is no truth of discourse—be it feminist or whatever. What the work moves towards and understands is writing, in the sense that writing can be not a discourse. All this is perceptible, for example, in Documentation III, with its record of the two-year-old child's conversations, juxtaposed with the mother's inner-voice commentary, and with her secondary revision (her diary-narrative), all inscribed over the child's scribbled marks, and with all those discourses set specifically into a pseudo-rational diary perspective schema. Or it's similarly clear in Documentation V which overlays information and traces concerning the child's gifts to the mother, the child's conversations, analyzed specimens of the gifts, statistical tables and manualized maps and descriptions of the mother's body.

But it is especially clear in "Documentation VI," the end of the work where the dissolution of image/narrative into writing becomes most importantly displayed for me. These magnificent slates, ironically appearing like the Rosetta Stone, where the child's "prewriting" (his inscription of the letter as it resists the imposition of the father's language), is analyzed by the mother; that analysis is itself juxtaposed with the diaries of the mother's search for a school for her child. Across these slates the mother-child-symbolic relationship is mapped so as to emphasize differentiation, to emphasize the interfering patterns of language that disrupt the unity of the social/symbolic world.

These slates present the gradated loss of the child suffered by the mother: the diary narrative is very much in the social world, the mother's inner-commentary is elsewhere and nearer to the child's prewriting, which is specifically a resistance to the patriarchal writing. In that resistance it's almost as if the child's marks constitute the very point of transgression which the mother's own language, her inner-voice, picks up on. The child inscribes the letter "i" and the mother replies:[7]

> i IS FOR INK. He calls it "a dot and an i." Sometimes he points to his eye but seems to know it's a pun. He's fascinated by it. Little"i"—the object watched by "I"—the subject. I IS FOR ALLIGATORS IMITATING INDIANS. I IS FOR AN IBEX IN AN INDIAN OUTFIT CHASING INSECTS ABSCONDING WITH AN ICE CREAM CONE. GOOD NIGHT LITTLE I IGOR ILLYCH IGUANA GOOD NIGHT LITTLE I. GOOD NIGHT.

And, too, it's almost as if it is not the mother who analyzes the child's writing, but the child's writing that analyzes the mother, producing within her language a similar resistance to the socially constricted language of the diary. So here, at the end of *Post-Partum Document*, is the beginning of writing where (and there is a lovely passage in Kristeva which talks of exactly this)[8] the adult is referred by the child (the child within the adult perhaps) to the fact that our language is never total, never the homogenous commodity of a unified subjectivity, never wholly rationalized: as the language, so the political structures and strictures. So there are moments of transgression and loss when it is possible to desire to speak and to dare to change.

(WHAT WILL I DO?)

s

I have no notion of what Mary Kelly's work will be doing next. But it does seem clear to me that she has begun to open up the space of a writing that is not a discourse; and this through a recognition of where it is that ideology works. In her art-practice there is now the theoretically-worked room for the subject's hopeful and happy writing, as that must now begin to assert its importance alongside the moral discourse of the desperate and melancholy protagonists/antagonists for whom discourse is truth.

NOTES

1. My title is taken from Julia Kristeva's *Polylogue* (Paris, 1977), p. 409. Kristeva claims—relevantly to this article—that the discourse of science "ne se préoccupe pas du sujet, de la mère terrain de ses opérations."
2. Quoted from *m/f*, nos 5/6, p. 145.
3. For Irigaray, women are both "interdites" and "inter-dites": both excluded, silenced, and told what their place is to be by reading between the lines of culture and language.
4. This view of the status of the photographic image is an extrapolation, in some ways, from Roland Barthes *La Chambre Claire* (Paris, 1980).
5. Peter Wollen, "Photography and Aesthetics," *Screen*, Winter 1978-9, vol. 19, no. 4.
6. For instance, the work of Suzanne Sontoro, operating at a political level which has the effect of identifying with the ethic it presumes to counter; this, in Irigaray's terms, is dreaming grammatically and symmetrically the inversion of patriarchal ethics—the changing of the guard.
7. *m/f*, nos 5/6, p. 133.
8. I'm thinking of *Polylogue*, pp. 473-6.

On the *Post-Partum Document*

Andrea Fraser
in: *Afterimage*, March 1986

Routledge & Kegan Paul's publication of Mary Kelly's *Post-Partum Document* marks perhaps the end of a period in which psychoanalytic feminist work was met with silence by the art-publishing industry.[1] Its publication in hardcover in 1983 roughly coincided with a special issue of *wedge* (no. 6, Winter 1984) entitled "Sexuality: Re/Positions," and with the New Museum of Contemporary Art's catalogue and traveling exhibition "Difference: On Representation and Sexuality," which evoked numerous articles and reviews. In 1985 *Post-Partum Document* was published in softcover. It seems that finally, in 1986, questions of the construction of sexual difference in ideology and representation, which have long been the focus of debates in independent film journals and among British artists since *Screen* took its psychoanalytic turn in 1974, are gaining currency in the American art world.

Post-Partum Document both emerged from and contributed to these debates. Kelly began work on her six-years, six-part, 135-piece interrogation of maternal femininity in 1973, the same year Laura Mulvey delivered "Visual Pleasure and Narrative Cinema" as a lecture and Juliet Mitchell completed *Psycho-Analysis and Feminism* for publication.[2] All three women participated in the same study group at the Women's Liberation Workshop in London. A year later *Screen* published its "Psychoanalysis and Cinema" issue, and Mulvey and Peter Wollen completed their film *Penthesilea* (Kelly and *Post-Partum Document* subsequently appeared in their 1977 film *Riddles of the Sphinx*).

The appropriation of psychoanalysis – particularly Jacques Lacan's re-reading of Freud through structuralist linguistics—by feminism and film theory satisfied the need for an account of the subject as something other than a biologically determined, autonomous individual. Lacan's theory of the construction of the subject in language (what he calls the Symbolic order), where it takes up a masculine or feminine position, thus became important for an understanding of how representation—and through it ideology—inscribes and continually reinscribes women in the subaltern position of passivity and dependence, as objects of masculine desire. Feminist film theory has primarily focused on specular relationships (usually understood to make up what Lacan calls the Imaginary order): the structures in film that seduce spectators into a narcissistic identification with the cinematic image/narrative, positioning viewers as the subjects of a gaze whose object, more often than not, is a fetishized image of a female body. *Post-Partum Document*—with Kelly's refusal to provide imagistic representations of the female body—examines instead the possibility of female fetishism and spectatorship. With objects and texts, Kelly poses the question of how women can represent themselves as the subjects, rather than the objects, of desire.

Post-Partum Document constitutes a theoretical study of feminine sexuality as important as any purely discursive text published in the last decade. But, as a transference of Kelly's maternal experience during the first five years of her son's life to her artistic practice, *Document* is also an intervention into the institutions of both motherhood and high art. Kelly's engagement in artistic practice ruptures ideological representations of maternity, which construct child care as the natural limit of women's responsibilities to the exclusion of all other interests and activities, thus enclosing feminine desire within an absolute being-for-another (child, husband, father). Conversely, Kelly's production of an artwork based on her maternal experience interrupts the foreclosure on the maternal function that sustains the procreative fantasy of autonomous artistic practice, in which the "painting" subject is characterized as the exclusive origin of "his" creative issue.

Post-Partum Document fragments the symbolic figures of mother and author, destroying their imaginary autonomy, their institutional antinomy. The subject of *Post-Partum Document* is at once the mother who finds both pleasure and anxiety in maternity and who collects memorabilia of the post-partum period in order to disavow her loss of narcissistic pleasure as the child becomes increasingly independent; the feminist who interrogates the construction of femininity in the social institution of motherhood; the researcher who analyzes the child's fecal stains and speech utterances; the artist who sublimates her lost maternal pleasure in the production of an artwork; and the author who produces the *Post-Partum Document* book.

Documents provided by Kelly's son—stained diaper linings, recorded and transcribed utterances, drawings, plaster hand casts, fragments of his blanket, natural specimens he presented to his mother as gifts, and examples of his prewriting alphabet—constitute the physical elements of each of the *Document's* six sections or "Documentations". Each section is framed by pseudo-scientific discourse (in the form of classificatory enumerations) and psychoanalytic discourse (represented by Lacan's graph of the structure of the subject, Schema R, with which every Documentation closes). Each is introduced by an explanatory text and concludes with an "Experimentum Mentis"—a psychoanalytic elaboration of the moment in the mother/child relationship recorded in the preceding Documentation.

Following Lacan's theory of the construction of sexual difference in language, *Post-Partum Document* traces the process through which a male child takes up a masculine position. All babies, whether they are born biological boys or girls, initially take their mother as a sexual object; all address to the mother their unconditional demands for love and the satisfaction of needs. This demand, Kelly writes in "Experimentum Mentis IV," "constitutes the mother as the Other who has the privilege of satisfying his/her needs and at the same time the whimsical power of depriving him/her of this satisfaction." In as much as the child receives the signifiers that constitute its demand from the field of the Other,[3] the needs articulated through these signifiers become irretrievably alienated, producing an unsatisfiable lack in the child that presents itself as desire.

But when the child tests the mother's "privilege" (as through the sexual inquiries recorded and transcribed in "Documentation V"), the child realizes that she too, being subject to speech, is also subject to desire, and therefore also lacking. The mother's lack in desire appears as castration, and the phallus becomes the signifier of desire. The phallus functions first as an image, a representation of what is lacking in the desired image of the mother, then it is positivized in the Symbolic order as the signifier of *jouissance*[4]—that which would satisfy the mother's desire. The phallus, which is now situated beyond the mother in the place of the symbolic father (who is introduced in "the mother's words" as the authority that "he calls upon to bear witness to the child's indiscretions," "Documentation III"), is raised from the signifier of a jouissance which is lacking to the mark of the law, which prohibits both the child's enjoyment of the mother and the mother's maternal enjoyment.

When the phallus becomes the signifier of desire, the paths of boys and girls separate, and the child must take up a masculine or feminine position. The child desires to satisfy the mother's desire as the condition of receiving the gift of her love. If the mother's desire is signified by the phallus, the boy "is content to present to the Other what in reality he may *have* that corresponds to this phallus"[5] (i.e., his penis). But the girl, who has nothing that corresponds to the signifier of desire except her own body, can only present herself and consequently must take up the position of *being* the phallus for the Other. And, as Kelly writes in "Experimentum Mentis VI," "being the phallus, she cannot have it; not having it she cannot represent herself as subject of desire."

While Kelly abides, in theory, by Lacan's account of the production of desire and construction of sexual difference in language, her shift in focus from the classical psychoanalytic study of the child to an analysis of the mother's experience constitutes a powerful critique. The material documents are not simply records of a boy's childhood, but are emblems of the mother's desire, memorabilia written over with her "inner speech" and diary entries, commentary, and analysis. Nor do the "Experimentum Mentis" texts simply reiterate psychoanalytic formulas as perhaps I just have; they supplement them with an analysis of the mother's experience, which doesn't complete but rather challenges the phallocentric assumptions of psychoanalytic theory.

Post-Partum Document problematizes mechanistic descriptions of the mother's function that ultimately naturalize a maternal femininity in which feminine desire, feminine jouissance, is already eclipsed. For Freud it is the mother who seduces the child, but only as a necessary condition of the sexual division of parental labor, only in the interests of good hygiene.[6] She does not enjoy the child. For Lacan the place of the mother is marked only by desire regulated by the phallic signifier. Her sexuality is set. Her jouissance is barred—always already replaced by proper pleasure, the function of which is to guarantee paternal authority by submitting to its mark, its name, its fantasy of exclusive possession.

Post-Partum Document presents a challenge to representations of women as passive conduits for masculine, paternal desire—the "properly feminine" function that supposedly culminates and comes to rest in maternity. The mother in *Post-Partum Document* is she who finds a jouissance in her relationship with the child, which, at least momentarily, transgresses the Symbolic Law-of-the-Father. But the mother also experiences anxiety, fear of failure, and guilt; for if this jouissance is not refused, psychosis will threaten the child. The mother is she who takes up the "masculine" position of *having* the child-as-phallus, a position that also paradoxically guarantees her maternal femininity, for, by functioning as a phallic substitute, the child supplements the mother's lack, allowing her to maintain a narcissistic image of fullness and completion. Thus, when the child recognizes the mother's castration and no longer subscribes to her image of maternal perfection, no longer invests in her exclusive privilege of satisfying needs, the mother must represent "a double loss—the child as phallus and the body as *feminine*" ("Experimentum Mentis V").

Mary Kelly writes in her preface:

> *Post-Partum Document* is not simply about child development, it is an effort to articulate the mother's fantasies, her desires, her stake in that project called 'motherhood.' In this sense, too, it is not a traditional narrative; a problem is continually posed but no resolution is reached. There is only a replay of moments of separation and loss, perhaps because desire has no end, resists normalization, ignores biology, disperses the body.

Post-Partum Document demonstrates that sexual positionality is never finally fixed—for mother or child—but is rather a problem continually posed and re-posed, an unstable relation to the signifier of desire that must be continually negotiated through language. The "traditional narrative" that *Post-Partum Document* disrupts is not simply an aesthetic one, but the narrative of a sexual development that achieves the final closure of a stable masculine or feminine identity. *Post-Partum Document* is thus a catalogue, not of the sexual development of a masculine subject, but of an intersubjective process including both mother and child, determined by the Symbolic order of a particular social information. The *Post-Partum Document* book, then, is a catalogue of a catalogue that similarly intervenes in the traditional function of art-historical monographs; the reconstruction of the artistic development of a masculine "painting" subject as a natural, subjective process of pseudo-maturation that culminates in the achievement of an individual aesthetic identity.

In her preface, Kelly parenthetically disclaims the book's monographic status. Instead, she refers readers to the collective struggles in which she participated: the British women's movement, psychoanalytic and feminist study groups, efforts to unionize women and improve day care for the children of working mothers. Yet, the book displays many of the conventional trappings of the monographic form: an introduction (by Lucy R. Lippard), a bibliography and appendix of selected reviews (two of which are quoted on the back cover of the paperback edition, alongside a short biography and photoportrait of "The Author"), a photograph of Kelly and her son (Kelly Barrie) during a recording session, and, most surprisingly, Kelly's signature, which is featured prominently on the book's cover, rather than her typeset name. In art-book etiquette, the artist's printed autograph is the authorizing, authenticating insignia of a monograph, a mark that ossifies the subject-in-collective-historical-process in a final maturity of unique self-possession.

Kelly's black scrawl—disintegrating into the book cover's silver ground like the crude coverage of a crayon or the remains of an antique inscription—is perfectly consonant with the eleventh piece of "Documentation VI," "Prewriting alphabet, exergue and diary," which is reproduced below her signature. With their tripartite strata of different scripts and their different discourses arranged on fragments of black slate, the works in this section have a form, Kelly writes, "analogous to the Rosetta stone."

If, following the Rosetta stone analogy, the three discourses that comprise the works in "Documentation VI" are different translations of the same text, Kelly's signature constitutes a fourth account of the subject inscription by language in the social order. But significantly, it isn't the last piece in "Documentation VI" that is reproduced on the book's cover, the piece with which *Post-Partum Document* comes to an end. Kelly Barrie's uncertain "hieroglyphs" finally give way to legible words; he achieves the writing of his proper name. Kelly's commentary on her son's first signature could be applied equally to her own, on the cover of a book that she doesn't think of as a monograph. For although "with the inscription of his proper name the child is [indeed] instituted as the author of his text," this moment is only a "replay of differences and separations already sanctioned in the structuring and dissolution of the Oedipus complex" ("Experimentum Mentis VI").

But, if Kelly's signature also functions not as the first or last articulation of a stable, self-possessed, constituting subject, but as a reduplication of the text of the process through which the subject is constituted, it is not simply a matter of bookcover semiotics. While *Post-Partum Document* is undeniably an artist's monograph, it doesn't contain the scholarly, chronological arrangement of a would-be-complete set of great works that the genre usually connotes. Although the 135 pieces presented in the book follow a certain chronology of production, it is not one in which you can trace the maturation of an artist's aesthetic that culminates in the achievement of a signature. They constitute only one work, and the changes that occurred in Kelly's project over the course of six years cannot be understood in the conventional terms of subjective development, but must be read, as Kelly writes in her preface, as "a kind of chronicle of feminist debate within the women's movement in Great Britain during the 1970s."

Perhaps the only monograph here is the one that I am engaged in writing. In her essay "Reviewing Modernist Criticism," Kelly notes that "criticism's function is to initiate that work which art history eventually accomplishes in the form of the biographical narrative, that is, as Griselda Pollock describes it 'the production of an artistic subject for works of art.'"[7] But the signification of a work and the subject that it produces is not only a condition of representation, or of art-historical representation, but is also contingent upon the structure of the practice in which the work is situated. Similarly, the ideological function of traditional monographs is not simply an order over-layed, but one that is allowed by an artist's assumption of a mode of production that presents its organization as immanent.

The labor that produced *Post-Partum Document* cannot be completely accounted for by institutional definitions that legislate the proper limits of artistic practice and that would allow the subject of its production to be articulated in the "form of the bourgeoise subject; creative, autonomous, and proprietorial."[8] The maternal labor on which *Post-Partum Document* is based, the intellectual labor that produced the theoretical texts, which supplant the institutional rhetoric that would otherwise frame the work, and the political labor that forms the social and historical context in which the work must be read, together constitute the heterogeneous field of Kelly's practice.

NOTES

1 This essay is dedicated to Carmen de Monteflores, writer, psychotherapist, and mother (mine).

2 "Visual Pleasure and Narrative Cinema" was published in *Screen* 16, no. 3 (Autumn 1975); reprinted in *Art after Modernism: Rethinking Representation*, ed. Brian Wallis (New York: New Museum of Contemporary Art, 1984). *Psycho-Analysis and Feminism* was originally published by Allen Lane (London, 1974) and is currently published by Penguin Books (New York).

3 In Lacanian theory there are two others. The *object petit a* (*a* is *autre* or other), whose status is imaginary, is both the object of the drive and the primordially lost object that causes desire (as, for example, the breast, imagined by the infant as part of itself), which is forever lost in the moment that the infant becomes a subject. The capitalized Other does not exist as such, but is rather the Symbolic locus of speech and language, a place that comes to be situated within the person to whom the subject addresses his or her demand for love, knowledge, or certainty.

4 The French word *jouissance*, translators claim, has no adequate English

equivalent. Lacan's translator, Alan Sheridan, notes: "'Enjoyment' conveys the sense, contained by *jouissance*, of enjoyment of rights, of property, etc. Unfortunately, in modern English, the word has lost the sexual connotation it still retains in French ... 'Pleasure' on the other hand, obeys the law of homeostasis ... 'Jouissance' transgresses this law and, in that respect, it is *beyond* the pleasure principle." *Ecrits* (New York: Pantheon, 1977), p. x.

5 Lacan, "The Signification of the Phallus," *Ecrits*, p. 289.

6 Ruminating on his long-abandoned seduction theory, Freud writes: "All of my women patients told me that they had been seduced by their father. I was driven to recognize that these reports were untrue ... And now we find the fantasy of seduction once more in the pre-Oedipal history of girls; but the seducer is regularly the mother. Here, however, the fantasy touches on the ground of reality, for it really was the mother who by her activities over the child's bodily hygiene inevitably stimulated, and perhaps roused for the first time, pleasurable sensations in her genitals." "Femininity," *New Introductory Lectures* (New York: W.W. Norton), p. 106.

7 In *Art after Modernism: Rethinking Representation*, p. 91.

8 *Ibid.*

Post-Partum Document, Mary Kelly

Edited by Sabine Breitwieser
for Generali Foundation
Vienna, Austria

Production Hemma Schmutz, Nadja Wiesener
Editing work Nadja Wiesener
Data entry of the English texts Barbara Schröder
Proof-reading Alix Sehr-Stewart, Amanda Peniston-Bird
Photos Ray Barrie
Photo CD Steve Lehmer
Graphic Design Dorit Margreiter

Paper Alster Werkdruck 100g